T0332857

Europe
BY TRAIN

Europe
BY TRAIN

Content

Previous page
A U-Bahn train
crossing Oberbaum
bridge, Berlin

Introduction

From the well-to-do embarking on a Grand Tour of the continent, to intrepid backpackers clutching their dog-eared Interrail passes, making a journey around Europe by train has enticed travellers for centuries. The charms of Europe's regions – Italy's art and architecture, Eastern Europe's storied cities, the Alps' adventure-packed resorts – are as attractive as ever, but the increase in low-cost air fares has, for a time, pushed the train journey from the forefront. Until now.

Europe is where train travel was invented and it's been busy reimagining it. Vintage icons like the *Orient Express* and heritage steam trains like *The Jacobite* still ply the tracks, but it's the new high-speed services, revamped sleeper trains and continued cross-border cooperation that's renewed people's excitement for rail travel. That wonderful moment when you arrive at your destination and step straight into a city street? It's only possible with rail travel. Watching constantly changing scenes from the comfort of your seat? You can't do that on a plane. And speaking of which, taking the train is a greener, friendlier alternative to flying.

It's never been easier to get from A to B: almost every corner of Europe is connected by track, helping you join the dots between some of the world's greatest cities and a supporting cast of destinations that you may never have thought to visit but will be glad you did. And that's what we encourage you to do. In *Europe by Train*, we've stitched together the best of Europe into 50 itineraries. Some crisscross the entire continent, others are devoted to specific countries or regions. You need not take a sabbatical to complete them: many can be covered in a week or fortnight, some in just a few days. Follow them rigidly or loosely and remember that journeys planned in advance are usually cheaper, but that sometimes you can't put a price on spontaneity. You're here for an adventure and in Europe, the possibilities are unlimited.

Inside King's Cross railway station in London

Practical Information

The following pages contain information to help you plan your trip around Europe, giving you steers on everything from ticketing to travelling with pets. For details about individual countries turn to the directory, which includes network maps for each nation *(p242)*.

Passports and visas

For entry requirements, including visas, check the government websites for the countries you are visiting, or consult your nearest embassy before travelling.

Citizens of the UK, US, Canada, Australia and New Zealand don't need a visa for stays of up to three months in the Schengen Area, but will need to register with the European Travel Information and Authorisation System (ETIAS) to be granted entry from late 2023. EU nationals do not need a visa or an ETIAS to travel to other EU countries.

The Schengen Area is a single jurisdiction, made up of 26 European countries, under a common visa policy. This means that there is no passport check or any other type of border control at any of their mutual borders. You will need to show your passport when you leave or enter the Schengen Area (immigration procedures typically take place at the station of departure), but once "inside" there are no hard borders between countries. In fact, it's often the phone network that first informs travellers they've crossed from one country to another, with a message informing them of new roaming rules.

All members of the European Union are also members of the Schengen Area, with the exception of Bulgaria, Croatia, Cyprus, Romania and Ireland.

Switzerland, Lichtenstein, Norway and Iceland (none of which are members of the EU) are also members of the Schengen Area. Monaco, San Marino and Vatican City, meanwhile, are not members of either the EU or Schengen Area but, as these city-states are surrounded by an EU and Schengen member country, they are de facto members of the Schengen Area.

ETIAS
www.etiasvisa.com

Government advice

Now, more than ever, it is important to check the latest travel advice from your own government and that of the country or countries you intend to visit. The UK Foreign, Commonwealth and Development Office, the US Department of State, the Australian Department of Foreign Affairs and Trade, and local government websites offer the latest information on security, health and local regulations.

Australian Department of
Foreign Affairs and Trade
www.smartraveller.gov.au

UK Foreign, Commonwealth
and Development Office
www.gov.uk/foreign-travel-advice

US Department of State
www.travel.state.gov

Insurance

Although EU citizens are entitled to emergency medical treatment anywhere in the bloc, they are not covered for search and rescue, repatriation or theft of personal property. It is therefore important to take out travel insurance even if you are an EU national.

Some countries have reciprocal health agreements with the EU. The UK Global Health Insurance Card (GHIC), for instance, entitles UK passport holders to emergency health care in the EU at a reduced cost or sometimes for free. However, it may not shield card holders from hefty medical bills and should therefore not be considered a replacement for travel insurance.

The US, Canada and New Zealand have reciprocal health care agreements with the UK, but not EU nations. Australia has reciprocal health care agreements with Belgium, Finland, Italy, Malta, the Netherlands, Norway, Ireland, Slovenia, Sweden and the UK. Once again, these agreements are no substitute for insurance.

GHIC
www.ghic.org.uk

Getting started

Forward planning will help you save time and money. If you're following one of the 50 rail trips featured in this guidebook, a lot of the advance work has been done for you – but you'll still need to figure out how to get to the starting point. Nearly all of the routes start and end somewhere that is accessible by plane or rail services, but always check ahead.

If you've been inspired by this book to craft your own rail trip, start by planning out your route using the directory maps. Once you're ready to book tickets, compare the cost of individual tickets to passes, check if you're eligible for any railcards and make sure to leave enough time between connections. Most online journey planners will do this automatically and you'll find lots of useful information for each country's ticketing system in the directory (p242).

Ticketing

Knowing where you are going is one thing, knowing how to get there is another. Rail travellers in Europe have two options: invest in a rail pass or buy individual train tickets for each leg of their trip. Which approach is best for you depends entirely on your route, budget and whether you value spontaneity or like to plan ahead.

To avoid fines or tricky exchanges with train guards, who might not speak your language, ensure that you have the correct ticket and a seat reservation if one is needed (high-speed trains often require one). Be aware that on some networks you must validate your ticket before boarding, too.

Flash sales can ease the cost of travelling around Europe by train. Rail operators often advertise special offers on their websites, as do third-party ticketing platforms. Interrail and Eurail also have sales which are usually announced via their joint news-

BOOKMARK THIS

TRAINLINE, RAIL EUROPE AND OMIO

Each country has at least one rail operator with its own ticketing website, which usually offers the lowest fares. However, third-party platforms such as Trainline, Rail Europe and Omio are good if you plan to take multiple trains in different countries and don't want to book them individually. A small booking fee is usually added.
www.thetrainline.com
www.raileurope.com
www.omio.co.uk

letter – sign up on the homepage of either site to receive it.

Those looking to make their euros go further could consider taking the scenic route. High-speed trains may slash travel times between cities, but older and slower regional trains are usually much cheaper. You'll also save money if you focus your route on Eastern Europe. Prices in this area are often lower than in the rest of Europe – not just for rail tickets, but also accommodation, activities and eating out.

Cancellations and delays

Passenger rights are robust in the EU. If a cancelled train means travellers will be more than an hour late to their destination, they are entitled to cancel their journey and receive a full refund. You can request a refund via the website of the train company concerned – note you may be required to upload a photograph or screen grab of your ticket.

Passengers choosing to continue their journey are entitled to transportation to their destination at the earliest opportunity, accommodation if they are required to stay overnight and assistance with meals proportional to the length of the delay.

In many cases, compensation is offered. If a cancelled train causes a delay of between one and two hours, passengers are entitled to 25 per cent of the original cost of the ticket. This rises to 50 per cent if the delay is more than two hours. Compensation is not available to passengers who opt for a refund, however.

If you miss your connecting train because of a late-running service or cancelled train, you should be able to travel on the next available train free of charge. However, travellers who have multiple connecting trains may not be able to travel with their existing tickets on later trains for the entire journey. If you have to pay for new tickets or accommodation as a result of a delay, you should be able to claim via your travel insurance. Note that the rail operator will only award compensation for the delayed service; expect to receive 25 per cent of the ticket value for a 60- to 119-minute delay, and 50 per cent for delays of 120 minutes or longer.

Personal security

Trains are generally safe to travel on in Europe, but it is important to stay vigilant and use your common sense. Keep an eye on your personal belongings and beware that while pickpockets are rare, they do operate in some places.

Some European nations have their own transport police to deal with crime on the railways. Others do not, so passengers should contact the regular police force to report a crime. Before you travel, it is worth familiarizing yourself with the appropriate emergency numbers.

Travellers with disabilities

If you have a disability or reduced mobility, you are entitled to free assistance when getting on and off the train and changing trains throughout Europe. To get the best assistance, contact the railway company or ticket seller 48 hours before your trip and explain what assistance you require.

Some networks have better facilities for people with specific requirements than others. The Netherlands, for instance, has the only rail network that is entirely accessible for visually impaired passengers, while some UK train stations have introduced British Sign Language announcements. Most other networks simply have dedicated seating areas for those with reduced mobility.

The European Disability Forum provides more information about accessible rail travel in Europe, including your rights.

European Disability Forum
www.edf-feph.org

Luggage allowance

There are generally no luggage limits on European trains, with one or two exceptions. Eurostar limits passengers to two pieces of luggage not exceeding 85 cm (33 inches) in any one dimension, though this is not strictly enforced. Ouigo, the low-cost French operator, only allows cases up to 55-cm (22-inch) x 35-cm (14-inch) x 25-cm (10-inch), plus a small handbag no bigger than 36 cm (14 inches) x 27 cm (11 inches) x 15 cm (6 inches).

If you have luggage that cannot easily travel with you in the passenger carriage, inform the rail operator so it can be registered in the baggage car. If your registered luggage is lost or damaged, you have a right to compensation. Train companies are required to pay up to €1,200 per piece of registered luggage, providing passengers can prove the value of its contents. If not, it's a maximum of €300.

Bikes

While European cities are among the best in the world to cycle around, taking a bike on a train remains frustratingly difficult.

Fold-up bikes will generally be treated like regular luggage, although it's advisable to transport them in a travel bag. Unfortunately, travelling with a normal bicycle is much less straightforward and rules vary depending on the operator.

Cyclists are often required to reserve a space for their bikes in the baggage car of the train for an additional fee. They may also be required to partly disassemble their bikes – for example, take a wheel off – to save space. Booking websites usually indicate whether it is possible to take a bike onboard a specific service.

Prams

Fold-up prams will generally be treated like regular luggage. However, if you have a pram that does not fold down, you may be required to reserve a space for it in the baggage car.

Travelling with pets

With a few exceptions, pets can travel with their owners within the EU, and from a non-EU country to the EU. However, the animal must be microchipped, have a valid rabies vaccination and in some cases have received tapeworm treatment. Pet passports or an EU animal health certificate are also required. Always check the rules of the country you're travelling to for any additional restrictions or requirements before you travel.

Most trains in Europe allow pets onboard, but check with the operator beforehand as some rail companies have different rules. For instance, only service dogs are allowed to travel on the Eurostar.

Small animals generally need to be kept in a carrier and can usually travel for free. Dogs will generally need to be muzzled, kept on a short lead and may even require a ticket to travel.

Sleeper trains

An endangered species until recently, European night trains are experiencing a revival amid rising demand for more sustainable travel options.

Leading the charge is Austria's state-run operator ÖBB, which has revived a handful of night-time routes including Paris to Vienna. Private operators are also getting involved, among them the Dutch-Belgian start-up European Sleeper, which is set to launch a night train between Brussels and Prague (at the time of writing, no launch date had been confirmed).

What to expect from sleeper trains depends where you are on the continent. While Central and Western Europe axed many of their night-time services, most of Eastern Europe's sleepers kept running and are starting to show their age. Central Europe's swanky new night trains, by contrast, are like hotels on wheels.

Even so, most sleeper carriages in Europe follow a similar design. Each cabin typically contains three beds, arranged one on top of the other, with a washbasin in the corner. Each carriage has an attendant and a shared lavatory. Cabins are always single-sex and have locks on the doors. Travellers may also come across couchettes, which are even cosier than cabins. They typically feature six foldout beds, with the bottom two doubling as seats during the day.

It is possible to book a normal seat in a regular carriage on a night train. Unsurprisingly, this works out cheaper than a bed but is far less comfortable.

Note that berths on night trains are sold individually, and that rail companies assign each passenger to a same-sex cabin – so expect to share the room with strangers. Solo travellers can book out entire cabins for themselves (at a cost) if they don't fancy bunking up with other passengers. Couples, who would otherwise be split up unless they are the same sex, could also book the entire cabin.

Some of the night trains entering service in Western and Central Europe feature luxurious cabins with private showers. In all cases, reservations are mandatory on night trains.

BOOKMARK THIS

YOUR EUROPE

The Your Europe website is one that you'll ideally not have to use. Outlining your rights as a rail passenger in the EU, it's the place to go if you have been inconvenienced by a train delay or cancellation in the bloc and are not receiving the help you need from the rail operator. It's available in multiple languages.
www.europa.eu/youreurope/index_en.htm

BOOKMARK THIS

EUROPEAN RAIL TIMETABLES

This regularly updated guidebook contains Europe's various train timetables, schedule information, maps and other details for those riding the rails. Check the European Rail Timetable website for the latest edition. Digital versions are also available.
www.europeanrailtimetable.eu

Rail
Trips

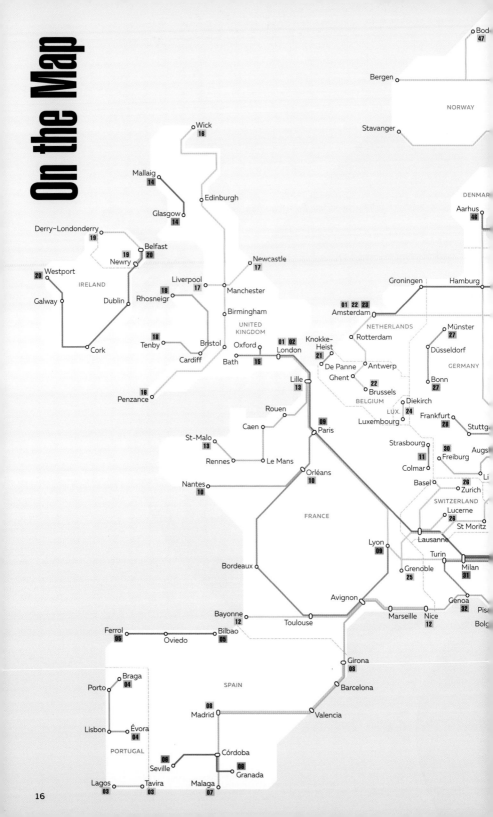

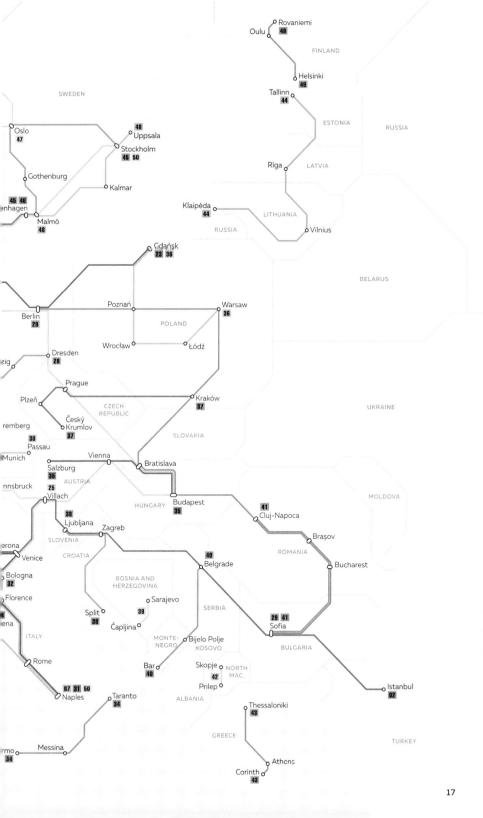

Rovaniemi 49
Oulu 49

FINLAND

Helsinki 49

Tallinn 44

SWEDEN

ESTONIA

RUSSIA

Oslo 47

Uppsala 48

Stockholm 45 50

Rīga

LATVIA

Gothenburg

Kalmar

Klaipėda 44

LITHUANIA

45 48
enhagen

Malmö 48

RUSSIA

Vilnius

BELARUS

Gdańsk 23 36

Poznań

Warsaw 36

Berlin 29

POLAND

zig

Dresden 28

Wrocław

Łódź

Prague

Plzeň

Kraków 37

UKRAINE

CZECH
REPUBLIC

Český
Krumlov 37

remberg 30

SLOVAKIA

Passau

Vienna

Bratislava

Munich

Salzburg 35

nnsbruck 25

AUSTRIA

Villach

HUNGARY

Budapest 36

Cluj-Napoca 41

MOLDOVA

Ljubljana 38

Zagreb

SLOVENIA

Brașov

erona

Venice

CROATIA

Belgrade 40

ROMANIA

Bucharest

Bologna 32

Florence

BOSNIA AND
HERZEGOVINA

Sarajevo

SERBIA

ena

Split 38

39

ITALY

Čapljina

Bijelo Polje

Sofia 29 41

Rome

MONTE-
NEGRO

KOSOVO

BULGARIA

07 31 50
Naples

Bar 40

Skopje 42

NORTH
MAC.

Istanbul 02

Taranto 34

Prilep

ALBANIA

Thessaloniki 43

rmo

Messina

34

GREECE

TURKEY

Athens

Corinth 43

17

01

The Grand Tour

From the 17th to 19th centuries, it was a rite of passage for the well-to-do to make the Grand Tour of Europe. Follow in their tracks on this version of the transcontinental journey, which stops in Europe's most iconic cities.

⏵ **LONDON** ENGLAND ◯ **AMSTERDAM** NETHERLANDS

✪ BUY AN INTERRAIL OR EURAIL GLOBAL PASS VALID FOR 10 DAYS OF TRAVEL WITHIN TWO MONTHS (P11).

🕐 21–24 DAYS ⦿ 4,980 KM (3,094 MILES)

London

2 hr 15 mins

Paris

10 hrs

Florence (Firenze)

1 hr 30 mins

Rome (Roma)

4 hrs

Venice (Venezia)

8–10 hrs

Vienna (Wien)

2 hrs 45 mins

Budapest

7 hrs

Prague (Praha)

4 hrs 20 mins

Berlin

6 hrs 20 mins

Amsterdam

London
ENGLAND

Traditionally, the Grand Tour was undertaken by British nobility, who set off on their voyage of discovery from London. And you, too, should start your journey here.

England's capital was founded by the Romans some 2,000 years ago on a loop in the wiggling and winding Thames. Over the following centuries, this river played a pivotal role in London's fortunes, serving as an international transport route in the Middle Ages and the trading hub of the British Empire in the 18th century. Today, the Thames is still central to the city and many of London's biggest sights can be found along its banks.

Walking part of the 298-km (185-mile) Thames Path is an excellent way to cover a lot of ground in a short space of time. The most well-trodden route shadows the river from William the Conqueror's imposing Tower of London in the east to the Palace of Westminster in the west, where you'll find Big Ben. Between these two sights, you'll pass Shakespeare's Globe theatre, the Tate Modern (a power station turned modern art gallery and wonderfully free) and the slowly spinning London Eye. By the end

Westminster Bridge stretching across the Thames to the Palace of Westminster and Big Ben of the walk, you'll have taken in nearly a millennia of history, and be ready for a slap-up meal and a show in the West End.

🚆 Trains from St Pancras International make the journey to Paris's Gare du Nord station approximately every hour.

_____

Paris
FRANCE

Paris has so many historic sights: the Louvre, Notre-Dame, the Eiffel Tower. See as many as you have time for, but make Montmartre, the hilly neighbourhood in the north of the centre, your base.

This former working-class area still has a village-like feel, with its cobbled streets, quaint houses and neighbourhood patisseries. Pick up a croissant – it's a must – and then make your way to place du Tertre to check out the ever-present buskers and artists' stalls. Since Matisse and Picasso's time, Montmartre has been a magnet for creatives, drawn by its low-cost housing, reputation for free living and breathtaking views. From the terrace in front of the Sacré-Cœur, you'll be able to see nearly all of Paris's famous monuments. Keep visiting the viewpoint again and again during your stay, especially at night when the Eiffel Tower sparkles spectacularly.

🚆 To travel to Florence, catch the train to Milano Centrale from Paris's Gare de Lyon station and change there for Firenze Santa Maria Novella. It's a long ten-hour journey.

_____

Florence
ITALY

Italy has always been given a lot of coverage on the Grand Tour

DETOUR
Fontainebleau

Take a break from the city streets in Fontainebleau, which is just a 40-minute train ride from Paris's Gare de Lyon station. Here, you can explore miles of hiking and biking trails through oak forests, and the 1,900-room Château de Fontainebleau with its lovely gardens.

and, with its good food and amazing art, who can blame your predecessors for wanting to spend so much time here?

First stop is Florence, the bastion of the Renaissance and art capital of Italy. Some of the country's best art museums and galleries are found here, including the Uffizi, Bargello and Galleria dell'Accademia. It's impossible to visit them all, especially during a flying visit, so stick to the Uffizi. Here, inside the former offices of the Medici (the family that ruled Florence for much of the 15th to 17th centuries), you'll find a vast treasure trove of Renaissance paintings. Highlights include Botticelli's _The Birth of Venus_, Raphael's _Portrait of Pope Leo X_ and Caravaggio's _Medusa_. To see Michelangelo's _David_, spend your time in the Accademia instead.

🚆 Fast and direct Frecciarossa and Italo services travel to Roma Termini from Firenze Santa Maria Novella every 15 to 30 minutes.

_____

Rome
ITALY

One remarkable relic after another is just around the next corner in the "Eternal City". As a result, there's never a need to plan

A cobbled street along a canal in Venice

out your time in Rome too strictly. Simply put on your comfiest shoes (the endless cobbles and marble floors can take a toll) and set off.

Most of the city's blockbusters (including the Trevi Fountain, Colosseum and Pantheon) are found on the east bank of the Tiber river, within striking distance of Termini station. Cross over to the west bank to visit the cylindrical Castel Sant'Angelo and vast Vatican Museums. The highlight here is undoubtedly the Sistine Chapel, which Michelangelo splashed with biblical frescoes in the 16th century.

Wherever you end up, you're bound to have worked up an appetite, which is no bad thing in this proudly foodie city. Fuel your sightseeing with the Roman street food of choice: *pizza al taglio* (a huge slice of pizza).

⊖ Direct Frecciarossa and Italo services from Roma Termini to Venezia Santa Lucia run hourly and take around four hours.

Venice

ITALY

Stretching across 117 islands, Venice is like no other place in Europe – or the world for that matter. Gondolas outnumber cars, the public transport system relies on *vaporetti* (waterbuses) and addresses are so bafflingly complex that even with a map and detailed directions you may struggle to find your way. Getting lost is inevitable, but also one of the great rewards, revealing some of this city's many secrets.

Leave plenty of time for aimless wandering, but don't neglect the major sights, which are all conveniently clustered around the Piazza San Marco – Italy's loveliest but busiest square. Here, you'll find the Palazzo Ducale, the 14th-century palace that housed the Doges (the highest official in the Venetian republic) and the Basilica di San Marco, with its Byzantine domes, glinting mosaics and lifelike

marble statues. Visit in the early morning or late evening to have the place (almost) to yourself.

➤ Trains travel from Venezia Santa Lucia to Wien Hauptbahnhof three to five times each day. Opt for the Nightjet sleeper service, so you don't waste any sightseeing time on the eight- to ten-hour journey.

Vienna
AUSTRIA

It's always hard to leave Italy behind, but Vienna will quickly win you over. First, head to one of the city's ubiquitous coffeehouses. Behind their awnings and signs, these grand buildings enclose a shabby-chic world of chandeliers, peeling wallpaper and chintzy paintings. The setting might sound a little touristy, but this is where the Viennese start their day with frothy cups of coffee and decadent multilayered slices of cake.

Vienna is also a visual feast. All architectural styles are represented here, from High Baroque palaces to Jugendstil U-Bahn stations. Don't miss the Secession Building, with its gilded dome, Stephansdom's tiled roof or the palatial Staatsoper. The scale of the city's opera house reflects Vienna's appreciation for music, a tradition that dates back to the 18th and 19th centuries when Haydn, Beethoven and Schubert were invited to perform at the Hofburg palace. Today, the city's calendar is packed with opera, music festivals and performing arts events, so round off your day with some music.

➤ ÖBB and Railjet services from Wien Hauptbahnhof to Budapest-Keleti depart hourly and take under three hours.

Budapest
HUNGARY

On to Vienna's Austro-Hungarian partner: Budapest. Perched on either side of the Danube, the Hungarian capital was actually two separate cities – Buda and Pest – until 1873.

Concentrate on the Buda side of the city, climbing up castle hill to the Budavári Palota, the city's vast palace. Here, you can explore its museum, get lost in the spooky underground labyrinth and look out over Pest from the romantic Halászbástya (Fisherman's Bastion). The framed view of Országház, perhaps Europe's grandest parliament building, will take your breath away.

➤ It's a long seven-hour journey from Budapest-Nyugati to Praha Hlavní Nádraží; direct ÖBB services depart every two hours.

Prague
CZECH REPUBLIC

Sometimes called "the City of a Hundred Spires", Prague positively bristles with medieval turrets, Gothic steeples and

Vienna is also a visual feast. All architectural styles are represented here, from High Baroque palaces to Jugendstil U-Bahn stations.

Baroque bell towers – vestiges of more than 1,000 years of history. Its UNESCO-listed historic centre and hilltop castle have made it a must-stop on the tourist trail, and its cheap-and-cheerful nightlife has sometimes brought out the worst in visitors. But don't let that put you off – its cobbled streets, statue-lined Charles Bridge and traditional pubs are unmissable for good reason.

⊖ Deutsche Bahn trains travel between Praha Hlavní Nádraží in Prague and Berlin Hauptbahnhof every couple of hours; the journey takes under four-and-a-half hours.

Berlin
GERMANY

The city on the Spree has seen it all: the rise and fall of fascism, wartime devastation and a wall that divided a people. As you'd expect from a city with such a storied past, there's an abundance of art and culture here.

Berlin literally has a whole island dedicated to museums, called, somewhat matter of factly, Museumsinsel (Museum Island). Despite war losses and Soviet looting, some of the world's finest collections are found here. The Altes Museum contains a huge number of classical antiquities, the Neues Museum is dedicated to Egyptology, the Alte National-galerie is all about the Romantics and the Bode-Museum has a little bit of everything, from Roman sarcophagi to Renaissance sculpture. But the pinnacle is the Pergamonmuseum, with its Pergamon Altar and deep-blue-tiled Ishtar Gate. It's one of Europe's best museums and you'll want to leave at least a couple of hours to explore it.

Dedicate another day to the Reichstag and Berlin's most important memorials: the profound Holocaust Memorial and the street art-splashed Berlin Wall, which signalled the beginning of a new era when it fell.

⊖ The hourly Deutsche Bahn service from Berlin Hauptbahnhof to Amsterdam Centraal takes over six hours.

Amsterdam
NETHERLANDS

Reflective waterways, gabled houses and cobbled canal paths: Amsterdam is one of Europe's prettiest cities. Shaped by centuries of immigration and still grappling with its colonial past, it also has a fantastic cultural scene. Old Masters in the Rijksmuseum are right around the corner from contemporary art pieces in the Stedelijk, 17th-century merchant's mansions sit across the water from post-industrial cultural hubs, like NDSM, and for every *gezellig* (cosy) pub there's a cool street food stall. It's the perfect place to end your journey around Europe's big hitters.

EXTEND
YOUR TRIP

Brussels

Not ready to go home? Continue on to Brussels (*p121*). The headquarters of the European Union, this multilayered and multilingual place seems like a microcosm of Europe as a whole. Must-dos include the EU sights, museum-hopping on the Grand-Place and sipping world-class Trappist ales.

02

DIY Orient Express

You don't have to fork out for an *Orient Express* ticket to have a trans-European adventure – make the most of a well-oiled public transport system instead and discover the lesser-explored side of Europe's most-visited cities.

● **LONDON** ENGLAND ○ **ISTANBUL** TURKEY

◉ FOR THE GREATEST FLEXIBILITY, BUY AN INTERRAIL OR EURAIL GLOBAL PASS VALID FOR TEN DAYS OF TRAVEL WITHIN TWO MONTHS (P11).

● 16–20 DAYS ● 3,490 KM (2,169 MILES)

London
ENGLAND

Since the *Orient Express (p30)* began steaming its way across Europe in the 1880s, London has been its northern terminus. Passengers of the luxury train might constrain themselves to swanky central and west London, but you should head south of the Thames (on public transport, of course). Like all of London, this quarter of the capital is a patchwork of distinct neighbourhoods and two of them are counted among the capital's coolest.

Start your day in Brixton. This district features not one but two buzzing markets, set just across the road from one another. Both Brixton Market and Brixton Village have stalls selling street food and vintage finds reflecting the area's Caribbean roots. The market was the first in London to be lit by electricity, inspiring Eddy Grant's 1982 hit song "Electric Avenue".

Brixton is separated from Peckham by leafy Herne Hill and East Dulwich, which seem positively sleepy in comparison. Peckham always seems to be on the move, with Rye Lane's ever-revolving roster of restaurants and a neighbourhood habit of turning disused buildings (including a multistorey car park and an old cricket bat factory) into multifunctional spaces.

🚊 The Eurostar to Paris departs from London St Pancras station every one to two hours. Arrive in plenty of time to go through passport control before boarding your train.

London

2 hrs 15 mins

Paris

3 hrs 50 mins

Lausanne

3 hrs 50 mins

Milan (Milano)

2 hrs 30 mins

Venice (Venezia)

26 hrs

Belgrade

25 hrs

Sofia

11 hrs

Istanbul

Paris
FRANCE

Instead of jostling with tourists around the Eiffel Tower or queuing for hours for the Louvre, make your first stop one of the French capital's most underappreciated sights. Set way out in the 20th arrondissement, the Cimetière du Père Lachaise is more of an open-air museum than a cemetery. Its ornate gravestones and memorials mark the final resting places of an eclectic line-up of celebrities, such as irreverent English writer Oscar Wilde, serious French author Marcel

Bustling Brixton Village, a reimagined covered market in south London

Proust, Parisian classical singer Édith Piaf and American rocker Jim Morrison.

Next stop: the nearby neighbourhood of Belleville. Having so far escaped mass-tourism, this multicultural pocket of Paris is a wonderful place to while away the afternoon searching out street art (try rue Denoyez or place Frehel) and loafing around the city's second Chinatown.

⊖ TGV trains leave Paris Gare de Lyon for Lausanne six times a day. Be aware that the last service leaves in the early evening.

―――――

Lausanne
SWITZERLAND

After the English and French capitals, Switzerland's small-scale Lausanne might seem a little provincial. Home to the country's second-oldest university, though, this lakeside city has a dynamic, youthful vibe and an outsized arts and culture scene that rivals much larger metropolises. Spend a day here, strolling the steeply stacked city centre and taking it all in.

⊖ Services from Lausanne to Milan Centrale run every two to three hours. On the way, the line runs through the Simplon Tunnel, along the shores of Lake Geneva and through scenic Swiss vineyards.

―――――

Milan
ITALY

It's true that Milan sees far fewer visitors than other Italian cities but the area around the Duomo still buzzes with people. It's easy to escape the throngs, though: just head off in any direction.

To the north is Porta Nuova, an intriguingly contemporary corner of the city. Here, architects and horticulturalists have joined forces to create the Bosco Verticale (Vertical Forest). Built in 2014, these two residential towers are covered in 20,000 trees and shrubs, sequestering carbon and forming an unusually biodiverse ecosystem in the centre of the city.

To the south is the picturesque neighbourhood of Navigli. Laced with canals, it has the looks of Venice but without the crowds. Come here to eat and drink – the waterways are lined with dozens of classic *osterie* serving an array of traditional Milanese food.

✪ Departures from Milane Centrale to Venice Santa Lucia are incredibly frequent, running every 30–60 minutes. At just two-and-a-half hours, the journey is also short in comparison to some of those to come.

Venice
ITALY

One of Europe's most popular destinations, Venice's many charms can easily be dampened by the hordes and hefty price tags. Find sanctuary on the little island of Burano, to the north of the city. Its reflective canals and pedestrianized streets are lined with some of the brightest, rainbow-hued houses you've ever seen. It's a wonderful place to amble, popping into artisans' studios as you go.

✪ Getting from Venice to Belgrade (the *Orient Express*'s usual next stop) will be the most logistically challenging part of your trip. Take an afternoon train from Venice Santa Lucia to Villach, Austria, and spend the night there. Then, board an early morning train to Zagreb, changing in the Croatian capital to travel onwards to Belgrade. The whole journey will take more than 24 hours.

DETOUR

Zagreb

As you have to change trains in Zagreb (p194) anyway, why not break up your journey with an overnight stop here? Stay in the Art Deco Esplanade Zagreb Hotel, which was built in 1925 to accommodate *Orient Express* passengers. Today, the cocktail menu pays homage to stops along the train route.

Belgrade
SERBIA

The Serbian capital, Belgrade, is one of Europe's most under-appreciated cities and its buzzy nightlife might just be the unexpected highlight of your trans-European adventure.

The most interesting corner of the city is Savamala, and if you only have time to visit one area of Belgrade (and you should really try to see more), make it this one. Sandwiched between the station and the Sava river, this area is home to historic sights, like Manak's House (this 1830 building is one of the last Eastern Balkan-style dwellings in Belgrade), and riverside warehouses, which have been converted into galleries, restaurants and clubs. Check out Breton Hala, an old customs house-turned-nightlife hot spot come evening and bring your time in Serbia to a close with a bang.

⊖ Another epic day-long journey lies ahead. First, ride a local service to the Serbian city of Niš. Overnight here, then catch a morning departure for Dimitrovgrad, Bulgaria. Trains run from here to the capital, Sofia, regularly.

Above
Food stalls at the docks in Eminönü, with Hagia Sophia in the background

Above right
A fish market in the Beşiktaş area of Istanbul

Right
The beautiful interior of Sofia's synagogue

Istanbul
TURKEY

Straddling the Bosphorus Strait, the continental dividing line, Istanbul has one foot in Europe and the other in Asia. Granted, the European side of the city is the most visited of the two thanks to big-name sights like the Hagia Sophia, Blue Mosque and Grand Bazaar. But there are still some unspoiled pockets here if you know where to look.

Swerve the bazaars and head to Eminönü's ferry port, where stalls whip up proper Turkish street food, or cross the Golden Horn to Beşiktaş. This waterfront district is a maze of narrow streets, dotted with little shops, laid-back bars and boisterous fish markets. It's a fitting end to your off-the-beaten-track, transcontinental adventure.

EXTEND
YOUR TRIP

Gebze

Istanbul's Marmaray train line runs under the Bosphorus, linking Europe and Asia. The 13.5-km (8.4-mile) undersea tunnel it speeds through is the deepest in the world, dropping to 60 m (200 ft) below sea level. The line ends by the Byzantine Eskihisar Castle, in Gebze, on the Asian side of the strait. Get off here to explore the castle and earn the bragging rights of having ridden the rails from Europe to Asia.

Sofia
BULGARIA

The Bulgarian capital's skyline is dominated by domed Orthodox churches and Ottoman mosques, but it's not just the competing influences of Christianity and Islam that have shaped Sofia. The city's Jewish heritage is a critical piece of its cultural jigsaw, too. The Jewish quarter, in the northern portion of the city centre, is home to the largest and probably most ornately decorated synagogue in southeast Europe. Next door is the Jewish Museum of History, which describes the dramatic last-minute rescue of Bulgaria's Jews during World War II. It's a great place to get to grips with a lesser-told side of the country's history.

🚆 An 11-hour sleeper train connects Sofia to Halkali station on the outskirts of Istanbul. From here, you can ride the Marmaray line to stations in the city centre, including Marmaray station itself.

Venice Simplon-Orient-Express

Ask someone to name a famous train and no doubt the *Orient Express* will be the reply. This historic service has been plying the continent in various iterations since the 19th century, the golden age of rail travel.

A grand suite, complete with a double bed and brocaded linen

When the *Orient Express* first hit the tracks in 1883, it only ran between Paris and Vienna but, as demand grew, so did the network, which soon stretched all the way from London to Istanbul. The journey fast captured the world's imagination and the train appeared in a succession of novels, including Bram Stoker's *Dracula* (1897), Agatha Christie's *Murder on the Orient Express* (1934) and Ian Fleming's *From Russia with Love* (1957).

Come the 21st century and high-speed trains and low-cost airlines saw the decline of the *Orient Express* – but it wasn't out of action for long. Hospitality company Belmond rescued and restored many of the original 1920s and 30s carriages, setting them to work as the *Venice Simplon-Orient-Express*.

The distinctive blue-and-gold carriages contain a world of opulence. Panelled with intricate marquetry, upholstered in velvet and replete with monogrammed linens, these Art Deco beauties live up to all of your preconceptions about this legendarily luxurious train.

There's still no finer way to travel from Venice to Paris. Sit back and let the stewards, dressed in smart navy uniforms or gleaming gold-button tunics, wait on you. Tuck into a decadent meal in one of the three dining cars, listen to whoever's tinkling the keys in the brocaded piano lounge or simply watch the world go by from your sleeping car.

THE PRACTICALITIES

The *Venice Simplon-Orient-Express* runs on multiple routes, but the classic overnight journey from Venice to Paris is still the most popular. There are regular departures from March to December, and tickets are available from Belmond and several travel companies. There are two classes of sleeping cars: Historic Cabins and Grand Suites. The former are cheaper and offer a more authentic experience, complete with a convertible sofa-berth, while the latter have a double bed and en suite.

www.belmond.com

03

Algarve Beach Hop

Algarve's seaside towns and cities are served by not one but four rail lines, making it easy to whizz along Portugal's sunshine-spoilt southern coast. Stop at these towns and beaches along the way.

▶ **LAGOS** PORTUGAL ⊙ **TAVIRA** PORTUGAL

🚋 BUY INDIVIDUAL TICKETS FOR EACH LEG OF THIS ROUTE AT STATIONS OR ONLINE (P249).

🕐 5–7 DAYS ⚲ 115 KM (71 MILES)

Lagos

With its irresistible blonde beaches, hemmed in by cinematic stacks of golden rock, Lagos is the perfect place to start your tour of the Algarve. The jewel in the town's coastal crown is Praia do Camilo, which is bookended by dramatic arches and honeycombed cliffs. These rock formations were carved by the robust Atlantic waves that have made this area a favourite haunt of surfers. And they're not the only fans – Lagos is one of the Algarve's most popular tourist destinations.

There's much more in the way of cultural attractions than you might expect from what is essentially a beach town. Walk the city walls, learn about Lagos's seafaring history at the Centro Ciêna Viva de Lagos and discover the region's grim connection to slavery at the Antigo Mercado de Escravos, where enslaved people were traded between 1444 and 1761.

 Trains depart from Lagos Central to Faro eight times a day. Try to sit by the window so you can soak up the scenery en route.

> DETOUR
> ## Portimão
>
> Just a 20-minute train ride from Lagos is the Algarve's second city, Portimão. Get to grips with the region's history at the cutting-edge Museu de Portimão, which explores how the sea has shaped the region.

Praia do Camilo, a beautiful beach to the south of Lagos

Lagos

1 hr 40 mins

Faro

40 mins

Tavira

Faro

Many travellers hurry through Faro, the capital of the Algarve, but this charming city is much more than just a transport hub. Stay a while and you'll discover Baroque churches and medieval mansions, lazy lagoons and perfect beaches.

Despite Faro's big-city feel, its compact centre is exactly that – compact. On the mosaic-paved pedestrianized streets, you'll find the Igreja de Nossa Senhora do Carmo, with its façade like a frosted cake topped with lemon, and the excellent Museu Municipal de Faro.

🚌 It's a short 40-minute hop from Faro Central to Tavira, with services departing hourly. The train's final destination is Vila Real de Santo António, so look for that on the station's information boards.

Tavira

Don't be surprised if you spend longer than planned in the pretty town of Tavira. Days vanish as you amble along the broad Rio Gilão or lounge on Ilha de Tavira's idyllic beach (a short ferry ride away). The town's churches are a delight, too: visit the art-filled Igreja Matriz de Santiago or the Igreja da Misericórdia, which hosts haunting performances of fado, Portugal's answer to the blues. You won't want your Algarve adventure to end.

Igreja Matriz de Santiago, one of the many white-washed churches in Tavira

Braga
30–60 mins

Porto
1 hr 15 mins–2 hrs

Coimbra
2 hrs 40 mins–4 hrs 40 mins

Sintra
45 mins

Lisbon (Lisboa)
1 hr 30 mins–1 hr 40 mins

Évora

04

Best of Portugal

On this week-long rail adventure around Portugal, you'll discover hilltop castles and hidden catacombs, *pastéis de nata* and port, and Porto and Lisbon – two of Europe's most captivating cities.

⦿ BRAGA PORTUGAL ◯ ÉVORA PORTUGAL

⦿ BOOK TICKETS AT LEAST 8 DAYS IN ADVANCE TO TAKE ADVANTAGE OF THE LOWEST FARES (P249).

⦿ 7-10 DAYS ⦿ 598 KM (372 MILES)

Braga

Dominated by the country's oldest cathedral, and characterized by its countless churches, Braga is Portugal's beating sacred heart and the perfect place to start your voyage of discovery. Spend even just a day here and you'll soon become aware of the weight of ecclesiastical power, embodied by an archbishop's palace built on a truly presidential scale and religious festivities that hijack daily life for weeks on end.

Perched on a hill 5 km (3 miles) to the east of the city centre is arguably Braga's most impressive symbol of devotion – the Santuário do Bom Jesus do Monte. To reach the sanctuary at the top of the slope, you must first climb the zig-zagging Baroque *escadaria* (stairway), which resembles the bellows of an accordion. The most pious pilgrims ascend the 577 steps on their knees.

⊖ Services bound for Porto's Campanha station, including fast Alfa Pendular express trains, depart every 30–90 mins from Braga.

DETOUR
Aveiro

Halfway between Porto and Coimbra is the charming coastal city of Aveiro. Famous for its network of canals, which are lined with brightly coloured houses and plied by equally vibrant barges traditionally used by seaweed foragers, Aveiro is a delightful place to wander.

Douro Historical Train

The steam-powered *Douro Historical Train* runs through the Douro Valley between Régua and Tua, to the east of Porto, from June to October. Onboard, passengers sip port and snack on local delicacies while listening to live music and soaking up wonderful views of the wine lodges and vineyards as they pass by the window.

Porto

Portugal's second city exudes the slightly ramshackle charm and maritime bustle of a working harbour town. And nowhere is that more apparent than in Ribeira. Despite being rejuvenated after Porto was declared European Capital of Culture in 2000, this riverside *bairro* (neighbourhood) has an olde-worlde feel with its pastel-hued, stacked houses and wooden *rabelos*. These traditional cargo boats still transport precious barrels of port from the vineyards of the Douro Valley to the wine cellars of Vila Nova de Gaia (technically a separate city, on the other side of the Douro to Porto), just as they have done since the 18th century.

It doesn't take long to explore Porto's higgledy-piggledy city centre, pausing to take in its biggest cultural attractions: the imposing cathedral and the history-spanning art collections of the Museu Nacional Soares dos Reis and the Fundação Serralves. But a trip to Porto isn't about careering around the sights – it's about slowly cruising along the Douro, sipping port at a historic winery like the Quinta das Carvalhas and taking your time over the city's favourite dish – the *francesinha*. A conglomeration of sausage, steak and ham, cocooned in bread and melted cheese, and doused in a tomato and beer sauce, this may just be the world's greatest sandwich.

🚆 Trains leave Campanha station twice hourly for Coimbra-B station, on the city's northern fringes. Change here for Coimbra station, which is in the city centre.

Coimbra

Although it's a lot smaller than Porto, Coimbra is no less steeped in history. It was the birthplace of six kings and served as the Portuguese capital from 1139 to 1256. It's also the site of the country's oldest university, the Universidade de Coimbra, which has sat on a hilltop overlooking the city since 1290. Don't miss the Biblioteca Joanina, the university's seriously inspiring library, which is decked out in dark woods and crammed from floor to ceiling with ancient tomes and treatises.

It's thanks to the university's lively 20,000-strong student population that the steeply stacked Old Town oozes joie de vivre as well as history. Here, *repúblicas* (student halls) are scribbled with street art, clubs

Above
A geometrically tiled cloister in the Universidade de Coimbra

Previous page
A metro train crossing over Dom Luís I Bridge, Porto

throng with youngsters making merry after handing in their latest assignments and gown-clad students croon Coimbra's jaunty version of fado (Portugal's answer to the blues).

🚆 Catch one of the regular departures from Coimbra to Coimbra-B, where you can change onto a train bound for Lisboa - Oriente. From here, slow but scenic Urbano services crawl to Sintra.

Sintra

Famed for its colourful catalogue of palaces and lush hillside setting, Sintra is a must-stop. You won't be alone, mind you; tourists throng the town, often overwhelming its charms. But don't let that put you off, the sights here are too good to miss.

The highlights include the Palácio Nacional de Sintra – a gleaming white mishmash of Moorish and Manueline architecture set in the pastel-hued Sintra-Vila (town centre). A short but winding walk takes you from here to Quinta da Regaleira, a romantic palace and grotto-filled park dreamed up by an eccentric millionaire. On the other side of the town is the Castelo dos Mouros, a precipitous castle built by the Moors. Topping them all is the Palácio Nacional da Pena, the emblem of Sintra. Like something straight out of a twisted fairytale, this medley of lemon-yellow, brick-red and purply-grey towers and domes rises from the forested slopes of the Serra de Sintra, a vast, untamed mountain range.

It's possible to hit all of Sintra's palaces in a day by jumping on and off the tourist bus, though

It's thanks to the Universidade de Coimbra's lively 20,000-strong student population that the steeply stacked Old Town oozes joie de vivre as well as history.

two days will make it easier to visit them early in the morning or late in the day when visitor numbers are at their lowest.

🚆 Every 5–30 mins, trains leave Sintra for Lisbon's Rossio station. The station is in the Baixa area, right in the centre of Lisbon, and is well connected to other parts of the capital (including Belém) by local Urbano services and the city's excellent metro system.

The fantastically colourful exterior of the Palácio Nacional da Pena, Sintra

Above left
Alfama, Lisbon's oldest neighbourhood, tumbling down the hill from the Castelo de São Jorge

Above right
Trams trundling through Lisbon's historic streets

Lisbon

Situated on a succession of hills (supposedly seven) on the northern bank of the Tejo river, Lisbon grew rich on transatlantic trade – slavery, in particular – in the 15th and 16th centuries. It's still grappling with this problematic history, but Portugal's capital is now largely a forward-thinking, socially conscious city, in large part thanks to the arrival of digital nomads from all over the world.

The city's terracotta-roofed and azulejo-crusted historic centre is compact and split into several neighbourhoods. The oldest part is Alfama, a lovely labyrinth of cobbled streets dating back to Moorish times that largely survived the devastating 1755 earthquake. Aside from its many *miradouros* (viewpoints), the main attraction here is the spectacularly sited Castelo de São Jorge. The castle grants amazing views of the nightlife-oriented Bairro Alto (upper town), which sits on a slope opposite. In the valley between these two hills is the Baixa (lower town) – a neat grid of grand 18th-century buildings that was erected when this part of the city was flattened by the earthquake. For a whistle-stop tour of the centre's highlights, ride the vintage Tram 28, which rattles through Baixa and neighbouring Estrela before trundling up Alfama's hills.

Beyond the centre, your time is best spent strolling around the riverside suburb of Belém, which is home to some wonderful museums, including the Museum of Art, Architecture and Technology (MAAT) and the contemporary art-filled Museu Coleção Berardo. It's also here

that you'll find the Mosteiro dos Jéronimos, which is decorated with symbols from virtually every corner of the empire and was funded largely through its spoils. A short walk away is Pastéis de Belém, which still makes custard tarts according to a secret recipe devised by Jerónimos monks in the 19th century. You can't leave Lisbon without having one.

🚇 Ride the metro from the city centre to Sete Rios in Lisbon's northern suburbs. Intercidades services run five times a day from here to Évora.

Évora

In a country replete with gorgeous historic towns, Évora eclipses them all. From the cinematic columns of the Roman Temple of Diana to the Moorish maze of tangled alleys, called evocative names like the "Alley of the Unshaven Man" and "Street of the Countess's Tailor", the past is palpable as you walk through this whitewashed, walled city. The ghosts of Évora's history are perhaps no more evident than in the Capela dos Ossos, an eerie 16th-century catacomb whose walls are covered with bones exhumed from over 5,000 graves.

This city is far from dead, however; thanks to a daily influx of excited visitors, it's always buzzing with hungry mouths looking to sample the bountiful produce of the Alentejo (the region that calls Évora its capital). Make your last meal of the tour a *carne de porco à alentejana* (a stew of potatoes, pork and clams) or *ensopado de Borrego*, a hearty lamb stew.

EXTEND
YOUR TRIP

Algarve

From Évora, continue south to the Algarve *(p.32)*, the famously sunny region that occupies Portugal's southern coast. It takes around three hours to reach Lagos, which has all the golden beaches you could hope for, as well as a fascinating historic core.

Bilbao

3 hrs

Santander

3 hrs

Ribadesella

2 hrs

Oviedo

7 hrs 20 mins

Ferrol

05

Slow Spain

Ride the narrow-gauge FEVE line to experience Spain's northern coast at a sightseer's speed. The train dawdles at over 100 stations and crawls by rolling hills, dramatic beachside cliffs, and dynamic towns and cities.

▶ **BILBAO** SPAIN ◯ **FERROL** SPAIN

⊕ UNMARKED ON MOST SPANISH RAILWAY MAPS, FEVE IS A DIVISIONOF STATE-OWNED RENFE (P249).

🕐 7-10 DAYS 📍 629 KM (391 MILES)

Bilbao

Bilbao is a Cinderella story if there ever was one. With the opening of the spectacular titanium-clad Guggenheim Museum in 1997, this smoggy city began a decade-long transformation into a beautiful, cultural metropolis, graced with architectural masterpieces and stellar street art. The centre is nestled in an elbow of the Río Nervión and surrounded by green mountains, earning it the nickname *botxo* (the Basque for "hole").

You'll need a few days to explore all Bilbao has to offer, and to settle into a rhythm of eat, drink, sightsee, repeat. The city is famous for its food, which ranges from Michelin star-studded dishes to humble *pintxos* (small eats). The labyrinthine Zazpikaleak, the medieval old quarter, hides some gastronomic jewels, including La Ribera market, Europe's largest covered food market.

🚄 Three FEVE services depart daily from Bilbao-Abando station to Santander.

Santander

Each summer, Santander sees
its population swell as well-to-
do city dwellers descend on its
beaches. This annual migration
started in the 20th century,
when King Alfonso XII and Queen
Victoria Eugenia built a summer
palace here. Marvel at their
English-inspired Palacio de la
Magdalena, which looks onto the
sunbathers on El Sardinero below.
This, the town's main beach, gets
its name from the huge quantity
of sardines fished from the cold
waters of the Bahía de Santander,
the protected bay that the city
envelopes. To sample some of the
bounteous catch, make a beeline for the Barrio Pesquero, the
fishing neighbourhood to the
south of the centre, come dinner
time (which is late in Spain). Here,
these fish are served straight
from the grill, garnished with
nothing but a dash of sea salt
and a bit of olive oil.

❷ There are two FEVE services to
Ribadesella each day.

Ribadesella

Due to its strategic position
where the Río Sella meets
the Cantabrian Sea, the small
town of Ribadesella has been
populated since Palaeolithic
times. Its outsized history is
depicted in six tiled murals by
Antonio Mingote, distributed
along the Paseo de la Grúa, the
waterfront promenade.
    Ribadesella is so small that
you'll easily scoot around it in a
morning, leaving you enough time
to explore the wild, snaggletooth

DETOUR
Gijón

Asturias' largest city, Gijón is just a 30-minute ride from Oviedo. Its highlight is the fascinatingly esoteric Museum of Asturian People, where you can brush up on the region's history.

biggest names on the scene is Nacho Manzano, who has three Michelin stars. Sample his cooking at Gloria, Nastura or NM.

It's over seven hours from Oviedo to Ferrol, so board the morning service to arrive at your next destination in the mid-afternoon.

peaks of the nearby Parque Nacional de Los Picos de Europa.

There are three or four departures for Oviedo per day, taking in some of northern Spain's most dramatic scenery en route.

Oviedo

Founded as a monastery in 757, the capital of the Asturias region is one of the few places in Spain never captured by the Moors. The Catedral Metropolitana Basílica de San Salvador sits on the site of the original monastery and is the starting point of the Camino Primitivo, the oldest route of the Camino de Santiago pilgrimage. Today, Oviedo attracts pilgrims of a different sort — hungry visitors seeking a taste of Asturias' rich and varied cuisine. One of the

Ferrol

Once a sleepy fishing village, Ferrol's fortunes changed forever when King Philip V chose it to be the site for a naval base in 1726. Engineers designed the Barrio da Magdalena, the ordered grid that acts as the city centre, at this time. In the early 1900s, Modernist architects reimagined the cityscape, adding the Jofre Theatre, Magdalena's Fish Market and the Town Hall. A self-guided walking tour takes in these marvellous buildings.

Ferrol can be seen in a day but, after being lulled into a leisurely pace by the FEVE, a few days may feel more apt. Then, you'll have time to explore the wild beaches north of the city. Start at wind-swept Praia de Lumebó, then wind your way up the coast, coming to a stop at the Cabo Prior lighthouse, which looks out towards North America It's a fitting place to end your journey on Europe's longest narrow-gauge track.

El Transcantábrico Gran Lujo

It may cover the same ground as the FEVE line *(p40)*, but the luxurious and fast-paced *El Transcantábrico Gran Lujo* provides a completely different experience. If you want to see northern Spain in style, this is the train for you.

El Transcantábrico Gran Lujo, operated by FEVE, rolling along the coast

Each year, hundreds of thousands of people trudge along the iconic Camino de Santiago or trundle across country on public transport to get from San Sebastián to Santiago de Compostela. Overtake them all on *El Transcantábrico Gran Lujo*, a sumptuous private train that glides effortlessly between the two cities.

The eight-day trip strikes the perfect balance between leisurely onboard time and on-the-ground sightseeing, with the train rolling into a new station each morning. Here, you can disembark and explore the stop, making sure to sample some local dishes while you're there. Northern Spain is home to some of the country's best produce, so food serves as a focal point for the trip.

The journey between stops is a world away from that onboard the FEVE. Settle into a plush window-facing seat in the lounge car with a cup of *café con leche* (coffee) or a refreshing gin and tonic, and watch northern Spain's verdant landscape roll by. Decked in darkwood and accented by stained glass and velvet upholstery, the lovingly restored 1923 blue-and-white Pullman carriages are reminiscent of Spain's old-school *paradores* (historical buildings turned five-star hotels). The train has all the modern comforts, though, with each of the 14 suites featuring sprawling private bathrooms with hydromassage tubs. There's really no more comfortable way to travel across northern Spain.

THE PRACTICALITIES

El Transcantábrico Gran Lujo runs from San Sebastián to Santiago de Compostela between April and October. Tickets are available directly on the Renfe site, as well as through the Reservation Centre (0034 91 255 59 12) and via email, trenesturisticosdelujo@renfe.es.
The sleeping cars are all called Gran Lujo suites and have their own sitting room, bathroom and sleeping area, and either double or twin beds.

www.renfe.com

06

The Spirit of al-Andalus

This week-long rail trip around Andalucía takes in some of Europe's most magnificent buildings. It's all the work of the Moors, who ruled much of the Iberian peninsula (then referred to as al-Andalus) in medieval times.

▶ SEVILLE SPAIN ○ GRANADA SPAIN

◉ RENFE RUNS SPAIN'S RAIL NETWORK (P249). IF YOU FIND THE WEBSITE DIFFICULT TO NAVIGATE, USE A THIRD-PARTY SITE (P10).

● 5-7 DAYS ◉ 324 KM (201 MILES)

Seville

Seville is both the perfect place to start your al-Andalus adventure and the worst – it's near impossible to tear yourself away from this city and continue your journey east. Andalucía's capital enchants with its near-constant sun, citrus-scented streets and sumptuous Moorish architecture.

After conquering the city in 712 CE, the Moors spent the next 500 years reimagining the cityscape. The Arabic rulers enlarged the principal mosque (later supplanted by the Gothic cathedral), erected La Giralda (a towering minaret that now serves as the cathedral's bell tower), and ornamented and enlarged the

Roman fortress now known as the Real Alcázar. Despite their work, the majority of the Real Alcázar complex seen today dates from the 14th century, when Christian kings rebuilt it using fragments from other Moorish buildings. With its intricately carved arches, gilded ceiling beams and jewel-like tiles, the result is a perfect marriage of Muslim and Christian architecture, known as Mudéjar.

Roaming Seville's streets, dipping in and out of these buildings and the city's many tapas bars, is a fine way to spend your time here. Be sure to try *montadito* (a small sandwich stuffed with Iberian ham and peppers), *espinacas con garbanzos* (a spinach and chickpea stew that

The Alhambra, Andalucía's most famous Moorish sight, perched high above Granada

Seville (Sevilla)

45 mins–1 hr 20 mins

Córdoba

1 hr 20 mins–2 hrs

Granada

candy-cane Caliphal arches, its interior still looks more like a mosque than a cathedral, despite the crucifixes. Keep returning to it throughout your stay; you'll find its beauty increases with each visit.

Nearby is the Alcázar de los Reyes Cristianos, a 14th-century palace-fortress that now hosts evening flamenco performances (Tue–Sun), so finish your day here.

🚉 There are two hourly departures from Córdoba Central to Granada. Maximize your time by boarding a direct service rather than changing in Málaga.

dates back to Moorish times) and gazpacho. This cold soup is just the thing on a sweltering Seville day.

🚉 Trains for Córdoba Central depart from Sevilla Santa Justa at least twice per hour. To save money, ride the slower service, rather than the AVE fast train.

Córdoba

The influence of Andalucía's Muslim and Christian heritage is also instantly recognizable in Córdoba. Its Old Town is full of Moorish-style whitewashed houses and mosques that have been turned into churches, but make your first stop the Mezquita.

Built as a mosque in the 8th century, when Córdoba was the capital of al-Andalus, this vast building became the city's cathedral almost overnight in 1236 when Christians took back the city. With its red-and-white

Granada

Your journey climaxes in Granada, home to one of the world's most beautiful buildings. The Moors set out to replicate paradise on earth in the Alhambra and, with its honeycombed stonework, reflective pools and ornately carved wooden ceilings, some would say they succeeded.

Built on the slopes of three hills, the rest of the city sits in the Alhambra's shadow and many visitors skip Granada's other sights all together. It's a pity as, unlike elsewhere in Andalucía, the trappings of everyday Moorish life seem to have survived here. The Old Town is peppered with fabric-strewn teahouses and restaurants serving up dishes like *remojón* (a salad of orange, spring onion, cod and olives). The spirit of al-Andalus still lives on in Andalucía.

07

The Med

The sun-drenched drama of the Mediterranean is best seen by following the train tracks in a banana-shaped arc from Spain to Italy. Expect a daily dose of art and architecture, fine food and laid-back life.

▶ **MÁLAGA** SPAIN ◯ **NAPLES** ITALY

🚆 TRAVEL BETWEEN SPAIN, FRANCE, MONACO AND ITALY WITH AN INTERRAIL OR EURAIL PASS (P11). CHECK THE DIRECTORY FOR INFORMATION ON EACH COUNTRY'S RAIL NETWORK (P242).

🕐 18-21 DAYS 📍 2,857 KM (1,775 MILES)

Málaga

5–6 hrs

Valencia

3 hrs

Barcelona

3 hrs

Montpellier

1 hr 45 mins

Marseille

3 hrs 30 mins

Monte Carlo

3 hrs

Genoa (Genova)

2 hrs 30 mins

Livorno

5 hrs

Naples (Napoli)

Málaga

SPAIN

Squishing southern Spain's biggest draws (boundary-pushing art, golden beaches and good food) into a few square kilometres, well-connected Málaga makes a fine introduction to the region.

The tangle of streets that make up the city centre radiates from the Plaza de la Constitución, the city's main square, which is lined with tall palm trees and stately 17th- and 18th-century buildings. Within this compact area is a series of interesting churches and museums, the Museo Picasso Málaga being a particular stand-out. The artist was born in Málaga, and here, in his former home, is an important collection of his works, ordered thematically

and chronologically. The Cubist paintings are particularly iconic and worth a closer look.

You'll easily scoot around the centre in a day, so spend the rest of your time exploring beyond its confines. To the west is the edgy Soho neighbourhood, filled with street art and skateboarders, to the east a string of sun-drenched beaches (16 in total), with cafés, restaurants and bars serving up refreshingly icy drinks and lip-smacking seafood fresh from the Med.

🚆 It's a long but picturesque ride from Málaga María Zambrano station to Valencia, but direct services are mercifully regular, with departures every two hours. Despite both cities being on the coast, the tracks cut inland to Córdoba and Cuenca before returning to the sea.

Valencia

SPAIN

From the birthplace of Picasso to the birthplace of paella. Spain's national dish originated in Valencia ("paella" means frying pan in *llengua valencia*, the regional language) and to come here without trying it at its most authentic would be a crime. Two things to remember: paella is a dish eaten at lunchtime not dinner, and chorizo never makes an appearance – instead expect a help-yourself platter of rice, topped with chicken, rabbit, green beans and whatever else is in season.

Paella aside, Valencia is known for being laid-back, cultured and cosmopolitan. Here, you're best doing as the locals do: hike or bike along the ribbon of green parkland that snakes through the centre, lounge on the (nearly always) sunny stretch of sand, and admire the city's remarkable architecture, including the ultra-modern Cuidad de las Artes y Ciencias and Baroque Palacio del Marqués de Dos Agüas.

🚆 Trains from the modernistic Valencia-Joaquín Sorolla station run along the sea towards Barcelona-Sants station every hour. Sit on the left-hand side for the best views.

Barcelona

SPAIN

After Málaga and Valencia, Barcelona can seem overcrowded and that's because it's a place

Overlooking Barcelona from Parc Güell, one of Gaudí's creations

of pilgrimage for so many. Those who appreciate architecture railroad in to see Gaudí's madcap cathedral, dream-like dwellings and fantastic Parc Güell. Football fans arrive to catch a game at the legendary Camp Nou stadium (conveniently located right by Sants station). And artists are caught between the galleries dedicated to Joan Miró, Pablo Picasso and Catalán contemporary art. The buzz of Barcelona can beguile visitors for weeks, so don't rush through it.

This is a city to savour, especially when it comes to mealtimes. Visitors dine out on *escudella i carn d'olla* (a winter stew of pasta, meat and seasonal vegetables) or *faves a la catalana* (a summertime salad featuring beans), all the while sipping sparkling cava or Barcelona-brewed Estrella. Better still, each district – or *barrio* – has its own flavour. Follow your nose to Gracia, to the north, full of vermouth bars and vegan cafés,

or make your way to Poble Sec, at the foot of Montjuic, for traditional tapas joints.

🚄 Each day, four direct trains speed between Barcelona-Sants and Montpellier St-Roch in three hours.

Montpellier
FRANCE

Montpellier provides a gentle introduction to France. Aside from a visit to the Musée Fabre art museum, take time here to appreciate life's simple pleasures. Read more of that book or watch the world go by as you sip a *café au lait* (coffee with milk) or iced *pastis* (anise-flavoured aperitif) in front of botanical gardens, honey-stone cathedrals and romantic *hôtels particuliers*, all sited in the tightly knit historic centre.

Whittle away further days on the soft sand beaches in striking distance of the city, diving, paddleboarding or kitesurfing, if you like.

🚊 Hourly trains from Montpellier St-Roch run through lagoons coloured pink by flamboyances of flamingos en route to Marseille St-Charles station.

Marseille
FRANCE

Hugging a sheltered bay, Marseille was first established as a Greek trading colony and has sat at a crossroads ever since. France's second city, it has direct train services to Spain and Italy, boats to Algeria and flights to Senegal. Its accessibility has gifted it diversity, especially when it comes to food, and the Noailles neighbourhood serves up some of the best.

Start your adventure at the area's Marché des Capucins, where stalls sell olives, dried fruit and spices. Then wind your way past little stores selling North African fabrics and ceramics, and more food stalls, to the nearby Vieux Port. Here, you'll find the Marché aux Poissons fish market, where you can learn how to make *bouillabaisse* (the city's soulful

seafood dish). You'll also find Mucem here, an interactive museum exploring the history of the Mediterranean and the people who have made it their home.

🚊 Marseille's subtropical station (complete with palm trees) has hourly services to Nice, from where connections to Monte Carlo depart every 30 minutes.

Monte Carlo
MONACO

Unless you have money to burn, don't plan on staying in a hotel or apartment in Monaco. Instead, treat this postcard-sized principality as a way to break up the long journey from France to Italy. It won't take you more than 45 minutes to walk across Monte Carlo, one of the four *quartiers* (sections) of Monaco – and that's all the time needed to prove that this city-state is one of the richest places on Earth. The Gare de Monaco-Monte-Carlo train station is glitzy enough but it's not a patch on the opulent hotels and casinos here, where gamblers bet thousands of euros each day. And then there's the Port du Monaco. At any one time, a billion

The grand exterior of the Casino de Monte Carlo

DETOUR

Cassis

Although it's only a 45-minute train ride from Marseille, Cassis feels a world away. This tranquil beach resort is enveloped by the Parc National des Calanques, a breathtaking land-sea national park. Take an e-boat ride to spot sea life or hike the park's fjord-like *calanques* (creeks). One walking trail runs all the way back to Marseille.

dollars worth of yachts are moored in this marina – some even have helipads, spas and submarines.

Connections from Monte Carlo to the Italian border town of Ventimiglia depart every 30-60 minutes, from where hourly trains hug the coastline on their way to Genoa.

Genoa
ITALY

Once a trading empire and one of the world's wealthiest cities, Genoa today feels a little rough around the edges, particularly after the glitz of Monte Carlo. It's still a working port (Italy's largest), after all. The old centre, to the north of the historic Porto Antico, is a web of *caruggi* (narrow alleys lined with tall, peeling dwellings). But reminders of the city's grandeur remain, hidden in plain sight. Find paintings by Caravaggio and Rubens in dimly lit churches and ceilings literally painted gold in museums like the Palazzo Reale.

Spend a day getting lost in the *caruggi* and another on the petite beaches of Boccadasse. Once a friendly fishing village, it's since been swallowed up by the city and become a sandy suburb.

Fast express trains and cheaper regional services meander along the Mediterranean coast from Genoa Piazza Principe station to Livorno Centrale every 30-60 minutes.

Livorno
ITALY

Two days is more than enough time to get acquainted with this beguiling port city, built around a series of forts and magnificent harbours. The compact centre is sandwiched between the sea and Venezia Nuova. Named after Venice, this district promises canals, bridges, boats and knockout seafood (look out for swordfish gnocchi).

Before moving on to Naples, make a day trip to Costiera di Calafuria. Buses take just 35 minutes to reach this scenic stretch of coast, where you can walk the pine-lined trails or swim in the beautifully clear water.

Fast hourly trains from Livorno Centrale station whizz down Italy's west coast to Naples, with a quick change in Rome.

Naples
ITALY

As tempting as it is to just get lost in this cacophonous city's labyrinth of streets – ducking down alleys, pausing to admire once grand façades and politically charged street art, devour pizza and sip spritz – make your way beyond the Centro Storico to the hilltop neighbourhood of Vomero.

Reached by funicular, the once genteel Vomero is a delight to wander, its ordered grid of streets and squares (often named after local cultural heroes) revealing glimpses of the city below. For the best views, make your way to Certosa di San Martino, perched atop the eponymous Vomero hill. This monastery-turned-museum grants sweeping views of Naples, the looming Vesuvius and the sweeping coastline, your con-stant companion on this tour of Mediterranean Europe's finest. On clear days, perhaps you'll make out a distant island – the beautiful Capri, Procida and Ischia beckon those tempted to extend their tour by another week.

Looking over Naples towards Mount Vesuvius from Vomero hill

EXTEND YOUR TRIP

Amalfi Coast

Continue south to Sorrento, the jumping-off point for the Amalfi Coast. With its charming seaside towns and rugged cliffs lapped by deep blue waters, the coastline feels a world away from Naples. Top pick of the towns is hilltop Ravello, where Villa Cimbrone's statue-lined belvedere grants fantastic views of the coast.

08

○ Girona

39 mins

○ Barcelona

35 mins

○ Tarragona

2 hrs

○ Valencia

1hr 50 mins

● Madrid

Essential Spain

Steep yourself in Spanish culture on this tour of the country's big hitters. Home to centuries of history and world-class museums – not to mention fabulous food and beaches – these cities never fail to delight.

▶ **GIRONA** SPAN ○ **MADRID** SPAN

● BUY INDIVIDUAL TICKETS FOR EACH LEG OF THE JOURNEY; PRICES VARY ACCORDING TO THE SPEED OF SERVICE (P249).

● 7-9 DAYS ● 822 KM (511 MILES)

Girona

With its colourful houses neatly arranged along the Onyar river, the medieval city of Girona almost seems out of place in Catalunya. It feels, instead, more reminiscent of Italy. Florence, perhaps. But a stroll to the heart of the old quarter leaves no doubt that this is a distinctly Catalán city.

Located at the confluence of four rivers, Girona became a hub for trade and intercultural exchange due to its strategic position. As a result, the city fell under the control of a succession of occupying powers – the Romans, the Visigoths and the Moors – whose influences you can see all around. Barri Vell, the Old

Town of Girona, is the most well-preserved Old Town in Spain, with over 2,000 years of history. Right at Girona's heart, it is a great place to begin the first day of your tour. Get a feel for the city with a stroll around the medieval streets, then call in to Girona Cathedral, an architectural wonder that took nearly 700 years to complete.

Just a short walk north, you'll find the 12th-century Moorish baths, Banys Árabs. When the Moors occupied Spain, they not only constructed a number of lavish palaces, but they also built ornately decorated bathhouses, a tradition from North Africa. This example is not only jaw-droppingly beautiful, but also the ideal place to unwind and relax after a day of exploration.

⊖ Trains for Barcelona-Sants, Barcelona's main train station, leave roughly every hour and run through the Catalán countryside.

Barcelona

Spain's second-largest city is often the first (or indeed the only) place on people's Europe wishlists. You need at least two days to experience Barcelona to the full, but even the time-crunched can get a taste for what it has to offer.

The highlight of this coastal city is undoubtedly the architecture of Antoni Gaudí, a Catalán architect who built a series of quirky masterpieces in the late 19th century. He was part of the Modernisme movement, an avant-garde form of artistic and literary expression that emerged in Catalunya around the same time as the Art Nouveau movement. You're probably familiar with Gaudí's La Sagrada Familia, an unfinished basilica in the Eixample district, whose 18 towering spires are visible from all corners of Barcelona. Then there's the colourful, cartoonish Park Güell, where a stroll around its natural trails reveals a reptile-shaped fountain and gingerbread-style houses. The park is perched on a hill in the Gaudí neighbour-hood, just north of Casa Batlló and Casa Milà, two further resi-dences that Gaudí constructed in the early 20th century. These multistorey, stone structures incorporate snake-like curves at every level, protruding balcon-ies, and rooftops with eccentric sculptures. Handily, the buildings are located just a five-minute walk from each other so you can easily see them both in one go.

Orange-hued houses along the bank of the Onyar river in Girona

Beyond touring Modernista architecture, your time in the city is best spent wandering the medieval streets of the Gothic Quarter, just south of Casa Milà. Here you'll discover over 2,000 years of history, with Roman buildings marked by the Visigoths, and dimly lit streets that carry an eerie and mysterious aura. Packed with family-owned bars and restaurants, this is also a great place to get a taste of Catalán cuisine.

🚆 Head to Barcelona-Sants station to continue your journey south. Trains for Tarragona leave around every 30 minutes.

Tarragona

Arriving in Tarragona, you might feel for a moment that you've been transported back to ancient Rome – until the whizz of cars and modern trappings of life jolt you back to reality. Once a colony of the Roman Empire, the city was originally known as Tarraco, from which the word Tarragona is derived. It may not be the only Roman city in Spain, but it was the very first and is arguably the most intact.

While there's a plethora of Roman structures dotted around the city, you can tick off the main ones in a day. Start at the Roman Amphitheatre, a magnificent, multilevel arena that could fit over 10,000 spectators in its heyday. Just down the street is the Roman Circus, where the locals held chariot races. This is one of the best-preserved circuses in Europe, despite the fact that new structures were built on top of it as the city industrialized.

🚆 You'll have to change at Barcelona-Sants station to continue your journey to Valencia. Trains leave approximately every hour.

Valencia

Besides being the birthplace of paella, the port city of Valencia is also home to some of the country's most pristine beaches. The city traces its origins back to the 1st century, when it was founded as a Roman colony.

The remarkable Ciudad de las Artes y las Ciencias complex in Valencia

Madrid may initially seem more subdued than Barcelona, but Spain's capital city is anything but dull.

Ruled by the Visigoths and the Moors before the Spanish Monarchs took over, the city today reflects myriad cultural and culinary influences.

Valencia's history has also been shaped by the Turia river, whose original path was diverted south after a devastating flood in the 1950s. To fill the vast swathe of land where the river used to flow, the Valencian government built Turia Gardens, the largest urban park in Spain. This green oasis contrasts sharply with the city's architectural attractions, which range from the historic Plaza de la Virgen and Lonja de la Ceda (a former silk market) in the Old Town to the strikingly modern Ciudad de las Artes y las Ciencias. This massive complex houses an array of over-the-top, futuristic buildings, including the largest aquarium in Europe, an opera house and a science museum.

🚆 Trains for Madrid depart from Valencia every 30–50 minutes.

Madrid

Madrid may initially seem more subdued than Barcelona, but Spain's capital city is anything but dull. With its lush green parks and distinct neighbourhoods, Madrid can keep you busy for months. Numerous national monuments and museums are found here,

including the Prado, home to the largest collection of Goya and Velazquez paintings, and the Reina Sofia, where you can view Picasso's larger-than-life master-piece, *Guernica*. The good news is that the must-see spots are clustered in the city centre, so you can easily cover them in a day or two.

Begin your tour of the city on Gran Via, the most iconic street in Madrid. It slices through several neighbourhoods and connects many of the city's main attractions, like the rooftop bar at Circulo de Bellas Artes, the historic city square of Plaza Mayor and the 3,000-room Royal Palace. El Botin, the oldest continuously running restaurant in the world, is on a side street – make a reservation to taste the restaurant's traditional Spanish dishes.

Madrid's bustling food markets are central to its food culture, so set aside some time for exploring them, too. Each market offers a window into the neighbourhood where it's located. Relax with a *tinto* (red wine) at Mercado de San Antón in LGBTQ+-friendly Chueca or sample Japanese fusion creations at the Mercado de San Ildefonso in offbeat Malasaña. Round off with some speciality cheeses at Mercado de la Paz, located further north in upscale Salamanca.

The ornate shopfront of a typical restaurant in Madrid's city centre

EXTEND YOUR TRIP

Andorra

Catalunya isn't the only place to discover Catalán culture. Make the epic one-day journey north from Madrid to the land-locked country of Andorra, a Catalán-speaking micro-state famous for its ski resorts and duty-free shopping. Spend a day or two in Barric Antic, the old town of Andorra la Vella, and explore its restaurants, bars and sculptures.

Plaza Mayor in the heart of Madrid

09

Best of France

Thanks to France's extensive rail network, it's easy to cover the country's highlights on a ten-day train tour. Between Paris and Lyon, you'll visit rolling vineyards, foodie hot spots and awe-inspiring castles.

⊙ **PARIS** FRANCE ⦿ **LYON** FRANCE

◉ BUY AN INTERRAIL OR EURAIL FRANCE PASS VALID FOR 8 DAYS OF UNLIMITED TRAVEL (P11) OR INDIVIDUAL TICKETS FROM SNCF (P246).

🕑 10-14 DAYS ⦿ 1,383 KM (859 MILES)

The unique exterior of the Centre Pompidou in the Marais, Paris

Paris

You can't claim to have seen the best of France and not visit its capital, which has become one of the world's favourite cities. With its beautiful cityscape, art-filled museums and enviable café culture, Paris lives up to even the most inflated hype. It's relatively compact as capitals go, but as each of Paris's 20 *arrondissements* are made up of village-like *quartiers* (districts), it's incredibly diverse. Instead of trying to tick off several neighbourhoods in a short space of time, stick to one and do it properly.

The Marais, which occupies much of Paris's 3rd and 4th *arrondissements*, is a good shout for first-time visitors. Here, you'll find the quintessential trappings of Paris: fashion boutiques, buzzing cafés, trendy art galleries and top-notch restaurants. Museum-wise, there's the excellent Musée Picasso, richly decorated Musée Carnavalet and thought-provoking Musée d'art et d'histoire du Judaïsme, which chronicles what daily life was like when this was the city's Jewish quarter.

On the Marais' western flank is the Centre Pompidou. Its inside-out exterior caused a furore when it first opened in 1977 – pipes, ducts and escalator tubes are all on the outside and colour-coded according to use. Inside, the fourth and fifth floors are occupied by the Musée National d'Art Moderne, the largest modern art collection in Europe. Among the 120,000 pieces are Marcel Duchamp's

One of the most sumptuous buildings ever constructed, the Palace of Versailles has become a must-do day trip from Paris.

Fontaine, Otto Dix's *Portrait of the journalist Sylvia von Harden* and Marc Chagall's *Les Mariés de la Tour Eiffel*.

After taking in all that art, you're bound to have worked up an appetite. Fortunately, the Marais has endless restaurant options, running the gamut from French classics to Middle Eastern treats. Don't feel like you have to try everything in one night; you can come back here tomorrow after your day trip to Versailles.

🚊 The easiest way to reach Versailles from Paris is to take the RER C train from Champ de Mars or Paris Austerlitz to Versailles-Château-Rive-Gauche station. Trains depart every 15 minutes and it's a 10-minute walk to the château from the station.

signed after World War I, and the grounds. Here, you can visit Marie-Antoinette's Petit Trianon palace, an extravagant wedding gift from Louis XVI, and her Hameau de la Reine, a little farmyard where the queen dressed up as a shepherdess and tended her flock.

Crowds of visitors, long queues and an excess of gold leaf can be exhausting, so it's worth spending a day visiting the palace and another exploring the grounds. Alternatively, stay on-site in the Airelles Le Grand Contrôle hotel, which offers after-hours tours of the château and grounds.

🚊 Take the train from Versailles-Chantiers station back to Paris Montparnasse 1 et 2, from where the TGV leaves every hour for Bordeaux St-Jean.

The Galerie des Glaces (Hall of Mirrors) in the Palace of Versailles

Versailles

One of the most sumptuous buildings ever constructed, the Palace of Versailles has become a must-do day trip from Paris. Originally a wooden hunting lodge, it took most of Louis XIV's long reign to turn it into a vast palace of gilded chambers and majestic staircases. It was only in 1682 that the so-called Sun King was able to move the French court, government and around 10,000 servants into the palace, where they remained until the 1789 Revolution.

The high points for many visitors are the Galerie des Glaces (Hall of Mirrors), which is where the Treaty of Versailles was

Bordeaux

A trip to France wouldn't be complete without sampling some of the country's world-leading

DETOUR
Arcachon

Fifty minutes by train from Bordeaux St-Jean station, Arcachon is popular with weekending Bordelais. The characterful resort is made up of four districts, each named after the seasons. (The main beach is unsurprisingly in the Ville d'Été – "town of summer".)

wine, and Bordeaux has long been the first word in the industry. Grapes have been grown here since Roman times, as you'll discover at La Cité du Vin. Located in the former docklands 3 km (2 miles) northeast of Bordeaux's centre, this interactive museum charts the wine region's history and has a fantastic top-floor tasting bar with amazing views across the Garonne river.

Wine will always be the main attraction here so set aside a few days to make the most of it. Hire a bike and cycle through the vines, board a tasting cruise along the river, take a tour of the city's wine bars – or simply enjoy it by the glass alongside a delicious dinner.

🚈 Trains depart every hour from Bordeaux St-Jean to Toulouse Matabiau, the city's main railway station.

Toulouse

Follow the Garonne river upstream to Toulouse. This sprawling city is known for its arts, aerospace industry and its pink-hued medieval centre, which has earned it the nickname La Ville Rose (The Pink City).

The pick of Toulouse's exceptional museums are the Musée des Agustins, which sees outstanding Roman statues and religious art housed in a former convent; the Hôtel d'Assézat, a dazzling Renaissance palace containing works by Tintoretto, Canaletto, Gauguin, Dufy and Bonnard; and, possibly the best of the bunch, the Musée d'Histoire Naturelle.

Beyond the buzzing social centre visitors will find Les Abbatoirs, an old slaughterhouse on the other side of the river now transformed into a decent art museum, and plenty of riverside *guinguettes*, or kiosks, ideal for a late-afternoon aperitif.

🚈 Trains depart from Toulouse Matabiau to Carcassonne every half an hour. The TGV takes 45 minutes, while the TER takes just over an hour.

Carcassonne

The turreted, fairy-tale citadel of Carcassonne is one of France's greatest medieval treasures and

Petit Train Jaune

The Little Yellow Train chugs between Villefranche-de-Conflet and Latour-de-Carol-Enveitg on the Spanish border, from where you can ride a broader-gauge track back to Toulouse. Opened in 1909 to connect mountain villages to the coast, the plucky electric train navigates the vertiginous Pyrenees through a series of viaducts and tunnels. It makes for a thrilling ride.

attracts countless visitors. A fortification has stood here since Celtic times, but the Château Comtal and Basilica of Saints Nazarius and Celsus were built by the Trencavel family in 1067. When Carcassonne later fell into the hands of King Louis IX, anyone who had supported the Trencavel family's claim to the citadal was expelled. The evicted population built a new settlement on the low ground by the Aude river, called the Ville Basse (Low Town).

Once through the citadel gates, knight-themed gift shops and café-restaurants cater for the coachloads of visitors who have booked tours to visit the Château Comtal. To escape the crowds, head down to the Ville Basse. The highlight here is the full-to-bursting Musée des Beaux-Arts, which has some notable landscapes by Corot and Courbet and a Cubist interpretation of Carcassonne by Henri Valensi.

An incongruous treasure 200 m (220 yards) from the Musée des Beaux-Arts, on the rue de Verdon, is the Maison Joë Bousquet. Bousquet was a Surrealist poet who was shot and paralyzed during World War I and forced to spend the rest of his life in bed. Trapped in his bedroom and with the shutters permanently closed, he received a string of guests, including German painter Max Ernst, Belgian artist René Magritte, French philosopher Simone Weil and Spanish Surrealist Salvador Dalí. The house has been preserved just as he left it in 1950 and makes for a fascinating visit.

🚌 Services leave Carcassonne every hour for Avignon Centre station.

Below
Looking towards Carcassonne's citadel from the Ville Basse

Right
Diners at a traditional *bouchon* in Lyon

Avignon

This tour is all about seeing the best of France, so stick to the must-see sights in Avignon: Les Halles d'Avignon market, the celebrated Pont St-Bénézet and the colossal Palais des Papes.

Built by Pope Clement V, who abandoned Rome in the wake of violent disorder after his election in 1309, this is the largest Gothic palace ever built. To sustain the Pope, his cardinals, and the various princes, dignitaries and artists who attended them, the area around Avignon was turned into one big garden. Today, olive mills still dot the surrounding countryside, fruity reds are produced in nearby Châteauneuf-du-Pape, and orchards and vegetable gardens cover Avignon's Île de Barthelasse (the largest river island in France). Fortunately, the local bounty is no longer hoarded by the papacy. Learn how to use these ingredients at Les Halles d'Avignon, where a local chef gives a demonstration every Saturday.

🔁 Make the short journey from Avignon Centre to Avignon TGV station. Then, hop on a Fast TGV service to Lyon Part-Dieu.

Lyon

Any tour of France should include the opportunity to sample its finest food. Lyon is France's culinary capital, supporting over 4,000 restaurants, from the Michelin-starred to *bouchons*. In these convivial, unfussy restaurants napkins weigh as much as jackets, tablecloths are chequered and the serving staff wear full aprons. Robust dishes like *sabodet*, a clog-shaped sausage in wine, or the *quenelle de brochet*, a dumpling of pike, are must-eats, enjoyed with an obligatory glass of Beaujolais wine. Pay a visit to Les Halles de Lyon, too, a huge market full of glass-fronted stalls, packed with the likes of cheese, charcuterie, chocolates and pastries.

Food aside, there's more to see and do in Lyon (although even the museums have excellent brasseries). Seek out the Musée des Confluences, an anthropology museum in the shape of a spaceship; the Institut Lumière, an Art Nouveau villa dedicated to photography; and the Musée des Beaux-Arts, whose art collection is second only to the Louvre's.

Food aside, there's more to see and do in Lyon (although even the museums have excellent brasseries).

EXTEND YOUR TRIP

Annecy

The pretty town of Annecy is just two hours by direct train from Lyon Part-Dieu, but it has a very different local cuisine. A gateway to the Alps, the town serves up hearty, warming dishes like raclette (melted cheese that is scraped off and ladled onto potatoes and meat) and *tartiflette* (layered potatoes baked with cheese, lardons and onions).

10

The Loire Valley

The Loire Valley is a land of fairy-tale castles, handsome medieval towns and fantastic wine. Discover the best of this French region on this journey from Orléans to Nantes on the Interloire train line.

▶ **ORLÉANS** FRANCE ○ **NANTES** FRANCE

⊚ DOWNLOAD THE LE VAL DE LOIRE VU DU TRAIN APP FOR INFORMATION ON INTERESTING SIGHTS SEEN ONBOARD AND AT STOPS; FOR TICKETS, USE THE SNCF WEBSITE (P246).

🕒 8–10 DAYS ⊙ 311 KM (193 MILES)

○ Orléans
35 mins
○ Blois
20 mins
○ Amboise
20 mins
○ Tours
60 mins
○ Angers
40 mins
● Nantes

Orléans

Straddling the Loire river at its most northerly point, Orléans was the chief inland port in France in the 18th century. Wine, vinegar and sugar from the colonies were shipped to the city before being refined and carried to Paris by road. You need only spend a couple of days here to sense both the city's close attachment to the capital (it's only an hour away by train) and the spirit of liberty and justice brought about by its most famous resident, Joan of Arc.

La Maison de Jeanne d'Arc belonged to Jacques Boucher, the Duke of Orleans' treasurer, who housed Joan during the 1429 Siege of Orléans. It's now a museum dedicated to her life with over 37,000 books, articles and items of memorabilia. Another must-see is the nearby Musée des Beaux-Arts, which contains the Le Nain brothers' masterpiece, *Bacchus discovering Ariadne on Naxos*.

🚆 Interloire services depart every hour from Orléans Centre station for Blois-Chambord.

Blois

A great base for visiting Chambord, Cheverny and Beauregard (three of the Loire's most sumptuous châteaux), Blois also has its own grand castle.

Chemin de Fer de la Vendée

The Chemin de Fer de la Vendée has been chugging across the three valleys (and viaducts) between Mortagne sur Sèvre and Les Herbier, to the south of Nantes, since 1865. During the two-and-a-half-hour return journey, passengers are treated to fantastic scenery and – in classic French style – a slap-up lunch in the Wagons-Lits restaurant cars, which date from the 1920s and 40s.

The grand façade of the Château Royal in Blois

Soaring above the town, the Château Royal is a flamboyant mix of Gothic, Classical and Renaissance architecture, with each of its resident seven kings and ten queens attempting to outdo their predecessors with the construction of extravagant wings, spiral staircases and secret panels. The castle has seen some gruesome murders over the course of their reigns, grisly tales of which feature in the *son et lumière* (sound-and-light show).

Opposite the château is the Maison de la Magie Robert-Houdin, a museum dedicated to magic and illusions. Attractions include a life-sized kaleidoscope, a submarine hallucinoscope and a six-headed dragon automaton, which bursts through the courtyard windows. Learning a few card tricks here is a must.

🜪 Trains leave -Chambord every hour for Amboise and take just 20 minutes.

Amboise

As is the case with almost everywhere in the Loire Valley, the main reason to disembark in Amboise is to explore its beautiful château. For much of the 15th and 16th centuries, the French court was based here and the Château d'Amboise is an interesting catalogue of each successive ruler's architectural predilections.

And there's more besides: the castle was visited by Leonardo da Vinci. The famed Italian artist and thinker was invited here by François I after his accession in 1515, and arrived from Rome with a handful of followers, his notebooks and his most famous painting: the *Mona Lisa*. He was gifted Clos Lucé, a brick manor house in the château grounds. Here, he spent his time preparing pigments in his private workshop and sketching inventions before his death in 1519. The designs have since been modelled into 3D versions and are displayed in the basement and gardens of Clos Lucé, which also has an immersive gallery exhibiting da Vinci's ideas.

🚅 Getting to Tours couldn't be easier: the journey only takes 20 minutes and Interloire services depart every hour.

Tours

Tours is the gateway for visits to the great châteaux of the Loire – Chenonceau, Villandry, Azay-le-Rideau and Langeais – so plan to spend a few days here. As well as making day trips to the châteaux, explore the city itself. A whistle-stop tour should include Tours' own modest castle, which hosts contemporary art and photography exhibitions; the cathedral; and the Musée des Beaux-Arts. In the museum's garden, you'll find Fritz. A performer in Barnum & Bailey's circus when it toured Europe in the early 1900s, this elephant escaped, was shot, stuffed and presented to Tours, where he has remained ever since.

A short stroll westwards along the riverbank leads to the medieval Old Town. Its social centrepiece is the place Plumereau, which is lined with half-timbered houses and filled with restaurant tables come summer. Like most of France, Tours is a magnet for foodies and has many specialities, including potted *rillettes* (slow-cooked shredded pork), *poires tapées* (dried pears soaked in Loire wine) and *nougat* (more like a cake than the sweet Montélimar version). The town is also known for its wines, particularly its crisp, white Chenin Blanc. Be sure to order a bottle to enjoy with your travel companions over a traditional dinner.

🚅 Trains make the 60-minute journey to Angers St-Laud every hour. Most trains are direct, but some services require a change at St-Pierre des Corps.

Angers

Vibrant and handsome Angers is located beside the Maine river, a tributary of the Loire. Once capital of the province of Anjou, it was the medieval seat of the Plantagenets whose hilltop château still dominates the city. It's not one of the valley's best castles architecturally, but it houses one of the world's most important tapestries.

The *Tapisserie de l'Apocalypse* was made for Louis I of Anjou in the late 1300s and depicts a bestiary-inspired Armageddon. Over 100 m (110 yards) still survives in six 4.5-m- (15-ft-) high sections hanging in the castle. Angers' second woven masterpiece is displayed in the Musée Jean Lurçat, a 12th-century Plantagenet hospital on the other side of the river. Created by Lurçat in 1959, the 10-section *Le Chant du Monde* presents a humanist, post-Holocaust alternative to the *Tapisserie de l'Apocalypse*.

🚅 Services for Nantes depart every 15 minutes or so from Angers St-Laud, so no need to rush back to the station.

The *Grand Éléphant*, a mechanical sculpture on the Île de Nantes

Nantes

The last major town on the Loire before it reaches the Atlantic, Nantes has transformed itself over the last two decades from an industrial port into northwest France's premier tourist destination. Star of the show is the 12-m- (40-ft-) high mechanical *Grand Éléphant*, which lurches around the Île de Nantes' esplanade spraying water from its trunk and amusing the crowds. You could easily spend a day on the island watching the Leonardo da Vinci-inspired machines, riding the vintage-style Marine Worlds Carousel and checking out the giant, steam-punk articulations in the Construction Gallery.

Everything after a ride on a mechanical elephant can feel a little ordinary, but Nantes' dynamic medieval quarter won't disappoint. It has a soaring cathedral, bustling main square and plenty of excellent restaurants, including La Cigale, a beautiful, Art Nouveau brasserie.

This historic area extends northeast from the Loire to the Château des Ducs de Bretagne. Built in the late 15th century by the last two rulers of an independent Brittany, François II and his daughter Anne, the castle has a moat, lawned gardens and ramparts. It's wonderfully free to explore and the last château you'll visit on your journey across the Loire Valley.

EXTEND
YOUR TRIP

Pornic

Take the hour-long train westwards from Nantes to Pornic, a resort on France's Jade Coast. The railway arrived here in 1875 and with it, the coast's first seaside holidaymakers. Today, visitors still come here to walk the cliffs, lounge on the fine-sand beaches and explore the brightly painted fishing cottages and turreted seafront château.

11

The Alsace Wine Route

Let the train take the strain as you sweep along the Alsace Wine Route. Services are slow, much like the idyllic days you'll spend sipping local wines.

◆ **STRASBOURG** FRANCE ◇ **COLMAR** FRANCE

◑ REMEMBER TO VALIDATE PAPER TICKETS IN THE YELLOW COMPOSTER MACHINES TO AVOID BEING FINED (P246).

◔ 6–8 DAYS ◉ 74 KM (46 MILES)

○ Strasbourg

50 mins

○ Dambach-la-Ville

10 mins

○ Sélestat

10 mins

● Colmar

Strasbourg

Linked by fast international train services to other cities around the continent, Strasbourg is the obvious place to start your journey (despite the fact that it isn't actually on the Alsace Wine Route). The city has such excellent rail connections because it's one of the European Union's self-styled capitals, home to the European Parliament and the European Court of Human Rights. Both are open to the public and worth a closer look if you have a few hours to spare, but you're really here for the historic centre, an eye-shaped island in the Ill river a mere five-minute walk from the station.

The island is dominated by the Gothic spire of the Cathédrale de Notre-Dame, which you can climb for an amazing panorama of Strasbourg, the Black Forest and the Vosges mountains. Back on the ground, revel in getting lost in the centre's narrow lanes, pausing at friendly *winstubs* for Alsatian food and, more importantly, wine.

🚆 Take the slow train to Dambach-la-Ville, travelling through scenic Alsace Wine Route villages like Obernai and Barr. It leaves Strasbourg station every hour.

Dambach-la-Ville

Your adventure begins in earnest when the train pulls in to the platform at Dambach-la-Ville, the undisputed star of the 70 something-thing villages on the Alsace Wine

Route. Its vineyards, which are set on the slopes of the Vosges mountain range, produce one of the region's finest vintages – the Grand Cru Frankstein, a fruity white wine.

Dambach itself is a beautifully preserved fortified village, known for its distinct half-timbered buildings which are almost entirely devoted to selling wine. Take your time here: explore more than one of the vineyards, compare (and sample) different vintages and stock up on bottles to take home.

🔁 Although it takes just 10 minutes to travel to Sélestat, plan ahead – there can be over an hour between services.

Sélestat

Sélestat's history is interconnected with the region's vineyards. The town became a major centre for the wine trade in the Middle Ages and the resulting wealth, coupled with the town's position halfway between the great intellectual centres of Italy and the Netherlands, led to a Latin school being built here in 1440. For the next century, Sélestat was at the heart of the Renaissance. Today, the only reminder of this trailblazing time is the Bibliothèque Humaniste, a library accumulated by a graduate of the school. Here, you'll find one of Europe's greatest collections of Renaissance manuscripts, including the *Cosmographiae Introductio* (1507), which is the first document ever to mention the word "America".

The nearby Château du Haut-Koenigsbourg is a worthy day

trip. Set on a forested slope, this medieval castle was heavily remodelled by Kaiser Wilhelm II, the last German Emperor, and reflects his romantic nationalist ideas. A shuttle bus runs from the railway station to the castle and back several times a day.

🔁 Trains depart every 30 minutes for Colmar. When you arrive, take some time to admire the 19th-century station, which is one of France's oldest.

Colmar

Bring your slow journey to a fitting close in the delightfully sleepy town of Colmar. With its pretty canals and picturesque streets lined with eccentric houses, Colmar rewards an unplanned, relaxed stroll. Perhaps you'll end up at the door of the Maison des Têtes. Topped with a bronze statue of a wine barrel-maker, and covered in 106 grotesque heads and masks, It's a symbol of the enduring importance of the Alsatian winemaking industry.

Rows of vines tumbling down a hill above Dambach-la-Ville

EXTEND YOUR TRIP

Mulhouse

Alsace's industrial power-house, Mulhouse is just a 20-minute train ride away from Colmar. Come here to check out the excellent Cité du Train, which displays steam locomotives, vintage carriages and modern TGVs, and to take advantage of the city's surprisingly active nightlife.

12

French Riviera

Touring the south of France is often associated with sports cars and gleaming yachts, but the extensive train network offers the same coastal views, beach resorts and good food for a fraction of the cost.

▶ **BAYONNE** FRANCE ○ **NICE** FRANCE

🚄 FOR INTERCITY AND TGV SERVICES IT'S WORTH BOOKING AHEAD, ESPECIALLY DURING THE SUMMER (P246).

🕐 16-21 DAYS 📍 992 KM (616 MILES)

Bayonne

Set in the very southwestern corner of France, and with the best rail connections in the area, Bayonne marks the start of this two- to three-week tour. As the city lies some 5 km (3 miles) back from the coast, it has historically been ignored – and most of the passengers disembarking here will get straight into a taxi bound for the nearby resort town of Biarritz. Before joining them on the beach, spend a morning exploring Bayonne's charming Old Town, with its colourful shutters and charming half-timbered houses.

🔄 Continuing your journey east to Toulouse is simple, with three or four trains each day.

Toulouse

Toulouse offers a change of pace after the sleepy charms of Bayonne. Home to one of the oldest universities in Europe, France's fourth-largest city has a lively, youthful vibe thanks to the presence of more than 100,000 students from across the country and beyond. There isn't a huge amount in the way of sights but factor in a night or two here. The city comes alive after dark, with bustling food markets serving inexpensive but tasty grub and some of France's best live music.

🚇 Catch the train to Narbonne from Toulouse-Matabiau station.

Narbonne

Narbonne was an important port until the Aude river changed course and left it marooned inland in the 14th century.

Today, it's a small and attractive city largely free of the tourist hordes that throng many of its southern counterparts.

The city centre is bisected by a narrow canal: the Canal de la Robine, which is lined with wide promenades perfect for strolling. On its southern side is the city's beautiful 1901 wrought-iron and glass market, Les Halles – a great spot for lunch. From here, cross over the canal to visit Narbonne's striking cathedral. This structure has been left in its skeletal, half-built state since the 14th century when it was discovered that the town's ramparts would have to be demolished for it to be completed. Nearby is the medieval bishop's palace, which houses an art gallery – don't miss the modern north African art on the top floor – and a spooky subterranean Roman warehouse complex, the Horreum.

🚇 Direct trains to Avignon depart hourly. There are also regular indirect services via Nîmes and Valence.

Bayonne

3 hrs 20 mins

Toulouse

1 hr 10 mins–1 hr 45 mins

Narbonne

2 hrs 15 mins

Avignon

2 hrs 45 mins

Toulon

1 hr 20 mins

Cannes

8–12 mins

Antibes

20 mins

Nice

Quai Galuperie, in Bayonne's Old Town, lined with shuttered houses

Avignon

Avignon has been on the tourist trail since it served as the headquarters of the Catholic Church during the early Middle Ages, and it's an unmissable stop on any tour of the south of France. The highlight is the old city, which hugs the Rhône river and is encircled by medieval walls that keep the sprawl of the modern city at bay. The area can be overwhelmed by crowds, particularly in summer. To escape the crush, explore the main sights, like the Palais des Papes (the fortified palace that housed the medieval popes), in the early morning or evening, when it's illuminated by an evocative son et lumière (sound-and-light show). Alternatively, forget the sights all together and use Avignon as a base to explore the surrounding vineyards and lavender fields.

❷ There are direct services every one to two hours, plus indirect services via Marseille.

Toulon

The site of a major naval base, the port of Toulon is often neglected by travellers yet it has an understated charm that might just make it your favourite stop on this rail trip. In a day, you can hit the highlights: a boat ride across the azure waters of the Mediterranean, a trip to the summit of the 584-m (1,916-ft) Mont Faron for superb views, and a visit to the comprehensive Musée National de la Marine, which offers an insight into the city's naval history.

❷ It takes just over an hour to reach Cannes and services are very regular.

Cannes

With its exclusive boutiques, yacht-filled marinas and annual celebrity-filled film festival, Cannes is synonymous with glitz and glamour. It's unsurprisingly expensive to stay here, so only plan on being here long enough to stroll along the glorious Promenade de la Croisette and browse one of the renowned parfumiers (perfume-makers).

❷ Getting to Antibes couldn't be easier: the journey only takes around 10 mins.

Antibes

Antibes has long attracted writers, musicians and artists – notably Pablo Picasso, whose works are exhibited in an eponymous museum right on the waterfront, and author Graham Greene, who considered it the most unspoiled corner of the coast.

   The town has escaped much of the overdevelopment seen elsewhere. To the south, beyond the cobblestoned streets of the Old Town, is Cap d'Antibes, an unspoiled peninsula jutting out into the Mediterranean. Take some time to explore its ornate villas, verdant gardens, and sandy beaches and coves, backed by shady pine trees.

❷ To reach Nice, simply hop on one of the fast and frequent direct trains from Antibes.

Nice

The capital of the French Riviera, Nice combines big-city grittiness with seaside-resort glamour. While there may be congestion and

Nice's port, full of gleaming motorboats and sailing yachts

urban sprawl, it's not hard to see why Nice was once one of the most fashionable destinations on the continent. Alongside a treasure trove of Baroque, Italianate and *belle époque* architecture, it has a vibrant cultural scene and some fabulous beaches.

The local cuisine, which combines French and Italian influences, is another highlight: don't leave the city without sampling a *pissaladière* (onion tart topped with olives and anchovies), *socca* (chickpea pancake) and – of course – a *salade niçoise* (a mix of hard-boiled eggs, anchovies, olives and lettuce). You'll find these dishes in abundance in Vieux Nice, the atmospheric Old Town, where you can mark the end of your trip with a splash-out meal.

Café tables on a pedestrianized street in Antibes Old Town

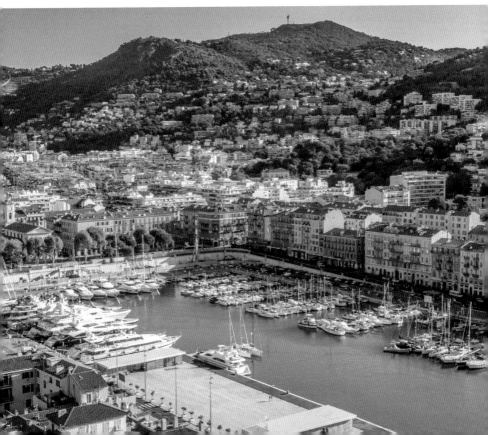

13

Northern France

The south may get all the glory, but the north is France's unsung hero – as you'll discover on this two-week-long train trip around idyllic beach resorts and historic country towns.

- ◑ **ST-MALO** FRANCE ○ **LILLE** FRANCE
- ◑ VALIDATE PAPER TICKETS MARKED "COMPOSTER" IN THE YELLOW MACHINES TO AVOID A FINE (P246).
- ◑ 14–18 DAYS ◉ 978 KM (608 MILES)

St-Malo

Poking out into the English Channel, and served by ferries from the UK and the Channel Islands, St-Malo sits on the very frontier of France. This fortified city-island has long had an independent spirit, declaring itself a republic in the 1590s and adopting the motto "Not French, Not Breton but Malouin!"

For decades, it was home to legions of corsairs, paid by the French king to attack enemy ships. Since France was at war with either the Dutch, English or Spanish for most of the 17th and 18th centuries, they had almost permanent employment. Statues celebrating their exploits are still found all over St-Malo and replicas of their nifty frigates

take visitors around the Breton coast on guided trips.

Another defining feature is St-Malo's grey-granite citadel walls. The *intra-muros* quarter, the tangle of streets within these walls, is the city's nexus, full of galette-bars, gift shops and fish restaurants – an ideal place for a spot of lunch.

⊖ Trains leave St-Malo station every 30-60 minutes for Rennes. On the way, the tracks pass through some scenic Breton towns and villages.

Rennes

Often voted the best place to live in France, the capital of Brittany has an attractive medieval Old

The fortified port city of St-Malo, with its sweeping golden beach

St-Malo
55 mins

Rennes
45 mins–1 hr

Le Mans
1 hr 45 mins

Caen
1 hr

Trouville–Deauville
1 hr 45 mins

Rouen
40 mins

Giverny
2 hrs 45 mins

Amiens
1 hr 20 mins

Lille

Town, a lively student population and a thriving foodie scene. Spending Saturday morning at the place des Lices, just north of the cathedral in the heart of the Old Town, is a must. Every week, 300 local producers stack their stalls here with the likes of fresh oysters, honey, cider, Coucou de Rennes (a rare breed of chicken) and Petit Gris de Rennes (an ancient variety of melon).

A 20-minute stroll away, on the other side of the Old Town, is the Musée de Bretagne. It's worth devoting an entire afternoon to exploring the museum's collection, which covers the region's history from prehistoric cave discoveries to the Dreyfus affair to the Allied landings on the Normandy coast in 1944. If you have more time to spare, spend a second day exploring nearby Fougères castle, one of Europe's best-preserved medieval fortresses.

🚆 Direct trains to Le Mans run hourly and there are several superfast inOui services, taking just 45 minutes, each day. It's a 25-minute walk or 15-minute tram ride from Le Mans railway station to the Old Town.

Le Mans

Known internationally for its 24-hour car race, Le Mans' prize attraction is unsurprisingly the Musée des 24 Heures, 5 km (3 miles) south of the centre. Tucked alongside the Bugatti circuit where the car race starts and finishes, the museum displays 140 racing cars and thousands of

Le Mans itself is much slower paced, although there are a handful of attractions to tick off in the Cité Plantagenet.

miniature models, and offers a self-guided tour of the track. Race day is at the end of June but there's a go-kart track nearby for anyone twitching to get behind the wheel.

Le Mans itself is much slower paced, although there are a handful of attractions to tick off in the Cité Plantagenet, the wonderfully preserved medieval quarter. Enclosed by the third-longest Roman wall in the world, the Cité fills the hillside above the Sarthe river and can be accessed via steep steps from the water's edge. At its centre is the Royal Palace on place St-Pierre, the birthplace of the future King Henry II of England and now the town hall. Down towards the river is a warren of cobbled lanes that look unchanged since the Middle Ages, with bruised pillars and half-timbered houses, complete with crooked window frames. Unmissable is the Maison Suspendue on rue St-Pavin-de-la Cité, which seems to hang unsupported above the street.

🚆 Trains to Caen take just 1 hour 45 minutes; there are six to eight departures per day.

Caen

Brutalized during the Battle of Normandy in 1944, Caen today

acts as a gateway for visits to the D-Day beaches. There are plenty of organized tours to the battle-fields from the city but a decent bus service, the Bus Vert de Calvados, helps those keen to go it alone.

After seeing where the Allies landed, visit the Mémorial de Caen, just north of the city on Esplanade Eisenhower. A com-bined ticket grants entry to the memorial, the 360-degree cinema at Arromanches and the Memorial de Falaise, a museum dedicated to stories of local people who survived the war.

➋ The journey from Caen to Trouville-Deauville takes just over an hour, but there can be gaps of several hours between services.

The historic fishing port of Trouville, a popular resort town in Normandy

Trouville—Deauville

At the halfway point of your tour of the north, you'll be ready for some relaxation and your next stop promises it in spades. Sharing a railway station, sister-resorts Trouville and Deauville lie just a mile apart on the Côte Fleurie (flowery coast). In truth the towns merge into each other along the harbourfront but Trouville has always been

DETOUR
Bayeux

Most people visit Bayeux (a 20-minute train journey from Caen) for one reason only: the legendary tapestry. Housed in the Centre Guillaume le Conquérant, it vividly recounts the Norman conquest of England and features battles, feasts and Halley's comet.

associated with the fishing industry while Deauville, with its prestigious annual American film festival, glamorous horse races and polo matches, and smart detached villas overlooking a vast expanse of sand, enjoys its reputation as part of the "Parisian Riviera".

With piers, carousels and fluttering flags, both towns are old-style seaside resorts and fun places to stay for a couple of nights.

➋ Catch one of the four or five daily departures for Rouen-Rive-Droite. The station is located right in the heart of Rouen.

Rouen

Rouen, the capital of Upper Normandy, is one of France's most historic cities. Straddling a curvaceous loop of the Seine, the city stands on the site of the Roman settlement of Rotomagus. The centre sits to the north of the river and, although it has the appearance of the medieval city laid out here in 911 by Rollo the first duke of Normandy, it was largely reconstructed after World War II bombing flattened the area. Another dark moment in Rouen's history: it was here in the 1400s, while the city was under English control, that Joan of Arc was tortured, burnt at the stake and thrown into the Seine.

Rouen has seen other famous faces since, including the 17th-century tragedian Pierre Corneille and 19th-century novelist Gustave Flaubert. Flaubert's birthplace is open to the public and is devoted to his childhood memorabilia and, somewhat randomly, the medical practices of the time. Visitors are treated

A bridge over a water lily pond in the gardens of La Maison de Monet, Giverny

tourist trail, attracting half a million visitors each year. You really can't come to northern France and miss the place – its Japanese-inspired water lily ponds, which Monet painted 250 times, are a sight to behold.

Nearby is the airy Musée des Impressionismes Giverny, which looks at the origins and legacy of the Impressionist movement. It has a substantial art and sculpture collection and a nice French brasserie in which to while away the afternoon.

⊖ To reach Amiens, you must first travel back to Rouen-Rive-Droite, providing another opportunity to enjoy the scenery. From Rouen-Rive-Droite, trains leave hourly for Amiens and take just 1 hour 20 minutes.

to apothecary jars, leech perches and a giant bed designed to sleep six patients.

Rouen isn't just about history, though. The city has a lively and cosmopolitan feel, enhanced by the rejuvenated riverfront, which is lined with parks, cafés and bars where you can try *pommeau* – a mix of cider and Calvados.

⊖ The journey from Rouen-Rive-Droite station to Vernon-Giverny takes around 40 minutes. Make sure to sit by the window so you can soak up the countryside that inspired Monet. A shuttle bus takes visitors from the station directly to La Maison de Monet.

Giverny

Gazing out of the train window one day in 1883, artist Claude Monet passed by the charming little village of Giverny and decided to rent a farmhouse there. He moved in with his companion Alice Hoschedé, his two sons and her six children, eventually buying the property and transforming the gardens into a floral paradise. Thanks to the artist's fame, Giverny is a must-stop on the

Amiens

With the Somme river passing through its centre, and a network of canals in the picturesque quartier St-Leu at its heart, Amiens has a dreamy, poetic feel that belies its commercial origins. From the 17th century, the city was the centre of France's velvet industry. Today, the canalside workers' district has been smartened up and taken over by trendy bars and restaurants.

On the must-visit list are the Cathédrale Notre-Dame d'Amiens, which is France's largest cathedral and twice as big as Paris's Notre-Dame, Jules Verne's house-museum and the Hortillonnages – magnificent floating vegetable and flower

The historic Vieille Bourse (Old Stock Exchange) in the Old Town of Lille

gardens that are only accessible by boat. On Saturday mornings, the *hortillon* farmers float their produce to the market in the place Parmentier.

🔁 Trains to Lille Flandres depart every hour and, as it only takes 1 hour 20 minutes to make the journey, don't feel like you need to cut your time in Amiens short.

———

Lille

Located on the main trading route between Flanders and Paris, Lille has been a merchant city since its inception. It's probably not surprising, then, that the lavishly decorated Vieille Bourse (Old Stock Exchange) is the symbol of the city rather than the cathedral. The Vieille Bourse sits on the eastern side of the place du Général de Gaulle, more commonly called the Grand'place, which acts as Lille's social focal

point and marks the southern boundary of Vieux Lille (the city's cobbled and labyrinthine old quarter).

The city's museums are all a short walk from the Grand'place, but there's no rush; Lille should be savoured for at least a few days. That way, you'll have time to stroll the beautiful medicinal gardens of the Musée de l'Hospice Comtesse, take in the Rubens at the Palais des Beaux-Arts, marvel at the taxidermied dodo at the Musée d'Histoire Naturelle and play school at the Musée des Écoles.

Just east of the Grand'place is a different side of Lille – the ultramodern business complex known as Euralille, where futur-istic towers in steel and glass surround plazas, shopping malls and the city's international train station. Here, you can jump on a train to almost every capital city in Europe and continue your journey across the continent.

EXTEND
YOUR TRIP

Roubaix

The industrial town of Roubaix is just a nine-minute train ride from Lille, making it the perfect day trip. It's home to La Piscine – an Art Deco swimming pool turned art museum, where graceful sculptures line the water, and art installations occupy the former showers and changing rooms.

Glasgow
2 hr 30 mins
Bridge of Orchy
1 hr 20 mins
Fort William
30 mins
Glenfinnan
50 mins
Mallaig

14

Wild Scotland

The west coast of Scotland is where the country gets its reputation for rugged beauty. Ride the West Highland Line to discover the region's soaring Munros, deep-dark lochs and quaint villages drenched in Jacobite history.

- ▶ **GLASGOW** SCOTLAND ○ **MALLAIG** SCOTLAND
- ⦿ BUY TICKETS FOR EACH LEG OF THE JOURNEY ON THE SCOTRAIL WEBSITE OR AT STATIONS (P244).
- ● 8-10 DAYS ● 258 KM (160 MILES)

Glasgow

It might seem strange to start your trip into the wild in Scotland's largest city, but Glasgow is wild in a different way. It has an unruly feel thanks in part to its famously rebellious locals, who top a statue of the Duke of Wellington in Royal Exchange Square with a traffic cone, earning it the nickname "Cone Heid". Everyone seems to be on first-name terms here, a tradition that stems from the city's close-knit shipyards.

Split in half by the Clyde river, Glasgow flourished during the 1700s when its port facilitated the transport of tobacco, sugar, rum and, regrettably, enslaved people from the British Empire to the Americas. Glasgow is still reckoning with its role in the Atlantic slave trade, something explored at the excellent Kelvingrove Art Gallery and Museum, which is worth a visit.

After enduring decades of economic hardship, Glasgow has become a cultural capital, with no real rival in Scotland outside of Edinburgh. The city is dotted with basement music venues, spoken-word clubs and inventive restaurants, serving up contemporary takes on Scottish classics, like haggis, neeps and tatties, and fish and chips.

🚉 Glasgow has two mainline stations – Queen Street and Central. The West Highland Line's four daily services depart from Queen Street.

Bridge of Orchy

Leaving Glasgow and its sprawling suburbs behind, the West Highland Line soon hits the dramatic scenery you associate with Scotland. As the track shadows Loch Lomond's shore and curves through scrubby glens, you'll understand why this has been proclaimed one

of the world's best train journeys. Too soon, the train pulls in to the platform at Bridge of Orchy.

Tempting passengers to disembark here is the promise of more wild scenery. This tiny village sits slap-bang in the middle of the West Highland Way, a legendary 154-km (96-mile) hiking trail that runs from Milngavie, near Glasgow, up to Fort William in the western Highlands. From the eponymous bridge, the Way snakes through pine forests to Mam Carraigh, a 200-m (656-ft) peak with brilliant views over Loch Tulla.

Following the West Highland Way in the other direction from the train station, walkers reach the village of Tyndrum within two hours. Here, you can grab a bite to eat before returning to Bridge of Orchy for the night.

🚉 Jump on one of the West Highland Line's four daily departures from the tiny Bridge of Orchy station.

Below
The train line shadowing Loch Eil, near Fort William

Previous page
A beached boat on Loch Linnhe, with Ben Nevis in the background

Fort William

Fort William's town centre is undoubtedly its historic High Street. Here, you'll find a statue entitled "Man with Sore Feet", marking the end of the West Highland Way, and the West Highland Museum, which displays Jacobite peculiarities, such as Rob Roy's sporran and Bonnie Prince Charlie's silk waistcoat.

The main reason to visit Fort William, though, is undoubtedly Ben Nevis, which at 1,345 m (4,413 ft) is the UK's highest mountain. The start of the Mountain Track (or "Tourist Track") is half an hour's walk from the High Street, near the brilliant Ben Nevis Distillery.

The wider area warrants a couple of days' exploration at east. The Nevis Range Mountain Resort is a short bus ride from the train station. Here, a gondola transports visitors the 650 m (2,132 ft) up Aonach Mòr, a mountain neighbouring Ben Nevis, which grants views of Loch Eil, the Great Glen and, on a good day, the Inner Hebrides.

🚋 Catch one of the four daily services to Glenfinnan. This section of the West Highland Line is considered the most scenic. Sit on the left-hand side for the best views, including when the train curves along the Glenfinnan Viaduct.

———

Glenfinnan

The Glenfinnan Viaduct became world-famous when the *Hogwarts Express* (aka *The Jacobite; p86*) chugged over it in the *Harry Potter* films. As impressive as it is when seen through the train window, it's best appreciated from the ground. It takes just 15 minutes to climb from the station to the Glenfinnan Visitor Centre. From the car park, you'll see the iconic viaduct and the poignant Glenfinnan Monument. Topped by an unidentifiable clansman, this 1815 monument commemorates the hamlet's role in the 1745 Jacobite uprising. Continue ten minutes onwards on the hiking trail to the signposted viewpoint for an even better view.

🚋 Glenfinnan Station has its own museum on the platform, where you can learn about the history of the West Highland Line, before catching the next service to Mallaig.

———

Mallaig

Marking the end of the West Highland Line is Mallaig, the gateway to Scotland's islands. From here, ferries leave for the small isles – Canna, Muck, Rhum and Eigg – and the famously beautiful Isle of Skye.

The town of Mallaig itself is a wonderful working fishing port, which flourished during the herring boom of the 1800s. A terrific 3-km (2-mile) circular walking route around the town is the best way to get your bearings and see some of the local sights. The trail starts at Mallaig East Bay car park, just five minute's walk from the train station, and grants great views out over the town to the islands and coastlines beyond. There's the option to detour to Loch an Nostarie, but continue on for views of Ben Nevis and over to the mountains of Knoydart, a remote peninsula that is home to Britain's most remote pub, The Old Forge. It doesn't get much wilder than that.

EXTEND
YOUR TRIP

Isle of Skye

Easily accessed via a 45-minute ferry from Mallaig, Skye is world-famous for its unique rock formations, such as the Old Man of Storr and Quiraing.

The Jacobite

Known to many as the *Hogwarts Express*, *The Jacobite* captured the world's imagination when it appeared in the *Harry Potter* films. Experience the magic for yourself as this spellbinding steam train chugs through the wild Highlands.

The Jacobite billowing pretty plumes of steam as it curves across the Glenfinnan Viaduct

From its inception as an extension of the West Highland Railway in 1901 to its transformation into a heritage route by West Coast Railways in 1995, the line between Fort William and Mallaig narrowly avoided closure multiple times. It's a fact that is hard to fathom today: *The Jacobite*, the 19th-century steam-powered locomotive that chugs and puffs along the tracks, is an international celebrity thanks to its starring role in the first *Harry Potter* film in 2001. The train will represent the *Hogwarts Express* forever more.

Many passengers buy tickets because of the train's wizarding connections, but the mesmerizing scenery through which *The Jacobite* trundles soon steals their hearts. During the 135-km (84-mile) journey, the train powers through some of Scotland's trademark landscapes, passing along the watery skirts of cloud-cast lochs and in the shadows of gorse-sprung mountains. Sit back in the plush, velvet-lined seats and watch the show, which is perfectly framed by the antique carriages' large picture windows.

The two-hour journey's most memorable moment is when the train pauses halfway across the 21 concrete arches of the hulking Glenfinnan Viaduct. For a minute or two of absolute magic, the curving carriages, billowing steam and rugged mountain landscape hang in view, before the train continues its westwards journey through the highlands.

THE PRACTICALITIES

The Jacobite steam train operates one morning and one afternoon service between May and September, and a single morning service in April and October. Tickets can be bought directly from West Coast Railways. First-class carriages provide a little extra leg room and complimentary tea and coffee, while Potterheads will appreciate the "HP" Compartment Carriage, a replica of those used to transport the students in the *Harry Potter* films.

www.westcoastrailways.co.uk

15

Quintessential England

If you're looking for the England as depicted in your favourite books and movies, you've come to the right place. London, Oxford and Bath are the country's three most recognizable cities.

Pulteney Weir, surrounded by grand Georgian buildings in Bath

 LONDON ENGLAND ⭘ **BATH** ENGLAND

🚆 GREAT WESTERN RAILWAY RUNS THE LONDON PADDINGTON-OXFORD AND OXFORD-BATH ROUTES AND CHILTERN RAILWAYS RUNS THE LONDON MARYLEBONE-OXFORD ROUTE (P244).

🕐 7–10 DAYS 📍 203 KM (126 MILES)

London

Combining a long, storied history with a dynamic, forward-looking outlook, England's capital receives more visitors each year than anywhere else in the UK. It would take a week or more to do it justice, but if you've only got a day or two to spare at the start of your trip, you'll need to be picky.

A great place to get your bearings is beautiful Hampstead Heath, which offers sweeping views of the skyline from its elevated position in north London. Seek out Kenwood House while you're here – you'll recognize it from Richard Curtis's 1999 film *Notting Hill*. Speaking of which, you really must visit the movie's namesake. It'll feel like you've stepped right into a scene in this pretty part of west London, with its famous antiques market, pretty pastel houses and, of course, blue-doored bookshop.

Just remember that London has much more to offer beyond these cinematic sights. The city is remarkably diverse – more than 300 different languages are spoken here – and one of the great pleasures of a visit is getting to know the real neighbourhoods behind the popular culture phenomena, and the communities who live in them.

🚆 Direct trains to Oxford depart every 10 to 20 minutes from Paddington and Marylebone stations.

London

50 mins–1 hr 15 mins

Oxford

1 hr 5 mins–1 hr 15 mins

Bath

dazzling art and artifacts – and the Bodleian Library.

To get to grips with the city and its university from a different perspective, hire a punt and take to the water. As you drift down the Cherwell or the Thames (known locally as the Isis), you're sure to be inspired to write your own screenplay or story.

🚆 There are frequent indirect trains to Bath Spa station, with a change at Didcot Parkway. As the train passes Corsham on its way in, the windows reveal pretty rolling hills.

DETOUR
Brighton

For a taste of the south coast, catch a train from London to Brighton. Here, you'll find a horde of Regency architecture to rival Bath, an attractive warren of shops, pubs and restaurants known as the Lanes, and a thriving LGBTQ+ scene.

Oxford

Follow the tourist trail along the tracks to Oxford. The city is, of course, renowned for its university, whose sharply pointed towers have resulted in the nickname "The City of Dreaming Spires". The backdrop for numerous films, books and TV programmes – from *Brideshead Revisited* to the *His Dark Materials* series – the centuries-old, honey-coloured colleges are evocative places for an idle stroll. Many of the university gardens and museums are open to the public: highlights include the Ashmolean – the UK's oldest public museum, home to

Bath

Bath's Roman heritage, exquisite architecture and rich cultural connections draw huge numbers of visitors. But don't be put off by the crowds – the city's A-list attractions and boundless charm shine through, making it a joyful place to end your trip.

Given its small size, it doesn't take long to explore the city, but savour every step. A short walk from Bath Spa station are the well-preserved Roman baths, which date back some 2,000 years. Continue north, heading steeply uphill beyond the Parisian-style arcade and covered market to the sumptuous Georgian townhouses of the Royal Crescent and the Circus. These areas look like they've tumbled from the pages of a novel by Jane Austen, who lived in the city and set *Persuasion* and *Northanger Abbey* here.

Looking out on Oxford's famous skyline from South Park

16

Land's End to John O'Groats

Wouldn't it be nice to say you've traversed the UK from Land's End to John O'Groats? Instead of cycling take the train. The UK's rail network whisks you from the sun-drenched beaches of southern Cornwall all the way to the wild north coast of Scotland.

◉ **PENZANCE** ENGLAND ◎ **WICK** SCOTLAND

◉ PURCHASE TICKETS FOR EACH INDIVIDUAL SERVICE; PRICES VARY (P244).

● 21–24 DAYS ◎ 1,564 KM (972 MILES)

Penzance
40 mins

Truro
1 hr 20 mins

Plymouth
1 hr

Exeter
1 hr–1 hr 20 mins

Bristol
1 hr 25 mins

Birmingham
1 hr 30 mins

Manchester
1 hr 45 mins

Kendal
2 hrs 15 mins

Edinburgh
1 hr 20 mins

Dundee
3 hrs–3 hrs 30 mins

Inverness
4 hrs 30 mins

Wick

Penzance
ENGLAND

A one-time fashionable resort for the moneyed Georgian classes, salty-aired Penzance retains much of its historic seaside charm. Here, locals stroll along the 19th-century promenade for sweeping views across Mount's Bay to St Michael's Mount, a tidal island topped with a castle, and swim in Penzance's landmark seawater lido, the restored Art Deco (and now geothermally heated) Jubilee Pool.

The Cornish town makes the ideal starting point for this country-spanning journey, though it doesn't technically count as the route's official beginning – that lies an hour's bus or taxi ride southwest in Land's End, where clifftop trails and stunning ocean views from England's western-most point await. A place of pilgrimage for walkers through the ages, Penn-an-Wlas, as it's known in Cornish, is the place to snap a photo of its famous sign: "John O'Groats 874 miles".

⊖ Catch the train to Truro; services depart every 30 minutes. It's a scenic journey, taking in coastal and countryside views.

Truro

ENGLAND

Diminutive Truro takes the title of Cornwall's only city – but buzzing metropolis it is not. Instead, the neat and narrow Georgian streets of this cathedral city lead visitors to a better understanding of Cornish culture. Head to the Royal Cornwall Museum to delve into photography collections that capture life in 19th-century Cornish mines and heritage objects exploring the region's industrial and cultural past.

➌ You've got plenty of time to make your train to Plymouth, as services leave every 30 minutes.

Plymouth

ENGLAND

Once a major port on England's southwest coast, Plymouth is a city shaped by the fortunes of the sea. Peer into the past at the waterside Barbican, Plymouth's old port, which is packed with

aged, cobbled streets and today lined with a stream of modern independent boutiques.

A short walk along the coast lies another of Plymouth's links to its seafaring history: Plymouth Hoe. This grassy park is scattered with landmarks, including red-and-white-striped Smeaton's Tower lighthouse and the Royal Citadel, a 17th-century fortress that defended Plymouth – and the rest of England beyond – from seaborne attacks.

➌ Spend a leisurely day in Plymouth before hopping onto one of the trains to Exeter, which depart every 20 minutes.

Exeter

ENGLAND

The former religious nexus of the county of Devon, Exeter is dominated by its striking 12th-century Gothic cathedral, featuring the world's longest uninterrupted medieval vaulted ceiling. The city centre is dotted with architectural relics of its Roman, Norman,

St Michael's Mount in Mount's Bay, near Penzance

93

Georgian and Victorian past, including remarkable 2,000-year-old city walls and Rougemont Castle, which dates to 1069.

This is a university city, though, and with that comes vintage stores, cosy coffee shops and nightclubs. Spend some time soaking up the youthful atmosphere before bidding Exeter and Devon goodbye.

🚆 Take your time exploring the picturesque streets of historic Exeter; trains to Bristol from Exeter St Davids leave half hourly.

Bristol
ENGLAND

Bristol might have filled its pockets through the 17th- and 18th-century transatlantic slave trade, but the city now trades in modernity, youthfulness and an abundance of culture. Set around the serpentine Avon river, Bristol has a sprawling centre, divided in two between the modern Shopping Quarter and the medieval Old City. On the outskirts of the latter lies the harbourside Arnolfini Arts Centre, with its contemporary art exhibitions, while the buzzy Stokes Croft neighbourhood – home to vintage boutiques and offbeat drinking holes – lies on the northern edge of the modern centre. Just northwest is the stunning suburb Clifton, which is well worth a visit for its statuesque townhouses and iconic suspension bridge.

Today, the city's most famous export is its street art. The enigmatic Banksy (believed to have been born nearby) has daubed walls across the city with his highly recognizable, and politically charged, graffiti; two-hour tours take in his work, as well as other contemporary pieces in the Bristol street art scene.

🚆 From Bristol's Temple Meads station, trains leave hourly for Birmingham.

Caledonian Sleeper

Rattling north from London into the emerald hills and glassy lochs of Scotland, the Caledonian Sleeper is an overnight train considered one of the UK's most iconic railway journeys. As the dark settles and the haggis, neeps and tatties of the dining cart are washed down with whisky, passengers are whisked through the night, awaking to breakfast and wild, Scottish scenery.

A fruit stall in the Rag Market, part of Birmingham's famous Bullring shopping centre

Home to more Michelin-star restaurants than any other UK city except London, Birmingham has a strong claim to culinary excellence.

Birmingham

ENGLAND

Birmingham is a case study in urban regeneration. Here, world-famous shopping malls and avant-garde architecture sit alongside over 160 km (100 miles) of canals – supposedly more than in Venice, Italy – which played a vital role in the city's thriving metal manufacturing industry in the 19th century. Today these waterways ring the city centre, which has Birmingham New Street station at its heart.

Home to more Michelin-star restaurants than any other UK city except London, Birmingham has a strong claim to culinary excellence and a visit here should be driven by your stomach. The city's most famed dish is the fiery balti, a curry dreamed up by the local Pakistani community in the 1970s and now a regular fixture on menus across the Balti Triangle, a neighbourhood in the south renowned for its curry houses. Wash it down in a taproom or historic pub on Stirchley Beer Mile.

Birmingham is also famous for its role in Britain's chocolate industry, thanks to Cadbury World in Bournville. A tour of this historic factory brings to mind Roald Dahl's fictional character Willy Wonka, as you learn about the history of the much-loved cocoa bean and sample plenty of tasty treats.

Plan ahead and keep an eye on the time: direct services to Manchester Piccadilly leave from Birmingham New Street station every hour.

Manchester

ENGLAND

Once the grimy, sooty heart of the Industrial Revolution, Manchester today is a dynamic city alive with a very different energy. A large population of students keeps this city young, while a pride in Manchester's self-made claim as the heart of British football sustains a warm and welcoming population. Head to the National Football Museum or take a tour of Manchester United's home ground, Old Trafford, to understand why Mancunians can't get enough of the beautiful game.

But Manchester isn't just a sports haven. This city has a strong claim to culture, whether in the industrial scenes at the quayside Lowry Museum or in one of the music venues that have incubated world-famous artists like the Stone Roses and Oasis.

DETOUR

Liverpool

Itching to delve deeper into Britain's musical history? Take a train from Manchester Piccadilly to Liverpool *(p98)*, the hometown of the world's most famous foursome: The Beatles. Avid fans will want to make a beeline for The Beatles' Story, the city's acclaimed museum dedicated to the rock band.

Tune into the pulse of the city's still buoyant music scene with a gig at the Deaf Institute or a concert at Bridgewater Hall. It's a fantastic way to bring your time in Manchester to a close.

🚆 From Manchester Piccadilly, non-direct trains to Kendal leave hourly while direct services depart four times per day.

———

Kendal
ENGLAND

The market town of Kendal couldn't have a more agreeable location. On the fringes of the Lake District, the UK's most popular national park, this picturesque town is the ideal base from which to explore the brooding scenery of Lakeland. Revered by centuries of authors, painters and poets, including Beatrix Potter and William Wordsworth, the landscapes here contain 214 fells and 16 sparkling lakes, with days of

Easy-going, well-heeled Edinburgh stakes its claim as one of the UK's most beautiful cities, with its Georgian buildings and historic castle.

hiking paths and biking trails weaving in between.

Make sure to save an afternoon for Kendal itself, though, if only to sample its most famous export: the hiking snack Kendal Mint Cake.

🚆 From Kendal, services to Edinburgh via Carlisle depart every two hours.

———

Edinburgh
SCOTLAND

A rich history of art culture underpins Edinburgh. Visitors in August will delight in everything from soul-swelling opera

to experimental theatre when the Edinburgh International Festival comes to town.

Outside of this month, easygoing, well-heeled Edinburgh stakes its claim as one of the UK's most beautiful cities, with its Georgian buildings and historic castle sitting high above the city on a rocky plinth. This city rewards exploration on foot. Stroll between classy coffee shops and raucous drinking dens along the Royal Mile that carves through Edinburgh's medieval Old Town, or head southeast of the centre to clamber up Arthur's Seat. This extinct volcano grants 360-degree views of the city from its 250-m (820-ft) peak.

The train to Dundee leaves every half hour from Edinburgh's central Waverley station.

Dundee
SCOTLAND

Firth of Tay-bounded Dundee makes a stark contrast from the picturesque seaside towns of Cornwall. Shipyards and transatlantic trade shaped this city, which lays claim to an important maritime past. The last of its vast boat-building workshops closed in the 1980s, but the memory of their triumph lives on in the RRS Discovery. This vessel was used by Captain Robert Falcon Scott during his 1901 voyage to conduct scientific research in Antarctica; it's now docked in the port and open to visitors.

Just next door, and inspired by the rugged local coastline, the V&A Dundee is a worthy stop along the revitalized waterfront, hosting the work of Scottish and international designers.

From Dundee, trains to Inverness via Aberdeen or Perth depart hourly.

Inverness
SCOTLAND

The capital of the Highlands, Inverness has a simply stunning location, straddling the Ness river that washes north from fabled Loch Ness. While Nessie's residence of this vast freshwater lake has yet to be confirmed, you can't visit here and not search for the legendary monster on a boat tour.

Continue south along the Caledonian Canal, which links Ness with three other lochs, for a fine introduction to sublime Scottish scenery.

Your final train departs from Inverness for Wick, with four services operating daily.

Wick
SCOTLAND

While the collapse of Wick's herring industry might have left a dent on this tiny coastal town, its raw beauty – characterized by windswept cliffs, tantalizingly empty beaches and winding coastal paths – has remained unchanged throughout.

Wick is as far as you can go by train, so you'll have to make the remainder of your journey by bus. It takes just 30 minutes to reach John O'Groats, Britain's northeastern tip, with its sign reading "Land's End 874 miles".

Above
The sign at John O'Groats, Britain's northeastern tip

Below left
Admiring the views over the Lake District from Loughrigg Fell

EXTEND
YOUR TRIP

Burwick

Scotland's wildness isn't confined to its shores. From John O'Groats, board a ferry across the often-turbulent waters of the Pentland Firth to reach Burwick on South Ronaldsay, part of the Orkney Islands. These Viking-influenced islands are fringed with stunning sandy beaches. On the way, look out for porpoises and dolphins playing.

17

Northern England

As well as being connected by the rail network, northern England's cities are linked by a history of cultural and economic rebirth. Explore the best of this reinvigorated region on this three-part tour.

- ◗ **LIVERPOOL** ENGLAND ◯ **NEWCASTLE** ENGLAND
- ◍ NORTHERN RAIL SERVICES AND THE TRANSPENNINE EXPRESS SERVE THIS ROUTE (P244).
- ◷ 4-6 DAYS ◓ 289 KM (180 MILES)

Liverpool

There's no better place to begin your trip around "The North" than Liverpool (although the proud residents of the other cities on this tour may beg to differ). Liverpool is a cultural colossus, with interactive museums, boundary-pushing art galleries and a world-famous live music scene. At the heart of the action is Royal Albert Dock's red warehouses. Once used to store goods before they were shipped out from here to the rest of the world, these iconic buildings now house the city's biggest attractions: Tate Liverpool, the International Slavery Museum, the Merseyside Maritime Museum and The Beatles Story. Talking of which, it's impossible to visit Liverpool and not feel the influence of this legendary band. A whole day could easily be occupied with Fab Four sights, from Penny Lane to the houses John Lennon and Paul McCartney grew up in.

🚆 Trains depart Liverpool Lime Street for Manchester Piccadilly several times hourly.

Manchester

English novelist George Orwell called Manchester "the belly and guts of the nation" because it was the engine of the Industrial Revolution – a legacy that's documented at the fantastic Museum of Science and Industry.

Liverpool
1 hr
Manchester
2 hrs 25 mins
Newcastle

Liverpool's Royal
Albert Dock, the
focus of the city's
cultural scene

There remains a visceral quality to the bold, brash capital of the north, but today its most famous exports are not machines but the twin glories of British culture – music and football. Manchester is home to two of the world's favourite football clubs (Manchester United and Manchester City) and has one of the UK's best nightlife scenes, centring on Canal Street's always-busy LGBTQ+ clubs.

🚆 There are regular services from Manchester Victoria to Newcastle.

Newcastle

Few places radiate local pride as brightly as Newcastle. For Geordies (people from around these parts), there's only one "Toon" (town) and it's Newcastle. This fierce sense of community is perhaps best represented by the city's symbiotic relationship with Gateshead. Separated by a mere sliver of the Tyne river, these two cities come as a pair, joined by a string of bridges and sharing the revitalized Quayside area. Here, you'll find enough attractions to fill a whole weekend: Newcastle's 12th-century castle, the BALTIC Centre art gallery and music venue Sage Gateshead.

Spend another day exploring beyond the cities, walking up to Anthony Gormley's sculpture *Angel of the North* – a symbol of the region's painful industrial decline and inspiring recovery.

EXTEND
YOUR TRIP

Glasgow

It's not just England's former industrial cities that are being transformed by exciting regeneration projects – Scotland's are, too. Continue north across the border to Glasgow *(p83)*; once a centre of shipbuilding, it's now a thriving arts hub packed full of independent boutiques and cool bars and restaurants.

99

Rhosneigr

1 hr

Conwy

2 hrs

Shrewsbury

1 hr 15 mins

Abergavenny

40 mins

Cardiff

2 hrs 50 mins

Tenby

18

Croeso i Gymru

***Croeso i Gymru* (welcome to Wales): the most overlooked country in Great Britain. On this rail trip, you're guaranteed to fall for this small but mighty land of craggy mountains, dazzling beaches and punchy cities.**

RHOSNEIGR WALES **TENBY** WALES

BUY TICKETS FOR EACH LEG OF THE JOURNEY ON THE NATIONAL RAIL WEBSITE (P244).

10–14 DAYS 529 KM (329 MILES)

Rhosneigr

WALES

After making your way to north Wales by air, train or ferry, your journey begins on wild and windswept Anglesey. Despite measuring just 673 sq km (260 sq miles), this is Wales's largest island and a stronghold of the Welsh language. You're guaranteed to hear the lilting sounds of Welsh here, particularly in Rhosneigr, a thriving little seaside village on Anglesey's southwest coast.

For a small settlement, Rhosneigr has an outsized number of beaches and a stay here is all about getting out onto the sand. Stretching to the east of the village is Traeth Llydan, which is backed by sand dunes and perfect for canoeing. To the north is Traeth Crigyll. Open to the elements, it's a favourite for wind- and kite-surfing. Both beaches are linked together by the Anglesey Coastal Path, which traces the island's 200-km (124-mile) coastline. If you have a day or two to spare, walking a section of the path is a wonderful way to kick off your adventure.

Plan your departure in advance – it's a long walk to Rhosneigr station and there are only eight direct services to Conwy each day.

Twr Maw
lighthouse o
the Anglese
Coastal Pat

Ffestiniog and Welsh Highland Railway

Heading deep into the craggy terrain of the Snowdonia National Park, the Ffestiniog and Welsh Highland Railway wiggles through some of north Wales's best scenery. Built in 1833–6, it's the world's oldest narrow gauge railway. Today it clatters along the 22-km (13.5-mile) journey from Porthmadog on the western coast to Blaenau Ffestiniog, a historic slate-quarrying town tucked beneath the Moelwynion mountains.

Conwy
WALES

Leaving Anglesey behind, trace Wales's scenic north coast to Conwy. Built by English King Edward I in 1283 to fortify his defence of a newly invaded north Wales, this city has a timeless quality, oozing medieval history from each and every pore. High above the silty shores of the Conwy river looms Conwy Castle, one of Europe's best preserved medieval fortresses and just one of Wales's 427 castles. Clamber to the top of one of its eight vast stone towers and you're treated to commanding views of both the river estuary and the sky-puncturing mountains of the Snowdonia National Park beyond.

The compact town below the castle doesn't take long to explore, and you'll get the measure of it in an hour or so if you walk the 1.3-km (0.8-mile) town walls. From Mill Gate, stride along the path, hopping down at the harbour for a quick guided tour of Quay House, which holds the eccentric accolade of being the smallest house in Great Britain. Close by is the Liverpool Arms, a fantastic riverside pub serving up refreshing pints and castle views.

🚈 Trains to Shrewsbury depart from Conwy every one-and-a-half to two hours. There are no border checks when you enter England.

Shrewsbury
ENGLAND

It's impossible to penetrate Wales's rugged mountainous interior by train so, to continue your journey south, you'll have to skirt into England. Break up the roundabout route in Shrewsbury, perhaps England's most Welsh town (it was built on the orders of the Welsh princes of Powys in the 5th and 6th centuries).

Much like Conwy, Shrewsbury has historic sights to spare – it's home to 660 listed buildings, running the full gamut from Norman to Art Deco. The highlight is the castle, an imposing 11th-century fortification on the Severn river.

Apart from its architecture, Shrewsbury's main attraction is its "shuts". Making the Old Town a delightful rabbit's warren, these narrow medieval alleyways are overhung with timbered gables and lined with independent shops.

🚈 You're in no rush to leave this pretty town – trains to Abergavenny leave from the central train station every 30 minutes or so.

Above
Inside the Royal Arcade, one of Cardiff's sheltered shopping streets

Left
The ruins of Conwy Castle, which was built in the 13th century

DETOUR
Portmeirion

The unassuming village of Minffordd, three-and-a-half hours by train from Shrewsbury, is the gateway to Wales's most curious settlement: Portmeirion. Built in 1925 by pioneering architect Sir Clough Williams-Ellis, this Italian-style village has pastel-washed buildings and a Mediterranean piazza.

Abergavenny
WALES

Crossing back into Wales, the rail tracks weave their way through mountainous terrain to Abergavenny, gateway to the Brecon Beacons National Park.

While Snowdonia has become overtouristed in recent years, the brooding, gorse-laid mountains and waterfall-slung valleys of the Brecon Beacons still feel wonderfully untramelled (though the paths are mercifully well sign-posted). Use Abergavenny as a base and strike out into the park. For hikers, the best trail is up the

perfectly conical Sugar Loaf, northwest of town. It's a gentle ascent to the 596-m (1 955-ft) summit, from where there are thrilling panoramas across the rounded hills and rolling fields of the Beacons. Cyclists, too, won't be disappointed. "The Tumble", the tricky climb up the western edge of Blorenge mountain, is often hailed one of the best cycles in Great Britain.

Its proximity to the national park isn't the only reason to stop in Abergavenny, though. This market town is famous for its traditional Welsh cheeses, including Y Fenni, a punchy mature Cheddar packed with fiery wholegrain mustard and Welsh ale. Try it in Welsh rarebit (toast slathered in a cheesy sauce) – it's the perfect pick-me-up for tired hikers and cyclists.

🚆 Ride one of the half-hourly services to Cardiff Central, from where you can explore much of the city on foot.

Cardiff
WALES

Wales's capital is a vibrant, metropolitan city, surrounded by sweeping valleys and imposing mountains. Although the city sprawls much further, the centre is compact and many of the sights are clustered in a fairly small area. The train station is a stone's throw away from the vast Principality Stadium, the nexus

Principality Stadium is the nexus of this rugby-obsessed city's fervour when the national team has a home game.

of this rugby-obsessed city's fervour when the national team has a home game (especially when it's against England). From here, it's a short walk to the shops. The city's seven Victorian arcades are ideal for an afternoon's retail therapy, especially if you can't resist an independent boutique. The best-preserved of all is the Morgan Arcade, with its Venetian windows and wooden storefronts enclosing high-end tailors and the world's oldest record store.

Further north is Cardiff Castle, an outwardly traditional medieval fortress with a surprisingly opulent and indulgent Gothic Victorian interior that shimmers with monumental quantities of gold leaf and Italian marble. It's worth at least an hour's exploration. Adjoining the castle is leafy Bute Park, from where water taxis potter down the Taff river to Cardiff Bay, 1.6 km (1 mile) to the south. A bustling port until the dock trade slumped in the 1930s, the Bay is now a buoyant waterfront area, home to reams of bars and restaurants, the stunning Senedd (home to Wales's devolved government), with its undulating roof, and the copper-coloured Millennium Centre. Dubbed "the armadillo" for its rounded roof, and built using materials reflecting the country's industrial past, it's Wales's premier concert hall.

Wales's musical prowess is legendary, with famous performers like Shirley Bassey, Tom Jones and the Stereophonics all hailing from this land. It won't come as a surprise, then, that the capital has a fantastic live music scene. Big-name acts play at the Millennium Centre and Principality Stadium, while up-and-comers perform at pint-sized venues all over the city. If you're looking to let your hair down midway through your Wales tour, Cardiff is the place to do it.

🚌 Departures for Carmarthen leave hourly from Cardiff Central station. Here, you need to change service (and potentially platform) to continue your journey to Tenby.

Tenby
WALES

Your next and final stop is Tenby, one of the most picturesque places in the entire country. This walled seaside town, with its pastel-hued port, romantically crumbling castle and golden sliver of sand, has graced countless postcards and social media posts. Despite its popularity with summer holidaymakers (especially in comparison with other stops on this tour), the crowds never seem to overwhelm its beauty, though. It's a gorgeous place to spend a few days.

Colourful houses lining Tenby's sheltered harbour

The town centre's undulating cobbled streets reward aimless wandering. On the way, you'll stumble serendipitously upon traditional pubs, independent boutiques and historic sights like the Tudor Merchant's House, with its faithfully reconstructed rooms.

Before you know it, you'll have reached the port. After soaking up the seaside scenes and snapping a few pictures of your own, climb up the hill to the castle ruins and adjacent museum and art gallery. From here, you'll be treated to far-reaching views over Tenby and Carmarthen Bay beyond on one side of the headland, and Caldey Island on the other.

This holy island is a popular day trip from Tenby, with boats running regularly from the port in high season. As well as the bright white monastery where Cistercian monks have lived a quiet life of prayer since Celtic times, Caldey is home to sheltered coves, a perfume and gift shop, and some fantastic footpaths.

Hiking is another of Tenby's many draws. The town is perched on the southeastern edge of the Pembrokeshire Coast Path – a 299-km (186-mile) walking route through the UK's only coastal national park. Few attempt to walk it all in one go, instead breaking it up into bitesize chunks. Don your boots and strike out from South Beach, a 10-minute walk from Tenby station, to Giltar Point and back. Your reward is a box of fish and chips on the seafront, before bidding *ffarwel* to Wales.

EXTEND
YOUR TRIP

Pembroke

Steeped in centuries of history, the town of Pembroke, a 20-minute train ride from Tenby, has another of Wales's finest castles and is the birthplace of King Henry VII. For a royal adventure, hire a rowing boat and paddle the 13th-century castle's glassy moat.

19

Best of Northern Ireland

The railway that runs along the Causeway Coast is supremely scenic, but this journey through Northern Ireland offers so much more besides great landscapes.

▶ **DERRY~LONDONDERRY** NORTHERN IRELAND
○ **NEWRY** NORTHERN IRELAND

⊕ PURCHASE AN ILINK ONE-WEEK TRAVEL CARD FOR UNLIMITED TRAVEL ON TRAINS AND BUSES (P244).

🕐 8-10 DAYS 📍 224 KM (139 MILES)

Derry~Londonderry

Sitting on the western edge of both Northern Ireland and the Causeway Coast, Derry~Londonderry has a long and complex history, from its repeated destruction by Viking invaders to the violence of The Troubles. The city is shaking off its past, but it's important to understand it. Get to grips with the history by joining a guided walk along the 400-year-old city walls to the Bogside murals.

Nowadays, the city's happier association is with *Derry Girls*, the TV show that's helped to shift how Derry~Londonderry is viewed on the world's stage. There's even a giant mural depicting the show's characters in the shadows of the city walls, often surrounded by a sea of selfie-takers.

It won't take you more than a day to tick off this fairly small city's main sights. But why rush? Two will give you a chance to experience Derry~Londonderry's thriving craft breweries, treasure-filled vintage shops and markets, and outsized live music scene.

🚌 Catch one of the hourly services from Derry~Londonderry to Coleraine from the North West Transport Hub. This section of the Causeway Coast railway is incredibly scenic. Sit on the left-hand side for the best views.

Derry~
Londonderry

40 mins

Coleraine

55 mins

Antrim

25 mins

Belfast

35 mins

Lisburn

30 mins

Newry

Coleraine

While the small town of Coleraine isn't without its charms, it really just serves as the gateway to the Causeway Coast. Take a day to explore the famous coast properly – the ten-minute train ride to Portrush is rewarded by the Caribbean-style sands of Whiterocks Beach, which looks out on the Skerries Islands. Not too far away (an hour-long coastal walk or 15-minute bus ride) are the Gothic ruins of Dunluce Castle, perched precariously on a cliff edge. Its rooms are now roofless and grass grows between the stone relics of what were once grand fireplaces and soaring arched windows.

✪ Trains for Antrim depart hourly from Coleraine railway station. After hugging the Causeway Coast, the line then cuts inland, taking in green fields.

Antrim

Set on the edge of Lough Neagh, Antrim town is surrounded by the kind of landscapes that make Northern Ireland such a joy, from the nine undulating Glens of Antrim to the forests and estates that formed the backdrop to many a scene in the TV epic *Game of Thrones*. There's not a huge amount to see in the town itself, apart from the 17th-century Antrim Castle Gardens, with its atmospheric listed buildings, contemporary art gallery and excellent tea room. But it's still worth hopping off the train here, even if it's just to break up the journey to Belfast.

✪ There's an hourly service from Antrim to Belfast Lanyon Place. The station is a 15-minute walk from Belfast's centre or catch the free shuttle bus using your train ticket.

DETOUR
Mussenden

The train line passes right underneath it on the Causeway Coast railway, but a jaunt up to Mussenden Temple itself is an absolute must. From Coleraine, the train takes just seven minutes to reach Castlerock, from where Mussenden is a 3-km (2-mile) hike away.

Derry Girls
mural by UV Arts
C.I.C in Derry~
Londonderry

The skeletal
remains of
Dunluce Castle,
near Coleraine

Belfast

Like Derry~Londonderry, Belfast
has long been tarnished by its
association with The Troubles.
For 30 years, between the late
1960s and 1998, Northern Ireland's
capital was besieged with sec-
tarian violence by unionists and
loyalists on one side, and Irish
nationalists and republicans on
the other. The city is still littered
with propaganda murals attes-
ting to this devastating time.
Discover the artworks and get
a handle on Belfast's turbulent
history on one of the many black
cab tours, with a knowledgeable
local at the wheel. Ask your driver
to drop you off at the Crumlin
Road Gaol, the prison that
detained both republicans and
loyalists during The Troubles.

You'll need at least two full
days to explore every corner of
Belfast's city centre properly,
which radiates out from the vast
Victorian City Hall in a series
of Georgian streets. In the north,
the Cathedral Quarter is a great
place to spend the evening, with
its centuries-old pubs sitting just
around the corner from Michelin-
starred restaurants and cobbled
streets splashed with street art.

Add another day to explore
the Titanic Quarter, where an
interactive museum is located in
the old shipyard, on the very spot
where the ship was built.

⊖ There are four train stations in Belfast, so
make sure you go to the right one – Belfast
Lanyon Place. From here, there are regular
departures for Lisburn.

Lisburn

After time spent in bustling
Belfast, slow it down with a
stop-off at the rather more
relaxed Lisburn, which is just
a 35-minute train ride away.

The heart of the city is
undoubtedly Lisburn Square, a
historic market place enveloped
by graceful white buildings. It's
the perfect place for a morning
coffee or evening drink. Every
Sunday, the square hosts a
popular artisan market. Another
of Lisburn's attractions is the
Lagan Towpath, an 18-km
(11-mile) off-road trail that follows
the Lagan river back to Belfast.

⊖ Trains run from Lisburn to Newry roughly
every two hours, with some services
requiring a quick transfer in Portadown.

Newry

This nondescript city might seem
like an underwhelming conclusion
to your tour of Northern Ireland,
but the awe-inspiring scenery of
the surrounding Mourne Mountains will quickly remedy that.
Once you've explored Newry's
centre, hit one of the many hiking
and mountain-biking trails that
lace this Area of Outstanding
Natural Beauty. One of the most
challenging climbs is up Slieve
Donard, the tallest mountain
in Northern Ireland. From the
summit, you can see a huge tract
of the island of Ireland and just
how far you've come.

EXTEND
YOUR TRIP

Omeath

A 15-minute bus ride
from Newry takes you
to Omeath, a tiny village
right on the edge of
Carlingford Lough. From
here, the Greenway (a
former railway line turned
cycle track) weaves along
the lakeshore to the marina,
where you can sample
some of the lake's prized
native oysters.

20

The Emerald Isle

The island of Ireland has a magnetism that makes every day feel like an adventure. Get ready for an epic two-week rail trip around The Emerald Isle, from Northern Ireland's capital to the very south and very west of the Republic of Ireland.

◐ **BELFAST** NORTHERN IRELAND ○ **WESTPORT** IRELAND

◐ AN EXPLORER TOURIST TICKET GRANTS 5 DAYS' UNLIMITED TRAVEL OUT OF 15 CONSECUTIVE DAYS ON ALL IARNRÓD ÉIREANN SERVICES IN THE REPUBLIC OF IRELAND (P244).

◐ 12-14 DAYS ◉ 1,015 KM (631 MILES)

Belfast
2 hrs 5 mins
Dublin
1 hr 30 mins
Kilkenny
40 mins
Waterford
3-6 hrs
Cork
1 hr 30 mins
Limerick
2-3 hrs
Galway
3-4 hrs
Westport

Belfast

NORTHERN IRELAND

Your journey around the so-called Emerald Isle starts in Belfast – the capital of Northern Ireland, which is part of the United Kingdom. It seems like there's always something happening here, whether it's a gig spilling out of a tiny old pub, or a gathering of people watching a local street artist at work. This is particularly true in the evening, when the busy bars, restaurants and clubs of the central Cathedral Quarter are jam-packed with revellers. During the day, things are a little more sedate but certainly no less interesting, thanks to the cutting-edge Metropolitan Arts Centre and scores of independent galleries.

With so much going on, you can easily fill a day with culture. Add more time to explore the neighbourhoods beyond the compact city centre. To the south is the Botanic Quarter, home to pretty gardens and chilled out restaurants, and to the east is the historic Titanic Quarter.

➊ Catch the train from Lanyon Place to Dublin, arriving into Connolly station. The city centre is about a ten-minute walk from here. Alternatively, ride the Luas tramline straight out to other areas of the city.

The quirky *Big Fish* sculpture by John Kindness on Donegall Quay in Belfast

Dublin

IRELAND

Just an hour outside of Belfast, the train crosses into the Republic of Ireland without any fanfare or passport checks. After another hour of beautiful Irish scenery, it pulls into Dublin, the country's capital and a famed nightlife spot. But, while the city isn't short of a pub or two, there's so much more to this place than trad sessions and lock-ins.

The Liffey river weaves through the centre of the city, dividing it into the Northside and the Southside, with residents battling it out over which side is best. Both areas are honeycombs of tiny but distinct neighbourhoods, such as cobblestoned Stoneybatter in the north and the sleek, portside Docklands, which straddles either side of the river. Spend your time taking in these neighbourhoods before deciding which side you prefer. As you explore, duck into Dublin's wonderfully free museums and art galleries, like the National History Museum and the Hugh Lane Gallery.

🚄 Services to Kilkenny leave from Heuston station, which is on the other side of the city to Connolly where the Belfast train arrived.

DETOUR
Sligo

Surfers descend on Sligo (a three-hour ride from Dublin Connolly) from all over the world. This town is all about getting outdoors: ride the waves, explore the pristine beaches and hike the lakeside mountains, before diving into the local seafood.

Kilkenny

IRELAND

Compared to the island's two vibrant capitals, Kilkenny might seem positively provincial. But

Merry crowds outside the Temple Bar pub, Dublin's most famous drinking hole

A viaduct crossing on the Waterford Greenway hiking and cycling trail

Waterford
IRELAND

More history awaits in Ireland's oldest city – Waterford – which is an amalgamation of Viking structures, Georgian townhouses and 18th-century churches. But the city's history isn't just tied up in architecture. This is where some of the world's most famous crystal is made, with pieces from Waterford Crystal forming chandeliers in London's Westminster Abbey, Masters Series shields and even New York City's Times Square Millennium Ball. Tour the factory to see behind the scenes, before purchasing your own crystal souvenir to take back home.

If you have time to linger here for more than a day, hire a bike and head off on the Waterford Greenway, a cycle trail and footpath that leads from the city out to the town of Dungarvan. Along the way, the route takes in towering viaducts, tunnels thick with dripping moss and the beautiful white-sand beaches of the Copper Coast.

⊖ The quickest way to get from Waterford to Cork Kent involves a transfer at Limerick Junction. There is an option to transfer through Dublin Heuston, though this adds a good two to three hours to the journey.

this town, which happens to be one of Ireland's oldest, has an outsized number of historic sights. The star of the show is the 12th-century Kilkenny Castle, which dominates the centre and acts as the starting point of the Medieval Mile, a walking trail that meanders from the castle to the cathedral along cobblestone streets, and past towers and friaries. It's the perfect introduction to the town.

Interspersed among the historical sights that line the trail are bougie boutiques, selling the likes of locally woven throws, hand-painted ceramics and glass-blown jewellery. There's also a strong vintage and consignment fashion scene, with stores stocking everything from 1950s ball gowns to retro Irish knits.

⊖ It's a short 40-minute train journey from Kilkenny to Waterford Plunkett station, but don't miss your planned departure – there's a big gap between services.

Cork
IRELAND

The Republic's second city, Cork stands toe-to-toe with Dublin when it comes to cultural attractions. Indeed, in many ways, Cork sees itself not in second place but as a rival to the capital. It produces its own national newspaper, *The Irish Examiner*, brews its own stout (don't expect

The Republic's second city, Cork stands toe-to-toe with Dublin when it comes to cultural attractions.

The swirling islands in Clew Bay, the bay on which the town of Westport sits

to get a glass of Guinness here) and has a thriving cultural scene of its own. Pop into any of the city's pubs and you'll hear trad music, with fiddles, whistles and the bodhrán drum playing into the wee hours. It's a wonderful city and might just be your favourite stop on this trip.

✪ There's an hourly service from Cork Kent to Limerick Junction, where you can change for Limerick Colbert. Be warned that Limerick Junction is a fair distance from the city – don't disembark here by accident.

Limerick
IRELAND

Over the past few years, Limerick has undergone something of a transformation, shifting from a lesser-visited city to a must-see. From the public artwork along the boardwalks of the Shannon river to the craft breweries in the Old Town, Limerick will keep you busy for at least a day. If you only have time for one thing, make it a stroll around the periphery of St John's Castle (the 13th-century fortress that forms the backdrop to the city centre), and then along the river, past higgledy-piggledy townhouses painted in various pastel hues.

✪ There are several direct services a day from Limerick to Galway station, which is right on the edge of Eyre Square – the city's focal point.

Galway
IRELAND

Sitting on the western coast of the country, Galway encapsulates the spirit of Ireland – it's pretty, it's full of character and it's a hell of a lot of fun. While the central zone around Eyre Square and Shop Street has its charms – namely the traditional pub Tigh Neachtain and the café-gallery hybrid Coffeewerk + Press – it can get a little crammed with tourists. Instead, walk the 15 minutes out from the centre to the Westend to have a pint, browse the second-hand bookshops or grab a bite to eat in peace.

Salthill Beach is a further 15-minute walk away. Locals come here to walk the length

of the prom and jump into the sea at Blackrock diving board, no matter what the weather is doing. If you join them for the stroll, be sure to kick the wall at the end of the 3-km (2-mile) promenade – it's a local tradition.

⊖ The fastest route between Galway and Westport necessitates a change in Athlone. Check journey times to avoid long waits here – typically, the afternoon service is best.

Westport
IRELAND

With its old stone bridges, colourful buildings and baskets of hanging flowers outside every shopfront, Westport may have the look of an Irish village, but it has the soul (and nightlife) of a city. Whether you're looking for a DJ-fuelled dance or a pint of Guinness in a cosy pub, you'll find good craic here.

During the daylight hours, use Westport as a springboard to explore the nearby islands of Clew Bay. The easiest island to reach is Achill: simply cycle along the Great Western Greenway, a decommissioned railway line turned mercifully flat off-road trail. The highlight here is Keem Bay, a little cove on Achill's north coast, which is frequently voted the best beach in Ireland. With its golden sand and bright green shallows, it's a stunning place to end your adventure around the Emerald Isle.

EXTEND
YOUR TRIP

Ballina

Catch the 50-minute train service (with one very quick transfer) to Ballina to explore Belleek Castle and the eccentric Jackie Clarke Collection, which contains more than 100,000 artifacts relating to Irish history. There are plenty of great hikes around, too, from gentle walks along the Moy river to longer treks in Belleek Woods.

21

Coastal Belgium

Utilize both the Kusttram (the world's longest tram-line) and the excellent train network to see some of the best bits of Belgium, stopping at sandy beaches, classic seaside resorts and the beautiful city of Bruges.

○ **DE PANNE** BELGIUM ○ **KNOKKE-HEIST** BELGIUM

○ AS THIS JOURNEY SHOULD TAKE YOU LESS THAN 10 DAYS, IT'S NOT WORTH BUYING A STANDARD MULTI TICKET (P251).

○ 5-7 DAYS ○ 88 KM (55 MILES)

De Panne

Belgium's 70-km (43-mile) coast-line is dotted with 15 separate resorts – a fantastic number when you consider the short distance between the French and Dutch borders. The starting point for the Kusttram tramline, and your journey, is De Panne. This small, easy-going city has seen its share of Flemish holidaymakers over the years including the Belgian royal family, who found safety here during World War I.

Despite De Panne's diminutive size, there's plenty to keep you entertained here for a few days. Explore the Westhoek nature reserve's wild, rolling dunes, try your hand at sand yachting (a sport that was invented here in 1898), relax in a retro, striped beach chair on the sandy beach (Belgium's largest) and tuck into *moules marinière* (a heaped bowl of mussels in a white-wine sauce) at a waterfront bistro.

● Trains make the trip inland from De Panne to Lichtervelde every hour. Change here for services to Bruges.

Bruges

It might be 14 km (9 miles) from the coast, but Bruges's history is intertwined with the North Sea. Thanks to its 12th-century canals, which still link Bruges to the sea, the city became an epicentre of international trade in the 14th century and its perfectly preserved medieval cityscape

It might be 14 km (9 miles) from the coast, but Bruges's history is intertwined with the North Sea.

○ De Panne

1 hr 10 mins

○ Bruges

12 mins

○ Blankenberge

30 mins–1 hr

● Knokke-Heist

dates from this heyday. A visit to Bruges is all about admiring these gabled buildings, sprawling market squares and Baroque churches. Instead of plotting a route around the city, enjoy wandering aimlessly along the intimate streets and narrow canals, popping into the ubiquitous chocolatiers and breweries along the way.

↔ Trains make the 12-minute hop to Blankenberge every 30 to 60 minutes.

Blankenberge

Famed for its Art Deco pier, this tiny town has been shaped by the fishing industry since the 11th century. The Huisje van Majutte, a beautifully preserved 1770s cottage and mini-maritime museum, shows what life was like for 18th-century fishers. But to best appreciate Blankenberge's reliance on fishing, head to one of its many seafood restaurants: De Oesterput serves up some of Belgium's best oysters.

↔ To avoid backtracking to Bruges by train, ride the Kusttram to Knokke-Heist. It runs every 10 minutes and shaves the journey to about half an hour.

Knokke-Heist

Knokke-Heist is the last stop on the Kusttram and your train trip. Affectionately described by Belgians as the "St-Tropez of the North", this resort is full of fashion boutiques, Michelin-starred restaurants and galleries. The best of the 60-plus galleries is Momentum, which houses cutting-edge sculptures. Surprisingly, you'll also find art in Knokke's casino, which is splashed with works by pop artist Keith Haring and surrealist René Magritte. It's a fun place to end your journey.

Blankenberge's Belgium Pier, an Art Deco construction stretching into the North Sea

22

The Low Countries

Ride the rails between some of Europe's most cyclable cities, hiring bikes to explore Amsterdam's canals, Antwerp's rejuvenated docklands areas, and the stately streets and urban art of Brussels.

▶ **AMSTERDAM** NETHERLANDS ○ **BRUSSELS** BELGIUM

◐ IF YOU PLAN TO TAKE YOUR OWN BIKE ON THE JOURNEY (P12), YOU'LL HAVE TO PAY A SUPPLEMENT IN BELGIUM AND ONLY TRAVEL AT SPECIFIC TIMES IN THE NETHERLANDS (P251).

● 12–14 DAYS ◉ 324 KM (201 MILES)

Amsterdam

NETHERLANDS

Where better to start your cycle trip than Amsterdam, the world's most famous bike-friendly city? The canal-ringed centre is laced by an enviable network of cycle lanes, which help you to safely whizz around the city's major sights: the magnificent Rijksmuseum, futuristic NEMO Science museum and the poignant Anne Frank House.

Beyond the centre, take your bike on the short ferry ride to Noord, a once-industrial area that has become a hipster haven. Alternatively, wheel along the Amstel river to Amsterdamse Bos, a forest park home to swimming ponds, Highland cows and plenty of cycling trails.

⊖ Trains depart Amsterdam Centraal for Utrecht Centraal several times hourly. If you're travelling with your own bike and there's no designated bicycle space available on a train, wait for the next departure to avoid a fine.

Utrecht

NETHERLANDS

With cosy cafés, and a labyrinthine network of canals and medieval streets pretty enough to rival the capital, Utrecht often seems like

Bikes on a bridge stretching over one of Amsterdam's ubiquitous canals

Amsterdam in miniature. But this city has usurped its doppelganger when it comes to cycling infrastructure - it claims to have the most extensive bike parking system in the world.

Bike rental shops are scattered all over the city but Bike2Go, just opposite the train station, is a convenient choice. Once you're n the saddle, ride the short distance across two canals to the city's most iconic landmark, the Domtoren. The mighty medieval tower is over 100 m (328 ft) tall and affords views all the way to Amsterdam. From here, walk (the one-minute ride isn't worth the effort of parking your bike again) to the magnificent Museum Cahterijneconvent, which houses an exquisite collection of medieval art that easily matches the Rijksmuseum's.

🚾 Services from Utrecht Centraal to Antwerpen-Centraal leave twice hourly. Passport and visa checks are carried out sporadically at the Netherlands-Belgium border so have your documents ready.

Antwerp
BELGIUM

Although it doesn't shout about it, Belgium is just as cycle-friendly as the Netherlands. In Antwerp, your first stop in the country, take

Above right
The strikingly modern exterior of Antwerp's MAS museum

Below right
Korenlei, a historic quay on the Leie river, which flows through Ghent

advantage of Blue Bike – Belgium's train station bike-hire scheme. After picking up your bicycle from the magnificent Art Nouveau train station, set off and explore this youthful and vibrant city. A good place to start is Het Eilandje, a rejuvenated area of the port, which is now home to fashionable restaurants and the eye-catching MAS museum. Be sure to check out Zurenborg, an elegant district of *belle époque* townhouses, too.

⊖ Return your Blue Bike to Antwerpen-Centraal station before boarding a train to Mechelen; services run every 20 minutes.

Mechelen
BELGIUM

Pick up a new Blue Bike at Mechelen's station (you can't take them on the train with you).

It won't take you long to wheel around the city centre, which is built on an island in the Dyle river, and hit Mechelen's major sights: the massive Sint-Rombouts-kathedraal and a pair of Rubens paintings in Sint-Janskerkhof church. Spend the rest of your time here exploiting Mechelen's status as a "Green Stop" – the starting point for numerous rural cycling paths.

⊖ Services for Gent-Sint-Pieters depart every ten minutes or so from Mechelen, so no need to rush back to the station.

Ghent
BELGIUM

Combining picture-postcard medieval architecture and a wealth of artistic masterpieces with a youthful student population and a buzzing music scene, Ghent has all the appeal of Bruges but without the crowds. The city's relative quietness and compact size make it perfect for cycling. Rent a bike from one of the many Donkey Republic points around the city and then shadow the canals. Sights to stop at include the turreted Gravensteen Castle, whose grisly torture chambers would test the resolve of even the most hardened historian, and Sint-Baafskathedraal, home to the *Adoration of the Mystic Lamb*, a sublime altarpiece by Hubert and Jan van Eyck.

❸ After returning your bike to a Donkey Republic point, board a train bound for Bruxells-Midi from Gent-Sint-Pieters station. There are four services an hour, so don't feel like you have to plan ahead.

Brussels
BELGIUM

Your journey comes to a close in perhaps the grandest city on this route. Brussels is the capital not just of Belgium but of the European Union, and it has the architecture and art to justify it.

The city centre is divided into two parts. The larger westerly portion comprises the Lower Town, fanning out from the marvellous Grand-Place, lined with stately civic buildings. To the east lies the smaller Upper Town, home to the rarefied Musées Royaux des Beaux Arts.

With a bike, you can explore beyond this polished centre and discover a more down-to-earth side of the city. Ride out to Marolles, a traditionally working-class neighbourhood now splashed with street art murals and full of café-bars and flea markets.

DETOUR
Bruges

From Ghent, it's just a short half-hour hop by train to bike-friendly Bruges *(p116)*, one of Europe's most photogenic medieval cities. Instead of plotting a route, see where the paths lead you – this city rewards spontaneity.

EXTEND
YOUR TRIP

Liège

Your journey so far has explored the Flanders region of northern Belgium. Continue west to French-speaking Wallonia, and the cycle-friendly city of Liège, which is an hour away from Brussels. This historic city hosts a one-day classic cycling race from Liège to Bastogne and back each April.

The light and airy main hall in the Musées Royaux des Beaux-Arts in Brussels, Belgium

23

Northern Europe

A train journey along Europe's northern coast joins the dots between pretty canal-laced cities, work-hard-play-hard ports and Baltic Sea beaches. It's an excellent alternative to the crowded Mediterranean coast.

⊙ AMSTERDAM NETHERLANDS ⊙ GDAŃSK POLAND

⊘ FOR THE GREATEST FLEXIBILITY, BUY AN INTERRAIL OR EURAIL PASS VALID FOR SEVEN DAYS OF TRAVEL WITHIN A MONTH (P11).

⊙ 10–14 DAYS ⊙ 1,485 KM (923 MILES)

Bright wooden houses lining Reitdiephaven, an inland port in Groningen

Amsterdam

NETHERLANDS

Built on the back of mercantile
wealth, Amsterdam is one of
Europe's great maritime cities,
as chronicled at the fantastic
waterfront National Maritime
Museum. You're never too far
from water here thanks to the
city's winsome canals, which
conveniently carve up the centre
into easily digestible chunks.

First-timers should stick to the
canal belt for the sheer novelty of
it. Pretty Jordaan is leafy family
territory, De Pijp young and cool,
and Oude Centrum has plenty of
canal-and-cobblestone charm.
If further afield appeals, hop on
the free ferry to NDSM, an old
shipyard turned cultural quarter
overlooking the IJ river. Wherever
you end up, you'll want to experience it like a local; that's to say

straddling a sit-up-and-beg bike
that'll shake your bones as you
rattle over the cobbles, taking
in the city as you go.

🚄 There are several services from
Amsterdam Centraal to Groningen each
hour, so there's no need to rush to the station.

Groningen

NETHERLANDS

With its pretty waterways,
crooked buildings and bicycle-
riding population, Groningen
looks remarkably like Amsterdam
and, indeed, many other Dutch
cities. Yet it has a lively and
infectious spirit that's all
its own, and it warrants more
attention than most tourists
give it. The most northern city
in the Netherlands, it was a key

Amsterdam

2 hrs

Groningen

2 hrs

Bremen

1 hr

Hamburg

2 hrs

Berlin

3 hrs

Szczecin

5 hrs

Gdańsk

trading centre in the Middle Ages; the lofty Martinitoren in Grote Markt square stands as a monument to this golden epoch. Today, Groningen is still an industrial powerhouse, but with a modern edge. Amid the canals and crooked houses are contemporary architectural flourishes that have echoes of super-stylish Rotterdam. The trippy Groninger Museum complex is the most eye-catching — you can't miss this brightly coloured mash-up of a building as you pull into the city on the train. Inside, the collection is just as impressive, featuring modern art from local, national and international artists.

🚆 Most services from Groningen to Bremen require a change in the German cities of Weener or Leer. As both the Netherlands and Germany are in the Schengen area, there's no border crossing.

Bremen

GERMANY

It's time to say goodbye to the Netherlands and follow the train tracks east into Germany. First stop is Bremen, a city made famous by the Brothers Grimm fairy tale in which a dog, donkey, cat and cockerel leave behind a life of hardship for Bremen, intent on becoming the town's musicians. Today, their image is hard to miss: a statue stands in front of the town hall, street entertainers in full costume regale the story and tourist trinkets depicting the quartet fill countless shop windows.

Bremen's (other) main attraction is its impressive architecture, a combination of medieval townhouses and civic buildings (funded in large part by rich Hanseatic merchants in

Right
On the approach to Hamburg's huge central railway station

Below
Bremen's pretty Schnoor district, lined with medieval buildings constructed when the city was a trading post

DETOUR
Copenhagen

Hamburg is linked to Copenhagen *(p221, p225 and p237)* by
the Green Belt Fixed Link rail
tunnel, which replaced the ferry
onto which trains used to roll.
The Danes have a long history
of seafaring, as explored at the
M/S Maritime Museum, and
Nyhavn harbour is still central
to life in the Danish capital.

Harz Narrow Gauge Railways

A Soviet legacy that's still
going strong, Harz Narrow
Gauge Railways serves
destinations in Germany's
Harz highlands, to the
south of Bremen and
Hamburg. Its coal-
powered steam trains chug
through forests come
sunshine or snow, ferrying
tourists and commuters
through a wild northern
European landscape.

the 11th century) and a madcap
series of Expressionist structures.
The latter were commissioned by
coffee magnate Ludwig Roselius
in the 20th century; head to
Böttcherstraße to see the gabled
Haus des Glockenspiels (its
carillon chimes on the hour 12–
6pm Apr–Dec) and the street's
decorated archway entrance,
among others.

Aside from admiring the city's
architecture, and perhaps paying
a visit to the Kunsthalle-Bremen
or the UFO-lookalike science
centre, the Universum Bremen,
time is well spent here on the
riverfront. Watching the world go
by as you tuck into traditional
German fare or sip on a beer is
one of the little things that make
a trip like this worthwhile.

🚨 Catch one of the two speedy hourly
trains from Bremen Hauptbahnhof to
Hamburg Hauptbahnhof.

Hamburg
GERMANY

A work-hard-play-hard port with
a buccaneering spirit, a Beatles
connection and notoriously
seedy underbelly, Hamburg
is one of Europe's great cities.

Germany's "gateway to
the world", it got rich through
shipping in the 13th century and
still flourishes as a trading hub
and tourist destination. It also
trades off its reputation as the
city where The Beatles cut their
teeth; the Liverpudlian band
played many gigs here before
hitting the big time.

Hamburg's louche maritime
spirit is embodied by the infamous
Reeperbahn red-light district, a
boisterous avenue of iniquity lined
with bawdy bars and brothels.
Little wonder locals call it *die
sündigste meile* — "the most sinful
mile". Too seedy? Hamburg has
wholesome diversions in the
form of grandiose churches, the
International Maritime Museum
and St Pauli night market.

🚨 Services from Hamburg Hauptbahnhof
to Berlin Hauptbahnhof are incredibly
frequent, with two services each hour.

Berlin
GERMANY

While it's true that Berlin is set
143 km (89 miles) inland, you can't
pass through eastern Germany

and miss this place. The stage for epoch-defining moments in history and Europe's wildest nights out, Berlin is one of the continent's most captivating capitals and a must-stop on any tour.

While its cultural attractions hog the headlines, the city is a surprising destination for an outdoor pursuit that's enjoying a post-pandemic revival. *Waldeinsamkeit* loosely translates as "forest loneliness", but more broadly means connecting with nature. There are many opportunities to do just that in and around Berlin, surrounded as it is by forests and lakes. Budget at least a few days here so you have time to take in the sights, hike the trails and lounge by lakes.

If your trip falls in summer, spend the evenings at Berlin's beach bars, which pop up along the banks of the Spree river each year. Here, mild nights, a scatter of sand and good company make for sultry, outdoor summer nights. Popular spots include Café am Neuen See in Tiergarten, Badeschiff with its floating lido and Capital Beach, which is conveniently found moments from Berlin Hauptbahnhof. It's the perfect spot for one last drink before hitting the tracks and swapping Germany for Poland.

🔁 Trains to Szczecin Główny depart from Berlin Gesundbrunnen several times a day. Look for "Stettin" (the German for Szczecin) on departure boards.

Szczecin
POLAND

Back on the coast, the railway line pushes on into Poland. Right on the border is Szczecin, a busy and in places gritty port that's firmly off the tourist trail (although German city-breakers are big fans).

Above
Capital Beach, a lively outdoor bar on the banks of the Spree river, Berlin

Below right
Baroque buildings, funded by the city's merchants, lining Ulica Długa in Gdańsk

Gdańsk

POLAND

Your journey ends in Gdańsk. Not that you'll be in a hurry to leave this Polish port; its elegant streets, waterside bars and moving museums will keep you occupied for a few days.

Unlike other Polish cities, but much like many of the stops on this tour, Gdańsk has been shaped by centuries of maritime trade. Its architecture owes much to the wealthy merchants who flourished here when it was the Free City of Danzig, a post-World War I city state under League of Nations protection. Find out more about the city's maritime history at the National Maritime Museum. On the opposite side of the water, the fantastic Museum of WWII describes how the city's fortunes changed with the first shots of the war. It's a sobering experience, but insightful nonetheless.

When you eventually feel like you've covered the centre, venture beyond to the Black Sea beaches. Jelitkowo and Brzezno are within the city limits and on the tram line, and provide a fitting conclusion to your coastal adventure.

EXTEND
YOUR TRIP

Warsaw

From Gdańsk, you can reach Warsaw (*p156 and p189*) in a little over three hours by train. As well as a hedonistic nightlife, regal architecture and excellent museums, the Polish capital offers beautiful beaches on the glorious Vistula river.

The centre was bombed extensively during World War II and the result is an assortment of architectural styles, which run the gamut from Art Nouveau buildings to ugly monuments to early-naughties consumerism. Perhaps the most striking is the partially buried, concrete exterior of the fantastic Upheavals Dialogue Centre. Part of the National Museum, this outpost is devoted to Szczecin's modern history from 1939 to 1989.

All of the city's main cultural sights are clustered nearby, making it easy to cover the city in a short space of time. Don't miss the maritime museum, philharmonic, Gothic cathedral or the castle, which was home to the dukes of Pomerania-Stettin from 1121 to 1637.

There are around half a dozen direct services from Szczecin Główny to Gdańsk Główny each day.

24

○ Luxembourg
   20 mins
○ Mersch
   25 mins
● Diekirch

Around Luxembourg

When it comes to budget-friendly railways, no country can compete with Luxembourg – all of its trains are completely free. It's a wonderful excuse to explore it.

▶ **LUXEMBOURG** LUXEMBOURG ◯ **DIEKIRCH** LUXEMBOURG

💰 ALL PUBLIC TRANSPORT IS FREE; THE ONLY EXCEPTION IS 1ST CLASS SEATS, WHICH HAVE A SMALL EXTRA COST (P246).

🕓 5-7 DAYS 📍 35 KM (22 MILES)

Luxembourg

Set on a lofty plateau above the confluence of two rivers, Luxembourg is one of Europe's most scenic capitals – so it's worth spending a couple of days here to soak it all in.

Luxembourg has been an important strategic location since the 10th century, when Siegfried I built a castle on the cliffs high above the Alzette river, and foreign invaders from Spain, Austria and France have all left their mark on the many fortifications. Here, history is quite literally written in stone, nowhere more so than the impressive mountain-carved Bock Casemates. This subterranean tunnel complex is full of centuries-old storehouses and barracks, which later sheltered 35,000 people from bombing during World War II. Above ground, just west of here, are the refined architectural icons of Luxembourg's old quarters, including the turreted Palais Grand-Ducal and the Late Gothic Notre-Dame Cathedral.

🚆 Trains depart from Gare de Luxembourg to Mersch Gare Routière approximately every 10 to 20 minutes.

Mersch

In the geographic heart of Luxembourg, the small town of Mersch slumbers amid the bucolic

landscapes of the Eisch Valley. Historic landmarks litter the countryside, from the prehistoric Menhir of Beisenerbierg to the ruins of a 1st-century Roman villa. Most visitors, however, have castles in mind. Mersch is the starting point for the Valley of the Seven Castles, a 37-km (23-mile) trail that winds through meadows and forests. Highlights en route include the Baroque Grand Château d'Ansembourg, with its beautifully manicured gardens, and Koerich, a crumbling, picturesque melange of Romanesque, Gothic and Renaissance styles. Allow at least three days here if you plan to walk the entire trail.

🚆 Direct trains run every 30 minutes from Gare de Mersch to Gare de Diekirch. With departures being so frequent, and the journey taking just 25 minutes, don't feel like you have to squeeze your time in Mersch.

Diekirch

Overlooking a tranquil stretch of the Sûre river, Diekirch has a delightful old centre, where flower baskets dangle from lamp posts and outdoor cafés enjoy fine vantage points of the town's steepled churches. Given the peaceful atmosphere, it can come as a surprise that Diekirch was the staging ground for Allied troops during the Battle of the Bulge in World War II. This pivotal confrontation, which ultimately led to the collapse of Nazi Germany, is recounted alongside other stories at the National Museum of Military History. After a visit, you can reflect on what you've learnt at nearby Café Beim Frank, toasting to brighter days with a glass of Diekirch's namesake beer – a refreshing lager that's been brewed in the town since the 1870s.

EXTEND
YOUR TRIP

Clervaux

Less than an hour's train ride from Diekirch is the small village of Clervaux. It has a fine combination of historic sights (like the 12th-century Château de Clervaux) and natural beauty, with trails that lead into the forests of the Ardennes.

Looking out over Luxembourg's old town from the Chemin de la Corniche

25

Alpine Adventure

Despite the mountains and frequent snowfall, traversing the Alps by train is remarkably straightforward thanks to some pretty spectacular engineering. Soak up the scenery as you journey from France to Switzerland to Austria on this tour.

◉ **GRENOBLE** FRANCE ◯ **VILLACH** AUSTRIA

◉ FRANCE, SWITZERLAND AND AUSTRIA EACH HAVE DIFFERENT TICKETING SYSTEMS; CHECK SPECIFIC ADVICE FOR EACH COUNTRY (P246 AND P256).

◷ 18-21 DAYS ◉ 1,334 KM (829 MILES)

Grenoble
FRANCE

In 2022, Grenoble's enthusiasm for cycling (undoubtedly thanks to its 60,000 students) and its climate plan gained it the title of European Green Capital. A fine accolade, but the city will always be better known as the self-styled French "capital of the Alps". Sitting at the confluence of the Drac and Isère rivers and haloed by mountains, it has a quintessential Alpine setting. For the best mountain views, ride Les Bulles (Grenoble's distinctive egg-shaped cable cars) up to Fort de la Bastille. On a clear day, you might be able to glimpse the white peaks of Mont Blanc from here.

On the other side of the Isère is the city's main cultural attraction, the Musée de Grenoble. Home to one of France's finest art collections, spanning everything from Egyptian antiquities to Warhol prints, the museum could entertain you for days on end, but try to contain it to an afternoon.

🚆 Grenoble's railway station was rebuilt for the 1968 Winter Olympics, so spend some time admiring it before catching your onward train to Annecy. Services depart every 30-90 minutes.

Annecy
FRANCE

From the capital to the pearl: the idyllic resort town of Annecy is the so-called "Pearl of the French Alps" because of its good looks and diminutive size. Constrained by Lac d'Annecy and Mount Semnoz, the town has escaped the sprawling development seen elsewhere in the Alps, remaining small and emininently walkable.

Les Bulles, climbing from Grenoble to Fort de la Bastille

133

As a result, you'll only need a day to scoot around the sights.

The highlight is the 12th-century Palais de l'Isle, an incredibly photogenic miniature castle on its own island in the river. In the past, it has been a prison and a courthouse; today it houses Annecy's local history museum.

🚆 Trains from Annecy to Geneva depart every hour. At the border, you may be asked to present your ID and, if necessary, visa.

Geneva
SWITZERLAND

Your first Swiss stop is Geneva, the country's cultural capital. There's no way you can tick off all of the city's 82 heritage sites, even if you stayed here for several days. The two must-visits are the International Red Cross and Red Crescent Museum, where artists explore how humanitarian action affects us all in rotating temporary exhibitions; and St Pierre Cathedral, the adopted church of John Calvin, leader of the Protestant Reformation.

It's because of Calvin's links with the city that Geneva was called the Protestant Rome from the 16th to 20th centuries. Although the church has since dimmed in importance, the cathedral still dominates the Old Town. Set on the southern bank of the Rhône, this area is an evocative place to explore, with its secret passageways and cobbled squares. Give yourself several hours, stopping for a glass of wine or generous portion of raclette as you go.

🚆 Services between Geneva and Zermatt are incredibly frequent: at rush hour they depart every 10 minutes.

DETOUR
Fribourg

Gruyère, the slightly salty Alpine cheese used to make fondue, comes from the Swiss canton of Fribourg. A short 90-minute train ride from Geneva, Fribourg town is full of dairies, cheesemongers and restaurants serving up the freshest fondue you've ever eaten.

Zermatt
SWITZERLAND

Sitting at the foot of the Matterhorn – the distinctive, pyramid-shaped mountain that was the inspiration for a certain triangular shaped confectionery – Zermatt has the Alpine setting that this journey is all about. Unsurprisingly for somewhere nestled below Switzerland's highest peak, Zermatt becomes a bustling ski resort during the winter months. The moguls on the Triftji piste have almost legendary status, but there are thankfully plenty of gentler ways to explore the ski area if your nerves or knees aren't up to that particular run.

🚆 Trains travel from Zermatt to Chur every hour but, as the journey takes around four hours, it's worth catching a service that departs in the morning or early afternoon.

Chur
SWITZERLAND

Chur is thought to be the oldest town in Switzerland, with archaeological evidence suggesting that this spot on the Rhine has been inhabited for at least 5,500 years. More than a dozen museums explore different

Bernina Express

The iconic bright-red carriages of the Bernina Express run along the highest railway in the Alps. Starting at Chur, Switzerland and finishing four hours later in Tirano, Italy, the line is an engineering marvel with 55 tunnels and 196 bridges. Toast the engineers who built it with a glass of Prosecco onboard.

aspects of Chur's history and cultural heritage; if you can only visit one, choose the Rätisches Museum. This attractive Baroque house dates from 1675, but the themed galleries cover prehistoric times, through the medieval and Renaissance periods, to the early 20th century.

🚋 Regular services depart for St Moritz every hour. Alternatively, you can ride the Glacier Express *(p138)* between Chur and St Moritz.

———

St Moritz
SWITZERLAND

After a brief historical interlude, you'll be ready to hit the slopes again. The next ski stop is St Moritz, one of Switzerland's most glamorous resorts. Apart from skiing, the must-do activity is bobsledding. At around 1.7 km (1.1 mile), the run here is the world's longest ice sculpture.

Nearby is Badrutt's Palace, often described as the birth-place of winter tourism because Johannes Badrutt was the first hotelier to promote spending the season in the area in the 1860s. For a taste of St Moritz luxury, treat yourself to tea or a cocktail at one of this opulent hotel's three bars.

🚋 St Moritz's station is right in the centre of town. Trains from here depart hourly to Filisur, from where you'll change for Davos Platz.

———

Davos
SWITZERLAND

Like St Moritz, Davos is synonymous with wealth but, although it hosts the World

A springtime Chur, nestled in a verdant valley

Economic Forum for five days each year, most of the time it seems like any other mountain health or ski resort. Enjoy Davos for free by taking to the hiking trails that stretch along the Landwasser Valley or making use of Europe's largest natural ice-skating field. Despite what you've heard, this resort can be enjoyed on a budget.

❸ There are two main stations in Davos. Trains bound for St Anton depart from Davos Platz (with changes at Landquart and Sargans). Border control will board the train to check your documents when you cross into Austria.

St Anton am Arlberg
AUSTRIA

A different country, maybe, but the landscape remains the same: expect snow-dusted mountains, bristly fir trees and bright white pistes. St Anton (no one calls it by its full name) is the "cradle of Alpine skiing" and the intertwined history of the resort and the sport is explored at the local museum, housed in a traditional log cabin.

Like so many Alpine resorts, St Anton isn't just a winter destination, though. In spring and summer, when the snow has melted, the pistes become hiking and biking trails. There are plenty of routes to choose from, including a flower-strewn path to Putzenalpe (an Alpine farm) and the family-friendly Mutspuren circular trail. Afterwards, refresh tired legs with a bracing swim in the Rosanna river.

❸ There are departures to Innsbruck every two hours but, as the journey can take the better part of four hours, it's best to plan ahead.

Innsbruck
AUSTRIA

The capital of Austria's Tyrol Region, Innsbruck has an enviable history of winter sports: it hosted the Winter Olympics in 1964 and 1976, the Winter Paralympics in 1984 and 1988, and the Winter Youth Olympics in 2012. Using the city as a base, you can ski in a different resort each day.

You don't have to be an active traveller to enjoy Innsbruck, though. The city has around 30 churches and a dozen museums, including the spectacular 16th-century Ambras Castle. The castle's Kunst und Wunderkammer ("Chamber of Art and Curiosities") has an extraordinary encyclopaedic collection of curios that will enthral you for hours. After working up an inevitable appetite, it's probably time for a slice of Sacher torte (a decadent,

The undulating slopes in Innsbruck, a popular spot for snowsports

multilayered chocolate cake). Café Sacher in the Hofburg Imperial Palace bakes the best in the city.

🚇 Arrive at Innsbruck station in plenty of time for your train to Badgastein. Departures are every four hours, so if you miss one you'll have a long wait.

built during Badgastein's heyday. Don't spend long here – a day is more than enough time to soak in the scenes and the spas.

🚇 Badgastein is served by the Tauern Railway, which runs from here to Villach every two to three hours.

Badgastein
AUSTRIA

A spa town since the 16th century, Badgastein became a centre for radon therapy after Marie Curie confirmed that the waters contained the gas. The health benefits of such treatments are debatable, but there's no denying Badgastein's beauty. The multi-drop Bad Gasteiner Wasserfall sits slap-bang in the middle of the town, tumbling among the grand, *belle époque* buildings that were

Villach
AUSTRIA

Your final stop on this Alpine adventure is Villach, the first place in Austria to be crowned Alpine Town of the Year. After speeding around the quaint centre, popping into the city museum and a coffee shop en route, head out to the Dobratsch Nature Park. Here, a series of viewing platforms grant far-reaching panoramas over the snow-dusted Alps – the perfect sight to end on.

EXTEND
YOUR TRIP

Ljubljana
It might not be in the mountain range, but vibrant Ljubljana (p194) has an important link to the Alps. The Slovenian capital, which is just 1 hour 40 minutes away from Villach, sits on the historic trade route that linked the mountains to the Adriatic Sea. It makes an interesting contrast to your slopes thus far.

Glacier Express

Trundling over Alpine passes and steep ravines, the *Glacier Express* proudly calls itself "the slowest express train on Earth". This journey is all about soaking up Switzerland's most spectacular scenery – something that can't be rushed.

The iconic red carriages of the *Glacier Express* curving along the Landwasserviadukt

Although public trains ply the same route between St Moritz and Zermatt every hour *(p134)*, riding the *Glacier Express* feels special. You don't have to contend with connecting services, life on-board is far more luxurious and – as the train rolls along the rails at the same speed as melting snow – there's a lot more time to soak up the scenery. It's a once-in-a-lifetime experience rather than a convenience.

Onboard, the bright-red train evokes the glamour of the 1930s, when the railway line first opened. The carriages are configured like restaurants, with fours seats arranged around a table. Here, passengers are served a multi-course menu featuring seasonal Alpine cuisine by well-dressed staff, who also point out sights on the route.

During the full-day journey between the well-heeled resort towns of St Moritz and Zermatt, the train takes in a storybook worth of scenery. The seat-to-ceiling windows frame clifftop castles and sleepy hamlets, plunging gorges and flower-strewn meadows. The most jaw-to-floor views, though, are those where you can appreciate the construction of the railway line itself. Proclaimed an engineering marvel when it first opened, the *Glacier Express* snakes across 291 bridges and through 91 tunnels on its journey. As the train curves along the six-arched Landwasserviadukt, you'll see the carriages in front of or behind yours suspended above the Landwasser river, before disappearing into a mountain tunnel.

THE PRACTICALITIES

The *Glacier Express* runs from mid-December to late October, with two trains making the seven-and-a-half-hour journey in each direction each day. Tickets are available to purchase up to two months in advance. Three classes are available: second, first and an even higher "excellence" class, which has plush leather seats, a private bar and concierge service, and iPads installed with an interactive map that illustrates highlights along the route.

www.glacierexpress.ch

The elegant
Fraumünster
church in Zurich

Zurich
1 hr
Basel
1 hr
Bern
1 hr
Lausanne
20–30 mins
Montreux
2 hr 15 mins
Interlaken
1 hr 50 mins
Lucerne

26

Best of Switzerland

Lakeside life, fantastic museums and Alpine experiences await on this high-altitude rail adventure around Switzerland's best towns and cities. Take your time: this is a country to explore at a leisurely pace.

○ **ZURICH** SWITZERLAND ○ **LUCERNE** SWITZERLAND

○ SAVE MONEY BY BUYING A SUPERSAVER TICKET. THE FURTHER AHEAD YOU BOOK (BETWEEN 1 AND 60 DAYS IN ADVANCE), THE CHEAPER THE FARE (P246).

○ 14-16 DAYS ○ 616 KM (383 MILES)

Zurich

Switzerland's largest city is the obvious place to start your tour around the country's highlights. Over the years, it's gained a reputation for being a banking powerhouse, and Bahnhofstrasse, the city's main street, is now lined with banks and luxury ateliers. But, despite the glinting wealth on display, Zurich's city centre hasn't lost its medieval mojo. The Old Town, which sits astride the Limmat river, is laced with cobblestone alleys and dominated by the towering twin steeples of the Grossmünster and Fraumünster churches. Niederdorf, the northeastern part of the Old Town, hosts a handful of Switzerland's greatest hits: artisan chocolatiers, candy box clock towers and avant-garde

Ask a local what the most enjoyable part of a train trip around Switzerland is and the reply is often a tongue-in-cheek "the return train to Basel".

galleries. Don't miss Cabaret Voltaire – ground zero for the surreal Dadaist art movement of the early 20th century.

For a taste of cosmopolitan Switzerland, head north to Züri-West on your second day in the city. Here, old factories have been turned into cultural centres and lively food markets now nestle beneath railway arches. It's the perfect counterpoint to the medieval streets Zurich is best known for.

➋ There's never a need to hurry in Zurich – the city's station, the Hauptbahnhof, is the country's busiest and trains for Basel leave almost every 10 minutes.

Basel

Ask a local what the most enjoyable part of a train trip around Switzerland is and the reply is often a tongue-in-cheek "the return train to Basel". Maybe they're right: this city offers the perfect balance of historic sights, fantastic museums and some of Switzerland's most exciting contemporary architecture.

Basel's position on the Rhine and its flourishing river port have long made it one of Switzerland's wealthiest cities. It's thanks to this booming economy that Basel has become a hub of contemporary art and architecture. There are countless art museums here, each with distinct collections.

The Kunstmuseum (which happens to be the world's oldest fine art gallery) runs the gamut from 15th-century to contemporary art, the Fondation Beyeler is a modern tour de force of Monets and Picassos, and the Museum Tinguely is dedicated to Swiss national treasure Jean Tinguely, who made sculptural machines from industrial waste.

Art isn't just confined to the museums though. Walk Basel's streets and you'll spot dazzling buildings by the likes of Renzo Piano, Mario Botta, Herzog & de Meuron, Zaha Hadid and Frank Gehry. Among these giants of modern architecture, you'll also find alleys emblazoned with murals and street art aplenty.

➋ Catch one of the frequent departures to Bern from Basel SBB, a Neo-Baroque masterpiece and one of Europe's busiest border stations.

Bern

Your next stop is the often-overlooked capital of Switzerland. The joy of Bern is to be found by simply ambling its streets. At the centre of the Old Town is the

Above
Looking over Lausanne towards Lake Geneva

Right
A slice of Basel's modern architecture scene, Messe Basel New Hall by Herzog & de Meuron

13th-century Zytglogge tower and its astrolabium – an astronomical calendar clock that tells the time, date and zodiac under which the sun currently sits. Start here, before zigzagging your way to the Federal palace, home of the Swiss Parliament, which looks out over the Aare river.

As well as being a hive of buttoned-down diplomacy and democracy, Bern has an art scene to rival Basel (namely, Zentrum Paul Klee, a homage to the Swiss-German Expressionist's wizardry) and fountains to rival Geneva. In fact, there are more than 00 beautifully sculpted waterworks here.

Fast trains heading west to Lausanne take just over an hour and, with 50 services a day to choose from, you can travel as and when you like. The scenery is at its best in the latter half of the journey, culminating with track-side views of Lake Geneva.

Lausanne

Nestled amid the tightly knit vines of the Lavaux region and the glittering water of Lake Geneva, Lausanne is Switzerland's culinary capital. Bustling food markets and traditional delicatessens serve up cheese from nearby Gruyères and tasty

are many ways to explore it, including swimming, kayaking and riding on a romantic *belle époque* paddle steamer.

🚊 The onward trains to Montreux depart several times an hour and take as long as it does to sink a glass of wine – about 20 to 30 minutes. The scenery is exceptional, though, so save the journey for daylight hours.

Montreux

Montreux is almost pure fantasy: a resort wedged between vineyard-lined foothills and riviera-chic lakeside. Aside from sampling wine and soaking up the sun, most visitors come here for Montreux's famous jazz festival, which takes over the city's cafés and clubs every July, and the Château de Chillon.

Switzerland's most iconic castle is just a short walk from town. With impenetrable walls set against a backdrop of snow-brushed mountains and shimmering waters, the castle's scenery is as postcard-worthy as it gets. Spend half a day exploring the echoey great halls and spooky dungeon, which inspired the English poet Lord Byron's epic narrative poem "The Prisoner of Chillon".

🚊 As efficient as the train network in Switzerland is, the national railway company still has the gigantic hurdle of the Alps to get around. This means that the trip from Montreux to Interlaken requires three trains and two changes, via Visp, Speiz and/or Brig.

Interlaken

After stopping in a succession of cities, you'll be itching to get out

Above
The rolling green pastures in the Lauterbrunnen Valley, near Interlaken

Right
The Rigi railway climbing from Lake Lucerne to the top of Mount Rigi

chocolate from Broc. Meanwhile, moody wine bars beckon passers-by with an array of local wines.

Aside from its culinary prowess, Lausanne is the home of the Olympics – the International Olympic Committee's global HQ and sister museum are both here. Inside the museum, state-of-the-art installations recount the history of the Olympics from its origins to today and memorabilia commemorate sporting highlights. There's also a lovely terrace café, overlooking Lake Geneva.

This huge body of water dominates the city and there

DETOUR

Gstaad

Glitzy Gstaad is only a 90-minute train trip (via the city of Fribourg and canton of Vaud) from Montreux. This glamorous mountain village is full of five-star hotels and champagne bars, but also ranks as one of the country's most beautiful glaciated valleys. It's worth a day trip, whatever your budget.

n the Swiss countryside you've seen so much of from train windows. Fortunately the next stop is Interlaken, an outdoor adventure playground. Plan to spend at least three days here, canyoning, paragliding or kayaking around lakes Thun or Brienz. f budget allows, you can even go skydiving above the notorious North Face of the Eiger.

Further afield, gushing waterfalls, wildflower meadows and sheer cliffs await in the picturesque Lauterbrunnen Valley. Alternatively, travellers with a head for heights can ride the funicular through the Jungfraujoch mountain massif. You'll disembark at the highest railway station in Europe (the aptly named Top of Europe), which stands, fortress-like, on the edge of the mountain. At a whopping 3,454 m (11,332 ft) high, it promises spectacular panoramas of Switzerland's glaciers and seismogram-ragged summits.

3 Trains to Lucerne are frequent, with around 20 departures per day, rather than ast. But you won't mind as the line snakes through some of Switzerland's most sublime scenery – it's a struggle to take your eyes off the carousel of natural drama out the carriage windows.

Lucerne

Clustered with medieval squares, frescoed houses and ubiquitous time-keeping clock towers, Lucerne is Switzerland at its most historic. This is the land of William Tell (the country's national hero), the Swiss army knife and Mount Rigi's historic cogwheel railway Europe's first mountain train. It's also where the Swiss confederation was established in 1291.

History aside, Lucerne is just as picture-perfect as the other stops along this trip. It sits either side of the Reuss river and is joined by the Kapellbrücke, a gorgeous wooden bridge fringed with hanging flowers. The river quickly flows into the über-blue Lake Lucerne, which stuns with its crystal-clear waters and scenic swimming spots.

In Lucerne's new town, wide boulevards host a number of excellent bars and restaurants. Join the locals here – away from the tourist throngs on the river banks – and treat yourself to a final feast of the country's culinary delights.

EXTEND
YOUR TRIP

Ticino

Most travellers are in some ways familiar with Switzerland's French and German parts, but what about the Italian? Ticino, an effortless 90-minute ride south from Lucerne, offers a taste of la dolce vita, with its café culture and tasty Italian cuisine.

27

Rhineland by Rail

The Rhine has made Germany's northwest cities some of the country's richest and most dynamic. Many visitors choose to cruise on the river between these cities but, thanks to Germany's excellent rail network, why not follow the Rhine by train instead.

- ◉ BONN GERMANY ◯ MÜNSTER GERMANY
- ◉ COMPARE THE PRICE OF INDIVIDUAL TICKETS (P251) WITH AN INTERRAIL OR EURRAIL ONE-COUNTRY PASS (P11); THE COST OF BOTH VARIES BASED ON WHEN YOU BOOK.
- ◉ 8-10 DAYS ◉ 197 KM (122 MILES)

Above
Hohenzollern
bridge, carrying
trains across the
Rhine to Cologne's
central station

Below right
The large bronze
statue of Beethoven
in Münsterplatz,
central Bonn

Bonn

From the moment you arrive on the banks of the Rhine in Bonn, Beethoven is everywhere. The legendary 18th-century composer was born in the city, living in what is now known as the Beethoven-Haus on Bonngasse, and his image and music seem to permeate every corner of his hometown.

Thanks to its most famous resident and its time as the capital of West Germany, Bonn has an air of grandeur and rarefied culture. Topping your must-visit list should be the Museum of Modern Art and August Macke Haus, both of which have world-class collections of modern and expressionist art. The Baroque Poppelsdorf Palace and its glorious botanical gardens are also worthy attractions. And, of course, no trip to Bonn would be complete without listening to some Beethoven in Beethoven-Haus's concert hall.

🚆 Bonn to Cologne is a breeze. The 25-minute station-to-station scoot can be done anytime, but you'd be best avoiding the rush hour squeeze.

Cologne

If there's one way to get your bearings in a new city it's by climbing to the top of a towering cathedral. Do just that at Cologne's 600-year-old Dom: views extend over the city, taking in the Hohenzollern (the busiest rail bridge in Germany) and the meandering Rhine below.

Located on the river's west bank, the oldest part of the city is a warren of shoulder-wide alleys, cobblestoned squares

and traditional dwellings. It's also home to some fantastic museums, including the sweet-smelling House of 4711 (eau de Cologne was first created in the city in 1792) and the Ludwig Museum, which houses pop art from the likes of Roy Lichtenstein and Andy Warhol.

Aside from cultural attractions, many of the half-timbered houses shelter beer halls. And a draft Kölsch (the local brew) is almost compulsory in this famously lively city, known for hosting Germany's largest carnival each February.

🚆 Düsseldorf is, as the Germans say, "ein Katzensprung" (a stone's throw away) from Cologne. There are almost 100 departures each day.

Bonn

25 mins

Cologne (Köln)

25–30 mins

Düsseldorf

30 mins

Essen

1 hr

Münster

Düsseldorf

Düsseldorf is one of Germany's greenest cities, thanks to a project that saw the road along the Rhine turned into a long park, and also one of its most arty. The centre is splashed with street art (seek out Kiefernstraße, where every house is adorned with a different mural), full of independent galleries promoting the newest names on the scene and home to an outsized number of excellent art museums. You'll find examples of almost every artistic period in the Kunstpalast, and Asian and modern European art in the Langen Foundation, a beautiful gallery designed by Japanese architect Tadao Ando. The pinnacle is the Kunstsammlung. Dedicate at least a morning to this modern art foundation, which is split across three different spaces: the K20, the K21 and the Schmela Haus.

Come late afternoon, Düsseldorf's bars beckon – and there are plenty to choose from. Earning it the nickname of the "longest bar in the world", the Altstadt (Old Town) has some 300. Visit a few to round off your day.

🚆 Catch the train from Düsseldorf's central station to Essen Hauptbahnhof; services depart every 30 minutes.

DETOUR
Duisburg and Oberhausen

To see more of North Rhine-Westphalia, add side trips to Duisburg and Oberhausen from Düsseldorf. Here, you'll find the Landschaftspark Duisburg-Nord, a repurposed 570-acre iron and steel smelting plant, and Gasometer Oberhausen, a monumental gas storage tank-turned-art space.

The Rhine, dividing Düsseldorf's Altstadt on the east bank (seen here) from the modern commercial areas to the west

Essen

Venturing inland from the Rhine, the train pulls into Essen. This city has come a long way since its smoggy industrial heyday. Following the decline of the mining and steel industries, the city has moved from mines to modern art, slag heaps to sculpture. You'll get the idea at Zeche Zollverein, an art complex that was once Europe's largest coal mine. Devote at least half a day to the precinct's Red Dot Design Museum, Ruhr Museum and outdoor pool in the colliery yard.

Aside from the ghosts of industry, Essen is a wellspring of Catholicism. Essen Minster and its Cathedral Treasury are home to the Golden Madonna of Essen, the world's oldest sculpture of Mary.

⊖ Your final train ride, from Essen to Münster, is the longest on this tour – but it only takes an hour. Services depart hourly.

Münster

Ironically, your rail trip comes to an end in Germany's cycling capital. Münster's credentials as a cyclist's city are justified: there are twice as many bikes here as there are people, the city's 60,000 students seem to cycle everywhere and the ancient walled centre is ringed by the Promenadenring, a 4.5-km (2.8-mile) car-free loop.

There's no better way to see Münster than by bike. Take to the saddle and wheel around the Promenadenring and city centre, popping into relaxed cafés and cute boutiques as you go. (Münster is full of them thanks to the young population attending its four universities.) As you cycle, you'll also get a whistle-stop run through 1,200 years of history: taking in the Gothic City Hall, picturesque Prinzipalmarkt and St-Paulus-Dom, the Romanesque cathedral with its astrological clock that runs anticlockwise.

Cycling through Prinzipalmarkt in central Münster

There's no better way to see Münster than by bike. Take to the saddle and wheel around the Promenadenring and city centre.

28

Explore Germany

When it comes to German cities, Munich and Berlin get all the attention. Swerve them both and ride the rails around central Germany to discover some of the country's lesser-visited cities.

▶ **FRANKFURT AM MAIN** GERMANY ○ **DRESDEN** GERMANY

🚏 BUY TICKETS FOR EACH LEG OF THE JOURNEY. TO SAVE TIME, BOOK INTERCITY EXPRESS (ICE) TRAINS; TO SAVE MONEY, BOOK INTERCITY (IC) SERVICES (P251).

🕐 8-10 DAYS 📍 795 KM (494 MILES)

Frankfurt am Main

Home to the country's largest international airport and one of its best connected rail stations, Frankfurt (no one really calls it its full name) is the ideal place to start your exploration of central Germany.

The city's skyline immediately makes it obvious that you've arrived in Germany's finance centre. Commonly referred to as "Mainhattan", this high-rise hub is where you'll find one of Europe's largest stock exchanges and the European Central Bank. But it's not all about the money here. Germany's fifth-biggest city also has a delightfully reconstructed Aldstadt (Old Town), plenty of quaint pubs serving golden glasses of *Apfelwein* (apple

wine) and the Museumsufer – a cluster of excellent museums along the Main river.

🚄 ICE services for Stuttgart depart every 30 minutes or so from Frankfurt (Main) Hauptbahnhof.

Stuttgart

If Frankfurt's reputation is built on money, then Stuttgart's has been shaped by fast cars. Home to the Mercedes-Benz and Porsche headquarters, and their associated museums (which are worth a brief visit), you'll see a fair number of their autos whizzing around the roads. And yet, Stuttgart is also a place to slow down and relax. Pore over a book in the

Römerberg square in Frankfurt am Main's reconstructed Altstadt

fantastically futuristic Stuttgart City Library, tramp one of the great inner-city hiking trails, soak in a spa supplied by local mineral springs and sip wine in a cosy *Weinstube* (a rustic wine bar stocked with bottles from the vineyards that surround the city).

🚄 On this trip's longest train journey, you'll cut across central Germany from west to east. There are only a few direct ICE services from Stuttgart to Leipzig each day, so you might have to change once or twice.

Leipzig

A haven for creatives pushed out of the capital by rising rents, Leipzig is often referred to as the "New Berlin". While noticeably smaller, it certainly packs a punch with an active arts scene, hip neighbourhoods and repurposed industrial buildings. Be sure to check out the Leipziger Baumwollspinnerei – an old cotton mill that now houses art galleries and studios.
    Another unmissable cultural sight is the Gedenkstätte Museum

in der "Runden Ecke", a museum exploring the city's East German past housed in the former headquarters of the secret police.

🚄 Trains to Dresden leave every 30 minutes from Leipzig Hauptbahnhof. ICE services take just over an hour, while IC and Regional Express (RE) trains are a bit slower.

Dresden

The city of Dresden's two distinct areas perfectly sum up central Germany's idiosyncratic character. On the south bank of the Elbe river is the Altstadt, which clings onto its historic beauty despite being almost entirely rebuilt post-war. Here, you'll find museums, quaint cafés and reconstructed "historic" buildings like the Residenzschloss, Zwinger Palace and Frauenkirche. On the north bank, the Neustadt reaches for the future, with its young multicultural population, politically skewering street art and alternative spaces. End your trip at Kunsthofpassage – five colourful courtyards filled with shops, galleries and places to eat.

Frankfurt am Main

1 hr 20 mins–1 hr 35 mins

Stuttgart

4 hrs 20 mins–5 hrs

Leipzig

1 hr 5 mins–1 hr 45 mins

Dresden

EXTEND
YOUR TRIP

Berlin

Can't resist the pull of the capital? Berlin *(p127 and p155)* is just a short ride away from Leipzig and Dresden and is the final piece in the former East German puzzle. Here the scars of the past form the backdrop to one of Europe's start-up capitals and a party scene that is second to none.

Stuttgart City Library, designed by famous architect Eun Young Yi

29

Eastern Europe

Eastern Europe's cheap fares and retro trains are evocative of a bygone era. But throw aside any expectations of cities stuck in the past: this region is thriving and well worth a lengthy tour.

● **BERLIN** GERMANY ○ **SOFIA** BULGARIA

○ AN INTERRAIL OR EURAIL GLOBAL PASS WILL GRANT YOU SEVEN DAYS OF TRAVEL WITHIN A MONTH (P11). IT MIGHT WORK OUT CHEAPER, THOUGH, TO BUY INDIVIDUAL TICKETS AT STATIONS.

● 14–16 DAYS ○ 2,824 KM (1,755 MILES)

Berlin

GERMANY

This tour takes you to the region's highlights but spend your time in Berlin exploring its alternative side. Built on the rubble of World War II, Germany's capital is constantly reinventing things, turning bomb shelters into techno clubs, factories into art galleries and disused industrial estates into lush parks.

To cover as much ground as possible, and make the most of the little time you have in the city, hire a bike. Wheel east from the Reichstag, in the Government District, shadowing the river Spree and dismounting at parks, markets, restaurants and museums whenever you fancy. (Definitely park up at the DDR Museum, which gives a fascinating insight into life in East Germany.)

You'll end up in Friedrichshain, perhaps the coolest of Berlin's cool neighbourhoods and an obvious choice if you can only explore one. Here, you'll find flea markets, organic food shops and alternative clubs, including Berghain. The ultimate test of whether you're hip enough for this city is if you can get past its famously selective bouncers. Don't worry: if it's a "nein", there are plenty of other bars and clubs to choose from.

✆ About a dozen trains depart for Poznań Główny from Berlin Hauptbahnhof (the city's main station) each day.

Cycling along the Spree river in the Government District, Berlin

Berlin	
3 hrs 15 mins	
Poznań	
3 hrs	
Warsaw	
3–4 hrs 30 mins	
Kraków	
6–7 hrs	
Bratislava	
2 hrs 30 mins	
Budapest	
16–17 hrs	
Bucharest (Bucureşti)	
9 hrs	
Sofia	

Poznań
POLAND

After Berlin, Poznań is bound to feel a little small. But this Polish city isn't just a convenient place to break the journey to Warsaw, it's a destination in its own right.

After rolling into the city in the late morning, spend the afternoon exploring the Old Town, gazing up at the colourful façades of Stary Rynek, popping into the excellent Poznań Historical Museum and stopping for *pierogis* (dumplings). It's the perfect introduction to Poland.

🚆 Six services run between Poznań Główny and Warsaw Zachodnia each day.

Warsaw
POLAND

Made up of an attractive melange of architectural styles befitting of its tumultuous history, Warsaw is a byword for resilience. It's endured the worst of modern history (Hitler ordered its complete destruction following the Warsaw Uprising in 1944), and has risen phoenix-like to become one of Eastern Europe's must-visit destinations.

The Polish capital is bisected by the Wisła (Vistula) river, with most of the main sights located on its western bank. The Royal Route, encompassing a series of connected streets, shadows the river from the 13th-century Royal Castle to the Wilanów Palace. Along its 11-km (7-mile) span, the route passes centuries-old palaces and manicured gardens. Walking it is an excellent way to orientate yourself and see a lot of the city in a short space of time.

🚆 Trains from Warsaw Zachodnia run to Krakow Główny almost hourly. Try to catch a fast service to shave 90 minutes off the journey.

Above
Colourful merchants' houses in Stary Rynek (Old Market Square), Poznań

Right
Sigismund's Column in Plac Zamkowy (Castle Square), Warsaw

Kraków
POLAND

The stately streets, soaring churches and grand palace of Poland's former royal capital have made it a fixture on most Eastern European itineraries. But don't let Kraków's popularity put you off.

Most visitors start in Stare Miasto (the Old Town) and you should, too. Ringed by Planty park and remnants of the city's medieval walls, this concentrated area is home to the city's big-ticket sights. Start at the 14th-century Wawel Cathedral, which contains the remains of most of Poland's 45 monarchs. Their tombs serve as an encyclopedia of European artistic movements. A short stroll away from the cathedral is Wawel Castle. Visitor numbers are restricted so book your ticket in advance to admire the opulent state rooms, private apartments and royal treasury. And don't miss Smok, the fire-breathing dragon statue.

Beyond Kraków, and accessible by organized tour or a two-hour public bus ride from the city centre, is Auschwitz-Birkenau. Approximately 1.3 million people were murdered by the Nazi regime in this complex of concentration camps, famously emblazoned with the words "arbeit macht frei" ("work sets you free"). It's a sobering but essential visit.

🚆 There's only one direct train from Krakow Główny to Bratislava Hlavná Stanica each day, departing mid-morning (check the exact time ahead) and taking six to seven hours to reach the Slovakian capital.

157

Bratislava
SLOVAKIA

Delightfully compact, Bratislava crams a city's worth of palaces, shops, cafés, pubs, restaurants, museums and churches into its pint-sized centre. As a result, it won't take you more than a morning to whizz around the big sights. Spend the rest of your time in the Little Carpathians, a vineyard-flanked mountain range full of cellar doors. You might not have tried, or even heard of, Slovakian wine before, but it might just become your new go-to order.

⊖ Trains make the two-and-a-half-hour journey from Bratislava Hlavná Stanica to Budapest Nyugati every couple of hours.

Budapest
HUNGARY

Straddling both sides of the Danube, and packed with monuments to the might of the Austro-Hungarian empire, Budapest certainly is a stunning city. But for all its pomp and grandiosity, and despite creeping gentrification, the Hungarian capital's beauty has faded in some districts, lending them a cool, alternative edge.

This is perhaps best epitomized in District VII, where once abandoned, dilapidated buildings have been turned into *romkocsma* (ruin bars). The most iconic is Szimpla Kert, an old apartment block and stove factory that now hosts movie screenings, live music, farmers' and flea markets and, of course, epic nights outs.

⊖ Board the sleeper train from Budapest Keleti. After a mammoth 16 to 17 hours, you'll wake up in Bucharest Gara de Nord.

Bucharest
ROMANIA

The Romanian capital has been slow to shake off its communist

Right
St Alexander Nevsky Cathedral, a Neo-Byzantine Bulgarian Orthodox cathedral in Sofia

Below
The glitter ball-festooned interior of Szimpla Kert ruin bar, Budapest

hangover. The skyline is still a
mass of concrete, Soviet-style
apartment blocks and the streets
are famously congested. But
away from the traffic, things are
changing. Once-derelict buildings
have reopened as chic hotels
and new restaurants suggest
a culinary awakening could be
on the cards.

This is your chance to see
Bucharest before it changes too
much and loses its messy appeal.
Stroll the tangle of wonderfully
ratty streets that make up
Lipscani, the only part of the Old
Town that escaped development
under Ceaușescu's communist
regime; browse the terrific yet
chaotic markets for communist
memorabilia; and watch the world
go by from a pavement café.

Only one train makes the nine-hour
journey from Bucharest Gara de Nord to
Sofia Central each day, so plan ahead. The
service is direct from June to October;
change trains in Ruse at other times of year.

Sofia

BULGARIA

With its onion-domed churches,
gilded cathedral and Ottoman
mosques, your last stop instantly
feels the most eastern of the cities
that you've visited on this tour.
It's all thanks to the Turks who
occupied the Bulgarian capital
from 1396 to 1878 and built a
series of mosques, including the
16th-century Banya Bashi, and
various bathhouses here.

The Russians, too, left their
mark on Sofia, most notably
with the golden-domed Russian
Church and nearby St Alexander
Nevsky Cathedral. Bulging with
domes and glittering with gold
leaf, this magnificent structure
was financed by public subscrip-
tion and built between 1882 and
1924 to honour the 200,000
Russian casualties of the 1877–78
War of Liberation. It's a stark
reminder of Russia's role in the
history of Eastern Europe.

EXTEND
YOUR TRIP

Thessaloniki

Greece's beaches are just
six hours south of Sofia.
Direct buses and a
temperamental train
service (check ahead to see
if it's running) connect the
Bulgarian capital with
Thessaloniki *(p213)*, which
promises a sandy end to
your eastern odyssey.

30

Romantic Germany

Marrying historic cities and enchanting scenery, this route shows off the very best of southern Germany. Hop aboard to glide past shimmering lakes and shady forests; hop off to explore characterful old towns and fairy-tale castles.

○ PASSAU GERMANY ○ FREIBURG IM BREISGAU GERMANY

◔ TICKET PRICES VARY ACCORDING TO THE CHOSEN ROUTE, TIME OF DAY, TRAIN TYPE AND CLASS (P251).

◔ 10–14 DAYS ◑ 749 KM (465 MILES)

Passau

Known as the "City of Three Rivers", Passau lies at the confluence of the Danube, the Ilz and the Inn. This fascinating natural phenomenon is best observed from the city's hilltop fortress Veste Oberhaus – from here, you can cleary see the different colours of each waterway merging.

Rivers aren't Passau's only draw though; this city is packed with Italian-style archways and buildings dressed in every hue imaginable. Take an afternoon to amble around, stopping by St Stephan's Cathedral, home to one of the world's largest pipe organs, and the eclectic mix of artist studios and galleries in creative Höllgasse. If art is your thing, it might be worth adding an extra day here to explore the Museum of Modern Art, too.

⊖ Direct Regional Express (RE) trains to Munich leave roughly every hour from Passau Hauptbahnhof.

Munich

The centre of southern Germany, Munich is an international hub with a strong local stamp. There's a lot that puts this city on the map – the world-class FC Bayern Munich football team and the iconic Oktoberfest, to name just a few – but there's even more to discover on the ground.

You'll need a couple of days to explore the city's cultural offerings. The cavernous Deutsches Museum is chockfull of science and tech exhibits, the BMW Museum documents the history of the homegrown car brand and the Lenbachhaus features a noteworthy German Expressionism collection. In the evening, theatres come alive with opera and ballet performances, and live music seeps from popular venues across the city.

And yet, it is also possible to visit the Bavarian capital and spend very little time indoors. Thanks to the Isar river, numerous parks such as the Englischer Garten, beer gardens and the locals' love of alfresco dining, a lot of Munich life takes place outside. Wherever you are, you'll never be too far from your next Maß – Oktoberfest or not.

⊖ Trains to Augsburg leave regularly from München Hauptbahnhof – for many this is a daily commute, so prepare for a busy train.

Passau

2hrs 10 mins–2hrs 45 mins

Munich (München)

30–50 mins

Augsburg

45 mins–1 hr 10 mins

Ulm

1 hr 35 mins–2 hrs

Lindau

3 hrs 50 mins–5 hrs

Freiburg im Breisgau

Augsburg

Founded by the Romans in 15 BCE, Augsburg is one of Germany's oldest cities. It's arguably not as quaint as some of the other stops on the Romantic Road, but it's refreshingly less touristy. The elegant Maximilianstraße and the huge town hall are the main draws. You can climb the Perlachturm (next door to the town hall) for sweeping views of the city, too.

Augsburg's more romantic side lies away from the big sights. Nip down narrow alleyways replete with cobblestone streets and ivy-covered houses; explore the network of picturesque canals in the Lechviertel, the former crafters' district; or hunker down in a café to indulge in the local plum cake, *Augsburger Zwetschgendatschi*. You'll find yourself waxing lyrical about Augsburg in no time.

No need to plan – direct services to Ulm run regularly from Augsburg Hauptbahnhof. The RB and RE trains take slightly longer than the Intercity options.

DETOUR
Füssen

Don't want to leave Germany without a snap of its fairy-tale castle? Hop on the train to Füssen for a bus connection to Neuschwanstein. Set within the gorgeous Bavarian Alps, this castle won't disappoint. The crowds might though, so arrive early or visit off season.

Ulm

Sitting pretty between Stuttgart and Munich, Ulm is often overshadowed by its famous neighbours, but that doesn't mean it should be ignored. Albert Einstein was born here and a number of places pay tribute to the legendary scientist – highlights include the quirky Einstein Fountain and a photo exhibition at the local Volkshochschule.

The rest of your time can be spent discovering the city's other claims to fame. Here you can see

Above
Half-timbered houses in the historic Fischerviertel district of Ulm

Right
Lindau's scenic harbour and lighthouse, with Bodensee (Lake Constance) in the distance

It's all about the setting in Lindau, with postcard-worthy shots of the surrounding mountains and views of nearby Austria and Switzerland.

...e world's tallest church (Ulmer Münster) and the world's most crooked hotel, found in the Fischerviertel (Fishermen's Quarter) where old mills and half-timbered houses line a tributary of the Danube. Come day's end, retire to a cosy inn for dinner and a nightcap.

🚆 Regional trains to Lindau-Insel leave Ulm Hauptbahnhof regularly. Alternatively, board a train heading to Lindau-Reutin and pick up a local service to the island from there.

Lindau

Connected to the mainland by two bridges, the Old Town of Lindau lies on an island in the beautiful Bodensee (Lake Constance). It's all about the setting here, with postcard-worthy shots of the surrounding mountains and views of nearby Austria and Switzerland.

Once you've lapped up the scenery, pay a visit to the historic harbour with its magnificent lighthouse and have an early dinner in one of the great restaurants. Just be sure to be back at the water's edge for sunset, when lights twinkle around the shore.

🚆 Bear in mind that the trip to Freiburg (Breisgau) Hauptbahnhof takes around 4–5 hours, and involves one or two changes and sometimes a border crossing.

Freiburg im Breisgau

After your island soujourn, head to Freiburg, or the "Capital of the Black Forest" as it's also known. This laid-back university town leads the way for environmentally friendly living in Germany – spot the futuristic city hall, the world's first public building with a net-positive energy balance, and the flurry of local cyclists.

It's also a balmy corner of the country, with endless sunshine doing wonders for local wine production. Visit the vineyards that surround the city or, if beer is more your thing, head to the beer garden at the top of Schloss-berg which overlooks the city's rooftops. A good view and a good brew, what better way to end your tour?

Höllentalbahn

If you're looking to venture into the Black Forest, take the Höllentalbahn (Hell Valley Railway) to the town of Donaueschingen. Along the way, the route swoops past rocky outcrops and the Ravenna Bridge, a soaring viaduct. Regular trains head to stops along the line, including the beautiful Titisee. Hop off here to take in the scenery and intercept the 3-Seen-Bahn (Three Lake Railway), which makes a detour to two further lakes.

31

Best of Italy

Milan (Milano)

2 hrs 30 mins

Venice (Venezia)

2 hrs 15 mins

Florence (Firenze)

1 hr 35 mins

Rome (Roma)

1 hr 15 mins

Naples (Napoli)

Hopping between the country's most iconic cities, this two-week tour has to be the ultimate Italian rail trip. You'll experience *la dolce vita* (the sweet life) everywhere you go as you travel from the north to the south.

- ▶ **MILAN** ITALY ○ **NAPLES** ITALY
- ◐ TO MAXIMIZE YOUR TIME IN EACH CITY, TRAVEL ON HIGH-SPEED FRECCIAROSSA SERVICES. BOOK AHEAD FOR THE BEST FARES (P252).
- ● 12–16 DAYS ● 1,002 KM (623 MILES)

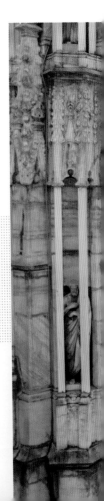

Milan

Financial powerhouse, fashion capital, cultural colossus – and the first chapter in your Italian odyssey. Milan is often ignored in favour of the other cities on this tour, but it shouldn't be. There's art and architecture in abundance here, including two of Italy's finest sights.

The city centre itself is relatively compact, and is best explored on foot. Standing at the heart of it all is the rather remarkable Duomo, a Gothic masterpiece with twisted pinnacles and spires soaring into the sky. It's arguably the most impressive cathedral in all of Italy – architecturally, yes, but also because it's one of the few where visitors are permitted to climb the rooftop. Enjoy the

surreal experience, and those sweeping views across the city below.

From here, you'll be able to see the dome of the Chiesa di Santa Maria delle Grazie, just a 20-minute walk away from the cathedral. This church's deceptively nondescript brick exterior conceals a world-famous painting: Leonardo da Vinci's iconic *The Last Supper.* Viewings are by reservation only so book ahead to avoid disappointment.

While you're here, you'll get your first taste of the Italian art of *aperitivo.* In the early evenings, *milanesi* sit back at stylish bars, sipping elegantly crafted cocktails and savouring finger food designed to whet the appetite. Do as they do, snacking on these little treats before planning your onward journey to Venice at a nearby restaurant.

🚄 Frecciarossa trains zip east from Milano Centrale to Venezia Santa Lucia, Venice's main station, every 30–60 minutes. The last part of the journey, when the train runs across the Venetian Lagoon, is particularly scenic.

Venice

Set over 100 islands, separated by a maze of canals and linked by over 400 footbridges, Venice and its unique watery cityscape continue to capture the world's imagination. Overtourism is a real problem here, so time your visit carefully and think about straying from the beaten path when you can.

Visitors inevitably gravitate towards Piazza San Marco, home to the Basilica di San Marco, the Palazzo Ducale, Galleria dell'Accademia and Punta della Dogana – not to mention the city's resident pigeons. Unless you've arrived out of season, set an early morning alarm to get a head start on your fellow travellers – queues can be lengthy and pavement space sparse as the day progresses.

The Piazza del Duomo, seen from the roof terrace of Milan's cathedral

Another way to escape the daily hubbub is to hop over to one of the other islands in the Venetian Lagoon. Burano, with its vibrant painted houses, and Murano, with its famous glassworks, are both fine choices. Even more off the beaten track is San Lazzaro degli Armeni, a small island that once served as a leper colony; monks give guided tours of the complex, which includes a church, museum and library.

🚆 High-speed Frecciarossa services run from Venezia Santa Lucia to Firenze Santa Maria Novella every hour.

Florence

Cradle of the Renaissance, Florence is famous for two things: art, and more art. The Medici family made their mark here, commissioning the most prominent artists of the time (Donatello, Brunelleschi, Michelangelo, to name a few) to embellish their properties and decorate city structures. And not a lot has changed since their heyday; the city is a living museum. The striped Cattedrale di Santa Maria del Fiore dominates the cityscape and visitors tend to begin days of sightseeing in its shadow. The Uffizi Gallery, Palazzo Pitti and the Accademia are all within striking distance, though to best appreciate the city's beauty the Piazzale Michelangelo is hard to beat. Dubbed the balcony of Florence, it's a favourite spot to watch the sun turn the city pink in the early evening.

A word of warning: to stave off the inevitable Stendhal syndrome (a psychosomatic condition brought on by so much beauty), make sure to break the day with quick bar-side coffees, drawn-out lunches and an evening negroni (invented here, no less).

🚆 Frecciarossa trains to Roma Termini run every 15–30 minutes from Firenze Santa Maria Novella.

Rome

With 2,000 years of history to cover, it's hard to squeeze all of Rome's delights into a few days. In the densely packed historic centre, ancient Roman structures are tucked away behind Renaissance fountains, richly decorated temples hide behind graceful piazzas, and restored *palazzi* (palaces) with frescoed ceilings harbour some of the world's most impressive historical artifacts and artworks.

The must-visits: the Colosseum, Roman Forum and Pantheon (which remains the world's largest unsupported dome). The Vatican Museums should make the list, too: the Sistine Chapel, decorated with magnificent ceiling frescoes by Michelangelo, is arguably one of the most significant pieces of art in the world.

Sightseeing aside, make time to do as the Romans do: enjoy a *passeggiata* (a leisurely evening stroll), the mandatory *aperitivo* and platefuls of hearty cuisine. You won't see all that Rome has to offer, but that's the joy: you know you'll be coming back.

🚆 Frecciarossa trains travel every 30 minutes from Roma Termini to Napoli Centrale.

Naples

With its narrow, densely packed streets, noisy street life and

The atmospheric remains of the Roman Forum, one of Rome's unmissable historic sights

DETOUR
Castel Gandolfo

Home to the Pope's summer palace, Castel Gandolfo makes a great summer day trip from Rome. Reachable in 40 minutes from Termini station, the town sits on Lake Albano, which is lined with beach clubs, restaurants and watersports rental stores.

ubiquitous droning mopeds, unabashed Naples is Italy stripped back to its most authentic. It's still to shake off entirely its reputation for crime and grime but stay a while and you'll be asking why.

While there are sights aplenty, not least the Museo Archeologico, with its spectacular finds from nearby Pompeii and Herculaneum (both worthy day trips), and the Cappella Sansevero, home to the astonishing *Veiled Christ* sculpture, plan your days around mealtimes rather than opening hours. Breakfast calls for two Neapolitan favourites: espresso and *sfogliatella* (a shell-shaped pastry filled with orange-flavoured ricotta or almond paste). Enjoy both slowly, surveying all of local life as it bustles around you. Street food vendors and bars make snack time a regular occurrence, with fried just about everything ensuring hunger never really makes an appearance. And for lunch and dinner? Naples serves the very best pizza – this is its birthplace, after all. Made with pillowy sourdough, creamy mozzarella and plump red tomatoes grown on the volcanic slopes of Vesuvius, a simple margherita might be the most delicious thing you've eaten on your entire tour.

EXTEND
YOUR TRIP
Sicily

Sicily *(p179)* is a timeless land of untouched beaches, little-visited sights, fiery wine and cheap street food. Getting to the island is a once-in-a-lifetime thrill in itself: trains from Calabria are driven onto a rail-ferry, which then chugs across the Straits of Messina, before shunting carriages onto the charmingly old-fashioned Sicilian network.

Right
A traditional *salsamenteria* (delicatessen) in Bologna

Below
Bologna's beautiful cityscape, dominated by the Torre degli Asinelli

Bologna
20–30 mins

Modena
30 mins

Parma
1 hr–1 hr 30 mins

Milan (Milano)
1 hr–1hr 50 mins

Turin (Torino)
1 hr 40 mins–2 hrs

Genoa (Genova)

32

Slow Food Italy

In northern Italy, trains are fast but food is slow – chefs take their time over dishes, putting local ingredients to good use. Speed between the region's foodie cities on this two-week rail trip, savouring dishes at each stop.

● BOLOGNA ITALY ● GENOA ITALY

● TICKETS FOR ALL SERVICES ARE CHEAPER IF YOU BOOK THEM IN ADVANCE ONLINE (P252).

● 10–14 DAYS ● 521 KM (324 MILES)

Bologna

The region of Emilia-Romagna is known for growing some of Italy's best produce so its regional capital, Bologna, is a good starting point for your slow food adventure. It's affectionately known as La Grassa ("The Fat One") for good reason – this is the city that gave the world lasagne (layers of green egg pasta, ragù, béchamel and grated Parmesan) and, of course, bolognese sauce. A heaped bowl of pasta is just the thing to perk up tired legs after a day spent climbing up the 97-m (318-ft) Torre degli Asinelli or strolling the Portici di Via San Luca, the seemingly endless porticoes that weave up to the Santuario Madonna di San Luca.

Making fresh pasta is an art in Bologna. Many *pastifici* (pasta shops) have huge picture windows so you can watch as the dough is slowly rolled out into wafer-thin sheets, stuffed with filling and tucked into little hat-shaped bundles. The best place

Parmesan or Parmigiano Reggiano cheese, one of Parma's many specialities

sweet nectar is surprisingly drinkable when it's this fresh.

Modena's cuisine isn't all about vinegar though. Other must-eats include *bollito misto* (tough cuts of meat like beef tongue and pig's foot slowly simmered in a rich broth), *zampone* (a mixture of pork meat, rind and fat stuffed into a pig's trotter) and *cotechino* (a deliciously tasty pork sausage stuffed inside a pig's bladder). You'll find these hearty dishes at most restaurants in the medieval centre, which radiates out from the beautiful Romanesque Duomo in concentric streets, though not at Osteria Francescana, Modena's much-lauded three-Michelin-starred restaurant. If you're after a splash-out, fancy meal midway through your trip, this is the place for it.

to catch the action is Le Sfogline, near the Mercato delle Erbe.

After watching the pros, try making pasta yourself. There are a plethora of classes available, usually ending with you tucking into your dish and sharing a bottle of wine with your classmates, Italian style.

🚆 High-speed Frecciarossa and Frecciargento (FR) trains zip from Bologna Centrale to Modena in only 17 minutes. Slower regional trains take 10-15 minutes more, but cost a fraction of the price.

🚆 Local Intercity (IC) and Regionale Veloce (RV) trains from Modena to Parma leave every 15–30 minutes.

Modena

Northwest of Bologna, the little town of Modena is known for its fast cars (Ferrari, Lamborghini and Maserati all have factories here) and slow food. Modena's balsamic vinegar is a household name and the town is peppered with historic factories, offering tours and tastings. This rich,

Parma

Think of "Parma" and "ham" undoubtedly springs to mind. The city is to thank for *prosciutto di Parma* (or Parma ham) – a leg of pork cured with nothing but sea salt, lending the meat a sweet and tender flavour. This may be the city's most famous cold cut but you shouldn't leave Parma without also trying *culatello di zibello* (a melt-in-the-mouth ham aged for a minimum of ten months) and *coppa* (air-dried pork neck stuffed in natural casings). Come lunch-time, pick up some bread and these meats from a traditional *salsamenteria* (delicatessen) and head to Parco Ducale. Here, you'll

Modena's balsamic vinegar is a household name and the town is peppered with historic factories, offering tours and tastings.

picnic surrounded by 16th-century sculptures and the Palazzo Ducale.

Italy's much-loved Parmesan, or Parmigiano Reggiano, is of course another of Parma's specialities. Spend an afternoon learning how this hard, dry cheese is made at the Museum of Parmigiano Reggiano in nearby Soragna. You won't be able to resist a doorstop chunk, probably accompanied by another round of cold meats.

⊕ High-speed Frecciarossa and local Intercity (IC) services to Milano Centrale leave every 30 minutes or so.

Milan

More often associated with fashion, Milan has an underestimated foodie scene. The cuisine here is heartier than elsewhere – butter is used more readily than olive oil, and risotto features on most menus. It's unsurprising, then, that the city's signature dish is *risotto alla milanese* (a comforting bowl of saffron-infused rice and onions simmered in an intense bone marrow and beef stock). It's like a warm hug in a bowl, so swerve the swanky restaurants and head to a family-run trattoria to try it. The central Navigli neighbourhood is full of good options.

This canal-laced area is also where the Milanesi go come *aperitivo* time – a typically Italian tradition that's all about warming up for dinner with a drink and some small eats. After a long day of sightseeing, there's really nothing better.

⊕ Ride one of the high-speed services from Milano Centrale to Turin Porta Susa or Porta Nuova to cut the journey time from nearly two hours to one.

A well-decorated traditional trattoria in Milan

Terraced vines in the Langhe wine region, near the city of Turin

Turin

Having historically flown under the radar, Turin increasingly features on itineraries due to its proximity to some of the best producers in the country. To the southeast of the city is the vineyard-clad Langhe region, known for its Barolo and Barbaresco varieties. Nearby, the town of Alba is the only place in the world where the much-prized white truffle is grown. This eye-wateringly expensive fungus is shaved onto *tagliolini* (the local pasta) in Turin's restaurants each autumn, invariably accompanied by some fine wine.

Aside from scores of restaurants, Turin's stately Baroque core is also home to delightful *belle époque* cafés serving all manner of sweet delights. Chocolate is the city's signature product, introduced in the 16th century by the Kings of Sicily who ruled this region. The famous boat-shaped *gianduiotti*, a delicious blend of chocolate and hazelnuts, make delightful gifts for foodie friends back home.

🚄 There are hourly Frecciarossa services from Porta Nuova in Turin to Genova Piazza Principe.

Genoa

It might be a little rough around the edges but Genoa's sprawling centre has plenty to keep you entertained for the last days of your trip. At the heart of the Old Town is the black-and-white striped façade of the Romanesque Cattedrale di San Lorenzo. Its fresco-filled interior is definitely worth an hour or so of your time. A short walk away from here are the Musei di Strada Nuova, three separate *palazzi* on Via Garibaldi that make up a sprawling art museum complex. The collection is one of the finest in Italy.

A little-known fact about Genoa: it gave the world pesto. The original recipe is said to use seven ingredients: pecorino, parmesan, olive oil, pine nuts, garlic, salt and a deliciously aromatic basil that gives it a delicate, intense flavour. There's a real art to it, and the Palazzo Ducale even hosts a pesto-making world championship every other year.

Fish also dominates menus in this port city. While you're sightseeing in the Old Town, pick up a *fritto misto*. This hearty mix of deep-fried squid, anchovies, prawns and other seafood is served in a portable paper cone, so it's perfect for eating on the go.

If you thought you didn't have room for any more food, Genoa is here to prove you wrong. For your last meal of the trip, head to Mercato Orientale, a multi-purpose market set in the old cloisters of a convent. Here, stalls serve up everything from pizza to sushi and an on-site winery pours more than 250 varieties. Take your pick and then join a table in the buzzy central food court.

EXTEND
YOUR TRIP

Sardinia

Hop on a ferry to Sardinia, making Arbatax, Cagliari, Olbia or Porto Torres your base. The cuisine is very different here to the mainland. Order a bowl of *fregola con arselle* – clams, saffron and *fregola* (Sardinia's unique take on pasta, which is more similar to couscous).

33

Tuscan Treasures

It's never been easier to travel around Tuscany by train. Ride the rails between the region's beguiling Renaissance cities and historic hilltop towns, taking in the cypress tree-speckled landscape as you go.

▶ **FLORENCE** ITALY ◯ **SIENA** ITALY

◉ TRENITALIA RUNS THE REGIONAL TRAIN SERVICES THAT PLY TUSCANY'S RAILWAYS (P252).

● 8-10 DAYS ◉ 323 KM (201 MILES)

Florence

Think of "Tuscany" and it's probably Florence that first comes to mind. And as the city is so well connected, with its three main stations, it makes sense to start your journey across the region in the Tuscan capital.

As the centre is relatively compact, it's entirely possible to tick off a few of the city's biggest sights in a day (the art-filled Uffizi, the vast Duomo, Santa Croce's sculptures and Michelangelo's *David* in the Galleria Accademia). Just two or three, though, will help you to get under the skin of this endlessly romantic city. With more time to explore, you can check out the Rose Garden, climb up to San Miniato al Monte to hear the Gregorian monks chanting each evening and discover the countless Renaissance frescoes hidden in all sorts of unexpected places (think pizzerias, bathrooms and the odd Airbnb).

It's not all history and art, though. Like almost everywhere in Italy, Florence offers unforgettable gastronomic experiences. During the course of your stay, be sure to try *Bistecca alla Fiorentina* (a particularly thick and juicy cut of steak), *lampredotto* (a surprisingly delicious tripe sandwich) and plenty of different flavours of gelato, which is said to have been invented here.

● Florence's main station, Santa Maria Novella, is a short stroll from the city centre. There are usually direct trains to Lucca every 30 minutes from here, but you may have to change at Pistoia.

Florence (Firenze)

1 hr 20 mins–1 hr 45 mins

Lucca

30 mins

Pisa

55 mins

Bolgheri

3 hrs 30 mins

Siena

Cattedrale di
Santa Maria del
Fiore, Florence's
beautiful Duomo

Lucca

Aside from having more churches than any day-tripper could possibly visit (100, to be precise), the small yet significant city of Lucca also happens to be home to one of Italy's most important music festivals. Since the 1990s, when Bob Dylan took to the stage for the first edition of the Lucca Summer Festival, everyone from David Bowie to Ennio Morricone has performed here. It's unsurprising, then, that the city punches above its weight when it comes to live music.

Lucca is also famous for its "round square", an oxymoron that makes more sense when you see it. Piazza Anfiteatro, the central square at the heart of the Old Town, is built on top of an old

Roman amphitheatre and has kept the elliptic shape. The Old Town is encircled by remarkably intact 17th-century walls. While walking these walls, you can count those church spires, before getting down in time to catch some live music.

🚉 Lucca station, found just outside the city walls, has regular departures for Pisa. The journey is particularly scenic, with the train speeding through rolling green valleys.

Pisa

It may be known for one thing and one thing only, but Pisa is so much more than its perilously leaning tower. Its unpolished yet characterful city centre and

175

vibrant student community make it a surprisingly diverting stop on any tour of Tuscany.

Of course, you can't come here without checking out the Campo dei Miracoli (Square of Miracles), home to the leaning tower, as well as a baptistry, graveyard and a vast white cathedral – relics of the city's Renaissance heyday. Make your visit brief, however, so you don't get swept up with the waves of tourists who flock here each day. Instead, head south through the maze of medieval streets to the Arno river, which cuts the city centre in two. On its south bank is the Giardino Scotto – an extensive fortified garden that dates from the 15th century. It's a good place to catch your breath away from the crowds, before heading to the station, which is a mere 15-minute walk away.

↔ Services from Pisa Centrale to Bolgheri run roughly every hour. Towards the end of the journey, vineyards shadow the tracks.

———

Bolgheri

Perched on a hill overlooking the Etruscan coast, this small village is a big name in Italian wine: Bolgheri DOC was the original Super Tuscan, marking a new era of Italian wine-making in the 1970s. A day is more than enough time to amble around the village centre, with its winding streets

and medieval cottages, before settling into a rustic trattoria to sample some of that wine.

↔ Regional trains chug along to Montepescali or Empoli every hour, where you'll need to change onto another service bound for Siena.

———

Siena

The journey between Bolgheri and Siena might be long by Tuscan standards, at a whopping three-and-a-half hours, but this stunning city won't disappoint. Within its impressively intact medieval city walls, you'll find some of the best-preserved Gothic buildings in the world. It's basically one big open-air museum and an essential stop on any Tuscan itinerary.

The physical and spiritual heart of the city is the scallop-shaped Piazza Il Campo, which hosts the historic and contentious Palio bareback horse race each summer. The square is dominated by the Palazzo Pubblico, one of the city's grandest Gothic buildings along with the Duomo di Siena, which is just a short walk away. Other must-sees include the Pinacoteca Nazionale, Museo Civico and Museo dell'Opera, which house some fantastic works of art.

The Piazza Il Campo and surrounding streets in Siena's golden-hued centre

EXTEND
YOUR TRIP

Montepulciano

Ride the rails through the Val D'Orcia to the hilltop town of Montepulciano, 60 km (37 miles) from Siena. With its narrow car-free streets, impressive churches and DOC wine, Montepulciano is a sedate place to end your trip.

34

Southern Italy

Southern Italy's roads can be rather exhilarating so, instead of getting behind the wheel, travel on the tracks. Relatively efficient train lines link the regions of Puglia, Calabria and Sicily.

Taranto
3 hr 30 mins–4 hr 15 mins
Cosenza
3–4 hrs
Messina
3 hrs
Palermo

▶ **TARANTO** ITALY ○ **PALERMO** ITALY

◐ SERVICES ARE NOT AS REGULAR HERE AS IN NORTHERN ITALY, SO PLAN AHEAD (P252)

● 5-7 DAYS ● 635 KM (395 MILES)

Taranto

If Puglia forms the heel of Italy's "boot", Taranto sits on the country's "arch". This coastal city has three distinct parts. To the north is the industrial area, which is only worth visiting when it's time to depart from the train station. Across the Ponte di Porta Napoli, on an island, is the Old Town, with its Byzantine cathedral and impressive castle. Once you've crossed off the Old Town's sights, cross the Ponte Girevole to the New Town. Here, you'll find the excellent Museo Nazionale Archeologico di Taranto (MARTA). Taranto was founded as a Greek colony and once abounded with temples and monuments. In the city's streets, there are few reminders of its former glory, apart from two ghostly columns from the Tempio di Poseidon, but an abundance of artifacts are housed in MARTA's collection.

➔ There are a couple of trains a day to Sibari, where you need to change for Cosenza.

Cosenza

Sun-kissed Cosenza sits in a valley in the heart of Calabria, the region that occupies Italy's "toe". Like the rest of Calabria, Cosenza welcomes very few visitors and that's part of the city's charm. The city's major sights are the Castello Svevo and, on the other side of the Busento river, the Museo all'Aperto Bilotti, or MAB. Rather than occupying a building, this museum is open-air, with

A restaurant on an atmospheric cobbled street in Palermo, Sicily

sculptures by the likes of Salvador Dalí and Giorgio de Chirico lining the pedestrianized Corso Mazzini.

✪ Two or three changes are required to reach Sicily. To cross the Strait of Messina, the train is embarked on a ship fitted with tracks.

Messina

Razed to the ground in the 1908 earthquake, Messina lacks the historic sights found in Sicily's other cities. But its earthly delights are just the ticket after a series of long train journeys. Tuck into freshly caught swordfish or a granita (a fruity iced drink) while looking back at the mainland.

✪ Services for Palermo leave roughly every couple of hours.

Palermo

After the slow pace and small scale of your stops in Puglia and Calabria, Palermo might quickly feel overwhelming. The city has Sicily's greatest concentration of sights, and a sprawling historic centre that comes second only to Rome.

You might very well get lost in its maze of alleyways, but that's the best way to get under the skin of this dynamic city. Pick an area (central Kalsa is the obvious choice), keep a few sights in mind (like the magnificent Cattedrale, La Martorana church and the Palazzo dei Normanni), and then just see where your feet take you. It might feel a little strange after days spent rigidly following the tracks, but Sicily famously doesn't play by the rules.

Ferrovia Circumetnea

The *Ferrovia Circumetnea* circumnavigates the base of Mount Etna, Europe's most active volcano. Connecting Catania and Riposto, the railway line was built at the end of the 19th century to link the Sicilian towns that lie at the base of the volcano. These days, the train has been usurped by road travel and is almost entirely ridden by tourists wanting to take in views of volcanic landscapes peppered with citrus trees, prickly pear and pistachio plantations.

35

Danube Delights

You don't need to take a boat to experience the beauty of the Danube – the cities along its banks are connected by rail, too. Climb aboard to discover Baroque palaces, Art Nouveau cafés and spa-loving neighbourhoods that have been going strong since the time of the Romans.

○ **SALZBURG** AUSTRIA ○ **BUDAPEST** HUNGARY

◐ TICKETS FOR EACH LEG ARE GENERALLY INEXPENSIVE, SO THERE'S LITTLE BENEFIT TO BUYING A RAIL PASS (P256).

● 9-12 DAYS ◉ 570 KM (354 MILES)

Right
The innovative Ars
Electronica Center
on the banks of the
Danube in Linz

Below
The Danube
river meandering
through the heart
of Salzburg

Salzburg
AUSTRIA

Straddling two graceful sweeps of the Danube, and surrounded by rolling mountains, Salzburg is a beautiful place to begin. Its natural beauty attracts many visitors but it's music, which seems as prevalent as the crisp mountain air, that has really put this city on the map. This was the stage for the first performance of Monteverdi's opera *Orfeo* outside of Italy, the birthplace of Mozart and the setting of one of Hollywood's best-known musicals.

Several museums serve as pilgrimage sites for Mozart fans, including the Geburtshaus where the composer was born and raised, and his later residence, the Wohnhaus, which displays his original fortepiano. If you're looking for places featured in the Julie Andrews classic, *The Sound of Music,* you might recognize Schloss Leopoldskron, the von Trapp family home; Nonnberg Abbey, which was Maria's convent; and Felsenreitschule, the place where the family sang goodbye to Salzburg. Now hosting concerts, it's a fitting place to end your own time in the city.

🚄 Trains from Salzburg Hauptbahnhof depart hourly for Linz/Donau Hauptbahnhof, which is to the south of the city centre.

Linz
AUSTRIA

Nestled in an elbow-shaped bend of the Danube, Linz has been an important trading post since the days of the Ancient Romans. The city's fortunes have ebbed and flowed over the years, from its 15th-century boom under Habsburg Emperor Friedrich III to the ignominy linked to Nazi Germany. Hitler went to school in Linz and oversaw the city's industrialization before and during World War II. After Germany's defeat, Linz confronted its troubled past, renaming many streets and opening the Jewish Historical Documentation Center, dedicated to documenting Nazi war crimes.

These days Linz is a forward-looking city with a well-preserved Altstadt (old town) on the south bank of the river, and a high-tech district on the north bank. One of Linz's blockbuster sights, the futuristic Ars Electronica Center explores artificial intelligence, neuro-bionics and other cutting-edge technology through hands-on exhibitions. Further back in time, the cobbled lanes of the historic centre lead past Neo-Gothic cathedrals, Renaissance-era buildings and medieval squares — like the café-lined Hauptplatz, one of the best places for enjoying an early evening pick-me-up.

🚄 Railjet services from Linz/Donau Hauptbahnhof to Wien Hauptbahnhof run every 30–45 minutes.

Vienna

AUSTRIA

The former capital of the Austro-Hungarian Empire from 1558 to 1918, Vienna has a remarkably intact historic core. Baroque palaces and grand squares have long captivated visitors, but they're only one small piece of the city's wide-ranging allure.

Allow at least two days here to explore hip enclaves like Leopoldstadt. Located a short walk northeast of the historic centre, it showcases the city's 21st-century eclecticism with a colourful jumble of creative cafés, eye-catching architecture (seek out the Hundertwasserhaus) and edgy boutiques, plus beach bars along the Danube Canal in the summer. Leopoldstadt is also home to the Prater, a large public park where locals go to walk the wooded paths, linger over drinks at shaded beer gardens or go for a spin on the iconic Wiener Riesenrad – going strong since 1897, it's the world's oldest still-operating Ferris wheel.

🚌 Head to Wien Hauptbahnhof for hourly trains to Bratislava Hlavná Stanica.

DETOUR
Graz

Though it lies on the gently flowing Mur river rather than the Danube, the city of Graz – a two-and-a-half-hour train ride from Vienna – is well worth visiting for its Renaissance architecture, abundant parks and vibrant arts calendar. Best of all is Graz's renowned culinary reputation, with award-winning chefs serving up Styrian classics.

Bratislava

SLOVAKIA

Lying in the foothills of the Carpathian Mountains in western Slovakia, Bratislava is one of the oldest continuously inhabited places in this part of Europe. Waves of conquerors have passed through over the years, including the Celts, Romans, Slavs, Moravians and Hungarians, the latter of whom made the city their capital from 1526 to 1784. During that time over a dozen royals were crowned inside St Martin's Cathedral, whose

The colourful Hundertwasser-haus in the Austrian capital of Vienna

85-m (279-ft) spire still dominates the city skyline.

History lurks around every
bend in the winding cobbled
streets of Bratislava's Old Town.
The 1785 Michael's Gate is a
surviving remnant from the 13th-
century walls that once encircled
the city, while the *hlavné nám*
(main square), with its Gothic
buildings and Baroque fountain,
seems little changed since the
day Napoleon laid siege to the
town back in 1809. There's even a
cannonball embedded in the old
town hall that dates from the
French bombardment.

On a hilltop just west of the
Old Town stands the city's most
famous landmark. Rebuilt many
times over the past 1,100 years,
Bratislava Castle offers unrivalled
views over town, particularly from
atop the 13th-century Crown
Tower. Here, the panorama takes
in no less than three different
countries (Slovakia, Austria and
Hungary) as well as the Danube
just below.

🚆 Trains from Bratislava Hlavná Stanica
leave every two hours to Budapest Keleti.

Playing chess in
the Széchenyi
thermal baths,
Budapest

Budapest

HUNGARY

The Hungarian capital has many
nicknames — Pearl of the Danube,
City of Bridges and Heart of
Europe — but for many Magyars,
Budapest will forever be known
as the city of spas. Pleasure
seekers have been luxuriating
in the thermal springs that
bubble up here ever since the
Romans built the first public
baths in Aquincum, a neighbourhood north of the centre, some
2,000 years ago. Expansive
baths were also built during the
16th and 17th centuries under
Ottoman rule, several of which—
including the elegant 1575 Veli
Bej Baths — still survive.

After spending a couple of
days exploring the city's major
sights – such as the artwork-filled
Royal Palace or grand houses of
worship like the Great Synagogue
– a rejuvenating visit to a spring-
fed bathhouse is just what the
doctor ordered. With over a
dozen different spas to choose
from, you won't lack for appealing
options. The famous Art Nouveau
Gellért Baths have a luxurious
elegance, but arguably the best
place to celebrate the end of your
Danube journey is the expansive
Széchenyi complex – its three
outdoor pools have a suitably
festive weekend atmosphere.

EXTEND
YOUR TRIP

Belgrade

You can keep following
the Danube as it heads
south across the border
and right through the
centre of Belgrade *(p203)*.
The exuberant Serbian
capital has an atmospheric
Old Town and fascinating
places to explore the
highs and lows of the past,
including the outstanding
Museum of Yugoslavia.

History lurks around every bend in the winding cobbled streets of Bratislava's Old Town.

Golden Eagle Danube Express

The most glamorous way to travel around Eastern Europe is undoubtedly onboard the *Golden Eagle Danube Express*. Luxury cabins, five-star service and private guided tours characterize your journey around this underrated region.

The Golden Eagle Danube Express curving over a viaduct, surrounded by rugged scenery

The *Venice Simplon-Orient-Express (p30)* might come to a halt at Venice, but your journey needn't end here. The *Golden Eagle Danube Express* takes up the mantle, swooshing through Eastern Europe in style. Like the *Orient Express*, this is a hotel-on-wheels, complete with deluxe sleeping cars, white-gloved waitstaff and wine-paired à la carte meals.

The only stressful part of the experience is picking your route. There are endless options: from Budapest to the Balkans, Belgrade to Bulgaria and beyond. The classic "Balkan Explorer" is the longest and most popular, gliding from Venice to Istanbul. During the 12-day trip, the train pulls into Eastern Europe's big hitters, including Ljubljana, Dubrovnik and Belgrade, as well as lesser-known cities like Mostar, Skopje and Plovdiv.

Although you're not in each stop for long (a day, max), you'll feel like you've really got under the skin of each city thanks to the knowledgeable guide that accompanies you on your journey and leads the tour of each stop. This onboard oracle is what sets the *Golden Eagle Danube Express* apart from other luxury train journeys. They're always onhand to answer questions, whether it's over your cooked breakfast, out for lunch at one of their recommendations or at cocktail hour in the sumptuous lounge bar.

THE PRACTICALITIES

The *Golden Eagle Danube Express* is a seasonal train that runs along various routes from April to October, with a special New Year's Eve trip from Budapest to Vienna to round the year off in style. Tickets are available from Golden Eagle Luxury Trains, as well as several travel companies. There are two classes of sleeping cars: superior deluxe cabins, with large picture windows and daytime seating areas, and deluxe cabins, which are much smaller but no less polished.

www.goldeneagleluxurytrains.com

36

Picturesque Poland

This scenic tour visits Poland's northern and central cities, from Gdańsk, Poland's historically pivotal northern metropolis, to Warsaw, the country's contemporary capital.

○ **GDAŃSK** POLAND ○ **WARSAW** POLAND

◑ AN INTERRAIL OR EURAIL POLAND PASS GRANTS UNLIMITED TRAVEL FOR A SET NUMBER OF DAYS WITHIN A MONTH (P11). FOR INDIVIDUAL TICKETS USE THE PKP INTERCITY WEBSITE (P258).

🕘 8-10 DAYS 📍 856 KM (532 MILES)

Gdańsk's historic waterfront area, where old and new boats sit side by side

Gdańsk

As one of the oldest cities in Poland, Gdańsk has seen it all. It was here where the Thirteen Years' War ended in 1466 with the defeat of the Teutonic Knights. It was here that World War II officially began when the Nazis attacked Westerplatte, a peninsula on the outskirts of the city, in 1939. And it was here at the Lenin Shipyard that the trade union Solidarity, which spearheaded the collapse of communism in Poland, was founded in 1980. It's fair to say that this windswept Baltic city has played a definitive role in European history. Today, after a century of sociopolitical convulsions, Gdańsk

is busy reinventing itself as the tourism epicentre of Pomerania, Poland's northern region.

Gdańsk's centre can largely be divided into two parts. To the north is the Old Town, which was reconstructed after being almost entirely destroyed by World War II bombs. Regardless of authenticity, the Brick Gothic churches, Renaissance city gates and narrow 18th-century merchants' houses still look the part. To the south and east is the bustling waterfront, with its jaunty, colourful dwellings. The main attraction here is the excellent National Maritime Museum, which includes the 15th-century Gdańsk Crane (the biggest in medieval

Europe) and the aforementioned Lenin Shipyard. Gdańsk's long history is palpable here.

🚊 Services depart for Poznań from Gdańsk Główny, on the outskirts of the Old Town, every two hours.

DETOUR

Toruń

En route from Gdańsk to Poznań is Toruń, once considered one of the most beautiful medieval towns in Central Europe. Today, it's more famous for its Museum of Gingerbread, which celebrates a baking tradition stretching back 1,000 years.

Poznań

The small city of Poznań makes an ideal overnight stop. If you arrive early in the day, there are several interesting sights to tick off, such as the cutting-edge Porta Posnania Interactive Heritage Centre and the Cathedral of St John the Baptist (Poland's oldest cathedral, set on the tranquil holy island of Ostrów Tumski). If you catch a train that pulls into Poznań well after the sun has set, however, you won't be disappointed by the city's energetic bar and club scene.

🚊 Trains for Wrocław from Poznań Główny run hourly.

Wrocław

Wrocław occupies an exceedingly picturesque location on the Odra river, complete with 12 islands, 130 bridges and countless riverside parks. The remains of a moat, which was redirected from the river, encircles the Old Town. This is the most charming part of the city, full of cobbled streets, and Gothic and Baroque buildings. At its heart is the market square, overlooked by fairy-tale-style buildings such as the quaint Jaś i Małgosia (Hansel and Gretel Houses), so-called because these 15th-century conjoined houses seem to hold hands. The scene is as photogenic as it gets and, as Wrocław sees

far fewer visitors than Warsaw and Kraków, you're likely to have it almost entirely to yourself.

Further afield is the Jewish Quarter, the University District, and the pretty river islands of Wyspa Piasek and Ostrów Tumski. While the Old Town oozes history, these areas seem spirited thanks to a considerable student population, thriving theatre scene and always-buzzing nightclubs.

 Move onto Łódź on one of the six daily trains from Wrocław Główny.

Łódź

Despite its substantial size, Łódź has somehow managed to remain a mystery to most travellers. Perhaps it's because it's a relatively young city, having grown up rapidly over the last 200 years from a small village to become Poland's third-largest metropolis. During its rise, Łódź picked up a couple of monikers. Its 19th-century textile boom led to the nickname "the Polish Manchester" and its film school, which tutored the directors Andrzej Wajda, Roman Polański and Krzysztof Kieślowski, has seen the city dubbed "Holly-Łódź" (pronounced "Holly-woodge").

There's a plethora of Art Nouveau architecture to keep you occupied for a few hours, but the city's main selling point is that

Above
Warsaw's Plac
Zamkowy, or Castle
Square, at night

Left
Strolling around
Wrocław's pretty
Old Town

breaks up the journey from
Wrocław to Warsaw. If there was
one destination to get the squeeze
on this itinerary, it would be Łódź.

Trains depart for Warsaw from Łódź
Fabryczna train station, 400 m (437 yds)
east of the city centre, up to twice an hour.

Warsaw

It seems only right to finish
your journey in Poland's capital.
At first glance, you might forget
that 85 per cent of Warsaw was
annihilated in World War II. The
city today is modern, fashionable
and thriving – everything you
would expect from a capital city.

At least a couple of days are
needed to get under the skin of
this multilayered city. Spend that
time taking in the must-see
sights: the UNESCO-listed Old
Town – reconstructed, but
charming nonetheless; the
enormous red-brick Royal Castle;
the haunting Jewish cemetery,
filled with over 150,000 tomb-
stones; the university and its
library's rooftop garden; and
Stalinist-era monuments such as
the Palace of Culture and Science
– a "gift of friendship" from the
Soviet Union. Then, there are the
museums. Too many to list here,
but if you visit just one, make it
the Museum of the History of the
Polish Jews, located in the midst
of the former ghetto.

Bieszczady
Forest Railway

The tiny hamlet of Majdan,
southeast of Warsaw, is the
terminus for the steam-
powered Bieszczady Forest
Railway. Trains first rolled
through the forest in the
late 19th century to
transport timber, but the
service halted with the
collapse of communism. In
1997, the 11-km (7-mile)
line was reopened by a
group of local enthusiasts
as a heritage railway.
It currently runs up to
five times a day during
the summer.

37

Alternative Central Europe

Swerve the region's better-known sights and journey through Poland and the Czech Republic's more intriguing corners. Here, you'll discover gorgeous medieval centres, fascinating museums and buzzing bars aplenty.

○ KRAKÓW POLAND ○ ČESKÝ KRUMLOV CZECH REPUBLIC

○ BUY A TWO-COUNTRY INTERRAIL OR EURAIL PASS OR PURCHASE INDIVIDUAL TICKETS FOR EACH LEG OF THE JOURNEY (P11).

● 8–10 DAYS ○ 803 KM (499 MILES)

Bar-restaurants
in Kraków's
Kazimierz district

Kraków

1 hr–1 hr 15 mins

Katowice

5 hrs 30 mins–8 hrs

Prague (Praha)

1 hr 20 mins–1 hr 30 mins

Plzeň

2 hrs

Český Krumlov

Kraków

POLAND

Poland's historic second city, Kraków deserves a couple of days at the start of your trip. This beautiful place packs a real punch, with a rich history, stately architecture and cultural clout to boot. If you've already ticked off classic sights like the Wawel Cathedral and Royal Castle, Rynek Główny (the Market Square) and Rynek Underground (its subterranean museum), it's well worth digging deeper.

Begin in the Jewish quarter, Kazimierz, which has an enchanting bohemian feel to it. Chic cafés have settled in among the historic synagogues here and well-worn buildings are covered in street art.

Across the river, the former industrial district of Zabłocie hosts the factory buildings once owned by German industrialist Oskar Schindler (immortalized by Steven Spielberg in *Schindler's List*). These structures now house a branch of the Historical Museum of Kraków, which explores the harrowing Nazi occupation. Once you've had your fill of history, look to the future at MOCAK (the Museum of Contemporary Art), which sits in the same complex.

🚆 You can keep your schedule in Kraków flexible, since trains from Kraków Główny to Katowice run every 30 minutes.

DETOUR

Warsaw

It takes just two-and-a-half hours to speed between Kraków, Poland's former capital, and Warsaw *(p156 and p189)*, the city that succeeded it. Warsaw's Old Town, reconstructed after World War II and the Warsaw Uprising, is a UNESCO World Heritage Site. Praga is arguably the city's coolest quarter.

Katowice

POLAND

In recent years, the former coal mining and metalworking city of Katowice has shaken off its grimy image and reinvented itself for the 21st century. Now, it's a vibrant hub of culture and sustainability, with a youthful, tech-savvy vibe.

Among the most compelling symbols of the new Katowice is

the Muzeum Śląskie (Silesian Museum). Occupying the site of a disused coal mine, this modern museum features historical and contemporary cultural exhibits; visitors can even climb the old mine headframe, which now acts as an observation tower.

🚇 There are around six direct trains from Katowice to Prague each day.

Prague
CZECH REPUBLIC

Most tourists who visit Prague converge on Karlův Most (Charles Bridge), the iconic 14th-century stone link between the Old Town and Prague Castle. Once you've done the obligatory crossing, escape the crowds by seeking out the city's lesser-known districts.

When the weather's kind, locals get together on the Náplavka riverfront, just south of the Old Town. There's a friendly farmers' market here on Saturday mornings, with purveyors selling cheese, local fruit and other goodies – live music also adds to the convivial atmosphere.

The hilly and happening Vinohrady and Žižkov districts, southeast of the railway station, also offer off-the-beaten-track adventures. Riegrovy Sady (Rieger Gardens), an English-style park created in the early 20th century, is an inviting place to stroll, and the cafés and bars near Jiřího z Poděbrad (George of Poděbrady Square) are always lively. The run-up to Christmas is a delightful time to be here: make your way to Náměstí Míru (Peace Square), which sparkles merrily from late November until Christmas Eve with its daily festive market in full swing.

For a local-style, beer-fuelled night out, the neighbourhoods

Pošumavská Southern Railway

Taking 90 minutes or so, the local line from Český Krumlov potters through picturesque forests and villages to Nové Údolí on the German border, where there's a treat in store. Here, enthusiasts maintain what they proudly call the shortest international railway in the world. Vintage carriages house a museum, and a replica steam train plies the 105-m (115-yard) track: a journey of under a minute.

of Žižkov or Vršovice, further southeast, make for a perfect base. A wander around these effervescent parts of town will quickly lead you to some of the city's best bars.

🚉 Trains cover the relatively short route from Prague to Plzeň every 30 minutes or so.

Plzeň

CZECH REPUBLIC

The elegant city of Plzeň (or Pilsen) is the birthplace of Pilsner lager, and most visitors make a trip to Pilsner Urquell Brewery their top priority. Here, you'll learn how beer is brewed and bottled, picking up trivia that's sure to be useful in your next pub quiz (the proportion of the world's beers that are named Pils, Pilsner or Pilsener, for example, is approximately two-thirds).

Don't spend all your time in the brewery, though; there are excellent art galleries, cafés and restaurants to check out. The compact centre lends itself to casual strolling, and with the spire of the Gothic cathedral soaring over the rooftops, it's impossible to lose your bearings – however many beers you've had.

🚉 Trains from Plzeň to Český Krumlov run approximately every two hours. You may need to change trains at České Budějovice.

Český Krumlov

CZECH REPUBLIC

One of Europe's best-preserved medieval sites, Český Krumlov is a popular day trip from other Czech cities. Its highlights can easily be squeezed into a day, but you may find the bewitching atmosphere tempts you to stay for two.

The Old Town, clustered on the Vltava river, is delightful to explore on foot: browse artisan gifts in the many boutiques and treat yourself to a *trdelník* (cinnamon bun) along the way. The main appeal is Český Krumlov itself, a castle that has stood here since the 1200s. Climb the tower – all 162 steps of it – to drink in the views from the top. If the river below looks appealing, hire a canoe and spend your final day floating gently downstream.

38

Adriatic Escapes

Combining sublime cities with spectacular scenery, this tour offers a snapshot of the head-scratchingly underrated Slovenia and Croatia, two countries worthy of your attention.

● **LJUBLJANA** SLOVENIA ○ **SPLIT** CROATIA

◉ IF YOU PLAN TO RETURN TO SLOVENIA AFTER VISITING CROATIA, BUY A DISCOUNTED CITY STAR TICKET (P252).

● 5-6 DAYS ◉ 563 KM (350 MILES)

○ Ljubljana
  2 hrs 15-2 hrs 30 mins
○ Zagreb
  6-8 hrs 30 mins
● Split

Ljubljana
SLOVENIA

Slovenia's dynamic capital doesn't tend to feature on European hit lists, but it really should. Ljubljana's green credentials are reason enough to visit. The city boasts an incredible 542 sq m (5,834 sq ft) of green space per inhabitant and the pretty centre is the largest car-free zone in the European Union. As a result, its cafés, bars and clubs tend to spill out onto the streets.

The city also offers an ever-growing roster of sights. With its beautiful Secessionist architecture, vibrant foodie scene and fantastic museums (don't miss the Museum of Modern Art and the Narodni muzej Slovenije, which covers Slovene history and heritage), the city could keep you entertained for weeks on end.

As hard as it is to leave Ljubljana behind, you must make a day trip from here to Lake Bled. With its glassy waters, forested mountain backdrop and the romantic island-bound Church of the Assumption, Bled is one of the most beautiful sights in all of Europe.

❸ There are four or five departures for Zagreb Glavni Kolodvor from Ljubljana each day. At Dobova, on the border, authorities will board the train to check and stamp passports; have your ID to hand.

Zagreb
CROATIA

Considered more straight-laced than its Slovenian counterpart, the Croatian capital nonetheless has a vibrant cultural scene,

encompassing historic art and architecture, alternative music, and independent cafés and boutiques. Nowhere sums up the city's dichotomies better than Donji Grad (Lower Town), aka Centar, where Neo-Baroque and Art Deco buildings are splashed with street art. Today, it's the city centre's hippest quarter.

You could whizz around the city centre in a day, but two will give you more time to take in the city's museums. If you only have time to visit one, make it the quirky Museum of Broken Relationships, in which everyday objects tell tales of lost love.

🕓 From January to September, three or four trains, including a sleeper, run from Zagreb Glavni Kolodvor to Split each day. From October to December, there's only one. Reservations are compulsory.

Split
CROATIA

The Roman emperor Diocletian fell in love with the Split peninsula in the third century, choosing it for his seaside retreat. It's easy to see why: with mild winters, sunny summers and a dramatic location between the Dinaric Alps and the sparkling Adriatic, this is a spot with huge natural appeal.

The remains of Diocletian's Palace are today Split's biggest attraction. Other highlights include Bačvice Beach, the old fisherman's quarter of Varoš and the Riva area, where you'll find plenty of seafront restaurants. Pick one of these for your last meal of the trip, slurping *Hvarska gregada* (fish and potato stew) and planning your return trip to the region.

The Church of the Assumption, set on an island in the middle of Lake Bled

EXTEND
YOUR TRIP
●━━━━━━━━○

Hvar

Split is at the end of the railway line, but you can continue your Adriatic adventure by boarding a ferry to Hvar. A favourite haunt of celebrities, the Croatian island has all the beaches and vineyards you could ever wish for.

39

Discover Bosnia and Herzegovina

Rich in historic architecture and natural scenery, Bosnia and Herzegovina is emerging from the aftermath of the Bosnian War as a promising tourism destination. While it has no international rail connections, it has a slow but reliable national network that makes it easy to explore.

○ **SARAJEVO** BOSNIA AND HERZEGOVINA ○ **ČAPLJINA** BOSNIA AND HERZEGOVINA

🎫 BUY ONE TICKET FROM SARAJEVO TO ČAPLJINA. YOU CAN STAY IN MOSTAR FOR AS LONG AS YOU WISH EN ROUTE (P252).

🕐 3–4 DAYS ◎ 164 KM (102 MILES)

Sarajevo
2 hrs
Mostar
25 mins
Čapljina

Sarajevo

Keen though Bosnia and Herzegovina is to look to the future rather than dwell on the past, Sarajevo will never forget the 1990s. During the Bosnian War, the city was besieged by the Yugoslav People's Army and the Army of Republika Srpska for almost four years: the longest siege of a capital city in the history of modern warfare. Several museums, including the moving War Childhood Museum, record those bitter times.

Over the last decade, post-war regeneration programmes have borne fruit, with the impressively restored Austro-Hungarian City Hall reopening in 2017 and new buildings such as the Avaz Twist Tower, completed in 2008, adding texture to the skyline.

As the centre is compact and Baščaršija and Ferhadija (the main market square and shopping street) are both pedestrianized, Sarajevo is best explored on foot. Fuel your sightseeing with a *sarajevski ćevapi* (a flatbread stuffed with sausage-shaped meatballs and raw onions). It's the quintessential Bosnian snack.

🚆 Only two or three trains run along the line from Sarajevo to Mostar each day. The journey is supremely scenic, so sit by a window.

Mostar

Mostar has a delightful historic centre, which hugs both banks of the Neretva river bridged by the supremely elegant Stari Most (Old Bridge). Much of its architectural character, including this stone bridge, was damaged or destroyed during the Bosnian War but has since been painstakingly restored. Its cobbled streets are once again lined with shops and bazaars, and traditional restaurants perch on both banks of the river.

Traditionally a peace-loving city, situated on the frontier of Christian Western Europe and the Muslim East, Mostar has always been culturally diverse. On the east bank of the river, which has historically been home to Mostar's Muslim community, minarets soar above the rooftops. On the west bank, meanwhile, church spires dominate the skyline. It's a fascinating place, and one that requires at least a day or two to get to grips with.

⊖ Two or three trains per day make the short journey from Mostar to Čapljina, from where you can take a taxi to the Kravica and Kocusa Waterfalls.

Čapljina

Set on the Neretva river, downstream from Mostar, Čapljina is a low-key town with few attractions apart from its proximity to the Kravica and Kocusa Waterfalls, two spectacular cascades found on the Trebižat river. Kravica is the taller, with water tumbling from a forested plateau into a 120-m- (394-ft-) wide lake, 26 m (85 ft) below. It's a glorious spot for a final swim or picnic – and reason enough to finish your journey here.

The centre of Mostar, straddling the Neretva river

The Kravica Waterfall on the Trebižat river, near Čapljina

40

Bar to Belgrade

The international railway line that runs from Bar, on Montenegro's Adriatic coast, to Belgrade, capital of Serbia, is famed for its beautiful scenery but its stops are just as diverting.

○ **BAR** MONTENEGRO ○ **BELGRADE** SERBIA

◉ BUY TICKETS AT STATIONS: ONLINE BOOKING IS NOT AVAILABLE IN EITHER MONTENEGRO OR SERBIA (P255).

🕐 6–7 DAYS 📍 469 KM (291 MILES)

Bar
1 hr
Podgorica
2 hrs 25 mins–
2 hrs 45 mins
Bijelo Polje
7 hrs 30 mins–8 hrs
Belgrade

Bar

MONTENEGRO

With ferries from Italy shuttling to and fro, the Adriatic port of Bar has a confident, cosmopolitan feel reminiscent of its Italian neighbour. The sunny streets are lined with pizzerias serving Neapolitan-style margheritas and the 19th-century palace built on the seashore by the last king of Montenegro, King Nikola, wouldn't look out of place in a Mediterranean resort.

After soaking up the city's sunny atmosphere, make the obligatory day trip out to Stari Bar (Old Bar), around 5 km (3 miles) inland. Surrounded by dramatic cliffs, this Byzantine settlement is as ancient as it gets. Pottery fragments suggest it was inhabited from at least 800 BCE right up to the 1970s, when an earthquake destroyed its aqueduct and made Stari Bar uninhabitable. Following restoration work, villagers are slowly returning and, today, it's an atmospheric place to explore, with its sturdy stone fortress, cobbled lanes and ancient archways.

⊖ The scenic trip from Bar to Podgorica is served by two long-distance trains bound for Belgrade, and around ten local services, each day.

Looking out on Stari Bar's Byzantine aqueduct from a ruined building

Podgorica

MONTENEGRO

One of Europe's smallest capital cities, there's an under-the-radar buzz to Podgorica. It has ambitions to be one of the continent's most eco-friendly cities and has set about constructing sustainable public buildings, street lighting, waste management and transport systems. There are plenty of trees and open spaces here including King's Park, northwest of the railway station, and Gorica Forest Park, just north of the centre.

Podgorica is also excellently placed for excursions into the Montenegrin countryside. A two-hour bus journey west of Podgorica is the medieval city of Kotor. A tangle of cobbled streets, quiet squares, red-roofed houses and pretty churches

perched about Kotor Bay, it makes for a supremely photogenic day trip. It's also easy to travel by bus from Podgorica to the pretty coastal town of Budva where – thanks to an abundance of beach bars, restaurants, folk events and music festivals – there's always something going on.

🚉 Seven trains, including the Bar to Belgrade service, make the journey between Podgorica and Bijelo Polje each day. Travel by daylight: the scenery is spectacular.

The Sava, one of two rivers running through Belgrade

Bijelo Polje

MONTENEGRO

Set in the Montenegrin highlands, Bijelo Polje's emerging slow food movement has brought it to the attention of gourmands. Hyper-

local produce such as pumpkin, honey and forest mushrooms are all celebrated in hearty dishes made to be savoured with a glass of Montenegrin wine. Take your time over dinner here, before leaving Montenegro behind and riding the rails into Serbia.

🚇 International trains between Bijelo Polje and Belgrade Centar run twice daily, one by day and the other by night. Passports are checked twice – once by Montenegrin authorities in Bijelo Polje, and again by Serbian authorities in Prijepolje.

Belgrade
SERBIA

Busy by day and positively hectic by night, the Serbian capital is the Balkan region's hippest party city.

Its club and bar scene is dynamic and diverse, so you'll need to tap into social media to seek out the latest hot spots. The centre's most emblematic hangouts are its *splavovi* ("splavs", for short): floating clubs, built on riverbank rafts, that open from the end of April to late September. More than 200 *splavs* can be found on the city's two rivers, running the gamut from intimate and classy venues to thumping, disco-ball bearing clubs. Come winter, when the *splavs* close, in-the-know locals converge on Cetinjska, a city centre street where a major brewery used to be located. Here, once-rundown spaces have been upcycled as edgy bars.

Once you emerge, blinking into the daylight, you'll find Belgrade an interesting city to explore on foot. It's a visual jumble, with stately 19th-century façades interspersed with chunky modernist masterpieces. The most prominent landmark is the Beogradska Tvrđava, a 3rd-century fortress at the confluence of the Danube and Sava rivers. Today, it contains numerous monuments and exhibits, including a clock tower, hammam, military museum and, in a surreal touch, life-size replica dinosaurs.

It may be far removed from Eastern Europe's medieval centres, but that's the beauty of Belgrade. Just like the other stops on this tour, it's an underappreciated city worthy of more time than most passengers on the Bar to Belgrade railway line give it.

EXTEND
YOUR TRIP

Novi Sad

With its top summer music festival and vibrant theatre, literature and poetry scenes (it was European Capital of Culture in 2022), Serbia's second city more than holds its own against the capital – and it's just a 35-minute train ride away.

41

Romania and Bulgaria

This rich and varied rail trip across two of Europe's lesser-visited countries takes in Transylvanian castles, the picturesque Southern Carpathian mountains and two of the region's most eclectic capital cities.

○ **CLUJ-NAPOCA** ROMANIA ○ **SOFIA** BULGARIA

◉ YOU MIGHT BE ASKED TO SHOW YOUR ID AND DOCUMENTS AT THE BORDER CROSSING FROM ROMANIA TO BULGARIA (P255).

● 10-12 DAYS ○ 1,046 KM (650 MILES)

Cluj-Napoca
ROMANIA

Thanks to its international airport, Cluj-Napoca has long been considered a convenient jumping-off point for exploring the Apuseni Mountains and the popular towns of southern Transylvania. That's all well and good, but it's also a delightful place to rest a while before beginning your eastern Balkans journey in earnest. Reserve a couple of days at least to explore the city's bohemian cafés, excellent nightclubs and live music venues, and notable architecture, including a Gothic church and medieval towers.

Another reason to spend a good amount of time in the city is that it's the unofficial capital of Romanian cinematography. In 1905, the country's first film studio opened in Cluj and the city boasts more cinema-goers than any other place in Romania, which is not that surprising considering it's the home of the country's principal film festival – the Transylvanian International Film Festival. Cluj has a creative buzz year-round but really comes to life when the ten-day showcase is in town in early June.

🚆 The main station is a 20-minute walk from the Old Town and has five trains a day bound for Sighişoara (roughly every three hours).

Sighişoara

ROMANIA

Think of Transylvania and it's probably Sighişoara that comes to mind. The city's saw-toothed skyline, with its needle spires and sinister battlements, is everything you'd expect from the birthplace of Romania's most famous historical figure: Vlad Ţepeş, also known as Vlad the Impaler or Dracula. But Sighişoara is so much more than its vampiric connection.

Perched on a rocky massif, high above the newer areas of the city, the Old Town is the worthy focal point of any visit to the city. Within its jumble of leaning, pastel-hued houses, you'll find enough welcoming cafés, boutique lodgings and creative craft shops to prove that Transylvania is both a vividly historic and modern region.

🚆 Sighişoara's train station is just over 1 km (0.6 miles) northeast of the historic centre and has several daily services to Braşov.

Turnul cu Ceas clock tower in Sighişoara, a quintessential Transylvanian city

○ DETOUR
Sibiu

Between Sighişoara and Braşov is the fascinating Transylvanian town of Sibiu. Its flamboyant Old Town, with its brightly painted gabled houses, looks distinctly un-Transylvanian and wouldn't seem out of place in Bavaria.

Braşov
ROMANIA

Braşov welcomes more visitors than anywhere else in Romania for good reason. Surrounded by forested mountains (ignore the incongruous Hollywood-style sign), the pretty city is bedecked with medieval watchtowers, Gothic spires and Baroque façades. At the centre of it all is the lovely main square, Piaţa Sfatului, lined with alfresco cafés.

Tourists also flock to Braşov because it's the jumping-off point for visits to Bran Castle, or Dracula's Castle – though Vlad only dropped by once in the 15th century. Add an extra day to your itinerary if you want to visit Bran (you'll need to take a bus or organize a taxi).

🚄 Jump on one of the hourly services bound for Bucharest, Romania's capital. The train passes through some of Transylvania's best scenery, so try to sit by the window.

Bucharest
ROMANIA

With the charms of Transylvania behind you, Bucharest may be a bit of a shock to the system. Here, huge concrete apartment blocks and monuments, as well as often-unfinished Soviet-style developments, rise up between arteries of traffic-clogged streets. But this is Romania's capital and with that distinction come the country's best museums (the National Art Museum, Museum of the Romanian Peasant and Village Museum are unmissable), galleries and restaurants. The city also has some interesting architecture, from 17th- and 18th-century Orthodox churches to the gargantuan Palace of Parliament – the world's heaviest building. When it's time to catch your train, you'll undoubtedly be sad to leave this city, and Romania, behind.

🚄 Only one train a day travels from Bucureşti Nord station to Veliko Tarnovo.

Left
A fountain-lined boulevard, leading up to the Palace of Parliament in Bucharest

Below left
Bran Castle peeking out of the forested slopes, near Brașov

When you cross the border into Bulgaria, guards may come onboard to check your passport and any necessary visas, so make sure you have them to hand.

Veliko Tarnovo

BULGARIA

There's no better introduction to Bulgaria than Veliko Tarnovo. You immediately get the sense that you're in a different country, with Bucharest's wide avenues and enormous buildings supplanted by the higgledy-piggledy lanes and stacked dwellings of this picturesque town.

Known as the "City of Tsars" it was capital of the Second Bulgarian Empire from 1185 to 1396), the town is rooted in history. Every visitor's hit list should include Tsarevets, the splendid medieval fortress that overlooks the town, and the Museum of the Bulgarian Renaissance and Constituent Assembly (where the first Bulgarian parliament assembled in 1879).

⊖ There are no direct trains between Veliko Tarnovo and Sofia; you'll have to change at either Gorna Orjahovica or Tulovo.

Sofia

BULGARIA

Many visitors bypass Bulgaria's capital, heading straight to the coast, mountains or airport, and at first glance Sofia can appear a little drab. There isn't much in the way of sights – apart from a motley collection of Ottoman mosques, domed churches and hulking Soviet monuments – but Sofia's café and bar scene is just as buzzing as Cluj-Napoca's. Spend a night or two partying – what better way to end your trip?

EXTEND YOUR TRIP

Black Sea Coast

Bulgaria's long Black Sea coastline is the natural next stop from the country's capital. There are regular services to cosmopolitan Varna and chic Burgas, from where you can hop to less-developed spots like medieval Nesebâr and ancient Sozopol.

42

North Macedonia

Skopje

35 mins–1 hr

Veles

1 hr 45 mins

Prilep

In the 20th century, North Macedonia's communist regime built dramatic concrete constructions around the country, including *spomeniks* (war memorials). Discover the country's unique architecture on this tour.

⊙ **SKOPJE** NORTH MACEDONIA ⊙ **PRILEP** NORTH MACEDONIA

⊙ PURCHASE A EURAIL OR INTERRAIL PASS TO HOP BETWEEN THE THREE CITIES AT YOUR OWN PACE (P11) OR BUY INDIVIDUAL TICKETS (P255).

⊙ 4–6 DAYS ⊙ 135 KM (84 MILES)

Skopje

The devastating earthquake that shook the North Macedonian capital to its core in 1963 led to a revolutionary shift in Skopje's architectural character. Under the creative leadership of Japanese architect Kenzo Tange, best known for his work in post-war Hiroshima, and with designs by others, such as Macedonian architect Janko Konstantinov, bold new Brutalist buildings emerged. Start your tour by seeking out such structures; among the most remarkable are the Post Office and Telecommunications Centre, designed by Konstantinov.

There's far more to Skopje than hard-edged concrete, however: the city's iconic Stone Bridge, which spans the Vardar river in the heart of the city, dates back to the Ottoman period. It connects Macedonia Square to the Old Bazaar, one of the largest and most historic markets in the Balkans. Much of the city's Byzantine charm has also survived. Wander the cobbled streets, and you'll spot minarets and hammams, along with the abundance of statues that has become the city's 21st-century trademark.

⊖ There are around ten trains per day from Skopje to Veles, mostly in the early morning and mid-afternoon.

Veles

Several rail routes, including the main line from Serbia to Greece, converge on Veles, but few passengers disembark here.

Those who do leave the station discover a picturesque city and one of the country's most beautiful spomeniks – Spomenik Kosturnica, on the northeastern edge of town.

Spomeniks are huge, sci-fi-like war memorials, commissioned by dictator Josip Broz Tito in the 1960s and 70s. North Macedonia is home to around 25 of them. They are in varying states of disrepair – some are valued city-centre landmarks, others stand on remote hillsides. In most cases, the concrete bears the streaks of time, but the striking curves of the Spomenik Kosturnica (which contains the remains of around 100 Macedonian Partisan soldiers who died here during Macedonia's National Liberation War in the 1940s) are bone-white.

🚉 Three trains per day (in the morning, afternoon and evening) wind southwest from Veles to Prilep.

Prilep

Like Veles, Prilep is an unassuming city with a remarkable spomenik. Known as the Burial Mound of the Unbeaten or the Partisan Necropolis, it commemorates the 800 or so Partisan soldiers who lost their lives while fighting for the liberation of Prilep from German and Bulgarian forces during the Second World War. Designed by the Serbian architect and designer Bogdan Bogdanović, and completed in 1961, Prilep's spomenik looks rather like a giant collection of outdoor chess pieces. The symbolism of the marble figures is a matter of debate: some see them as urns, others as dancers or even nymphs. Whatever your interpretation, it's undeniably impressive, just like the other architecture you've seen on this tour through the heart of North Macedonia.

The curvaceous white walls of the Spomenik Kosturnica in Veles

Athens'
magnificent
Acropolis, an
enduring symbol
of Ancient Greece

43

Historic Greece

Dive into the myth and history of Greece on this unforgettable train tour. As you travel, revel in the juxtaposition between vibrant, modern cities and a plethora of ancient sights.

▶ **CORINTH** GREECE ◉ **THESSALONIKI** GREECE

💳 BUY TICKETS ON THE HELLENIC TRAIN WEBSITE OR AT STATIONS. THERE IS NO PRICE ADVANTAGE TO BOOKING IN ADVANCE (P255).

🕐 5–7 DAYS 📍 580 KM (360 MILES)

Corinth

The story of Jason and the Argonauts, and their quest to capture the legendary Golden Fleece, is one of the most enduring tales of Greek mythology. The hero Jason was said to have lived in Corinth, an ancient city-state halfway between Athens and Sparta and one of the most prominent powers in Ancient Greece. Your journey begins here, among an impressive collection of ruins, including the remains of the old marketplace and a Doric Temple of Apollo, dating back to the 5th century BCE. Myth and legend hang heavy in the air – it's here that Sisyphus, the city's founder, was condemned to roll a boulder uphill for eternity. And it's said that Pegasus, the winged horse, would drink regularly from the Pirene Fountain, which you can still see in the east of the complex.

Corinth is rich in verifiable history, too. The site is home to both Roman and Greek amphitheatres, and the excellent

Archaeological Museum of Ancient Corinth, which pieces together the history of the site using recovered statues, pottery and inscriptions.

Ancient Corinth, where the historic sights are, sits around 7 km (4 miles) southwest of the modern city of Corinth, where you'll get off the train; take a taxi between the two.

🚇 Catch the hourly service from Corinth's station to Athens , a mere hour away. At various points along the journey, the tracks run right beside the sea.

Athens

Follow the footsteps of ancient philosophers to Athens, one of the world's oldest cities and the birthplace of democracy. Start at the Acropolis, an ancient citadel which still dominates the Greek capital some 2,500 years after it was built. The complex's time-worn shrines, temples and amphitheatres are some of the most recognizable sights in the world, particularly the elegant Parthenon, a former temple to Athena. Make sense of the sprawling site at the Acropolis

Museum, which brings the remains to life with reconstructed ancient neighbourhoods and unearthed statues and artworks.

Another unmissable ancient site in Athens is the Agora, which was the heart of the old city's political and commercial life. Walking amid the ghostly grounds of its Odeon (auditorium), which is presided over by now-headless statues, is a rather eerie experience. In contrast, the magnificently preserved Temple of Hephaestus, a short walk away, still appears almost complete.

In your exploration of ancient Athens, don't neglect the modern city, which is one of the most vibrant in Europe. Go to the glamorous Glyfada area for glitzy bars and high-end restaurants, to Exarcheia for colourful street murals, to Kolonaki for designer shopping and to Psirri for boisterous nightlife.

🚇 There is one train per day from Athens to Kalambaka, departing at around 7am. From Kalambaka train station, it's around a ten-minute taxi or bus journey to Meteora.

The dramatic setting of the monastery at Meteora, near Kalambaka

DETOUR
Delphi

In between Athens and Kalambaka is the town of Amfikleia. From the train station, it's a short taxi or bus ride to Delphi, one of Greece's most important archaeological sites. Here, the Oracle's prophecies influenced the course of the classical world.

Kalambaka (for Meteora)

Meteora is a sight that has to be seen to be believed: a complex of ancient monasteries, perched in defiance of gravity on top of vast columns of rock, as if placed there by a giant. The rocks are so smooth and strange, resembling great whalebones, that it's hard to believe they occurred naturally – let alone that monks were able to build monasteries here. But that's exactly what they did in the 14th century.

Back then, it was much more difficult to access the monasteries. To return to their home and place of worship, the monks had to scale long ladders and nets, which were withdrawn every time they wanted to be cut off from the world. (This was a handy feature: when the monasteries were first built the monks were fleeing persecution from the invading Ottomans.) Nowadays, the monasteries (of which six remain of the original 25) are much easier to reach – the journey from the nondescript town of Kalambaka takes just ten minutes and staircases have been carved into the rock faces. Agios Stefanos is the only monastery that is wheelchair-accessible.

Spend a day here, exploring the monasteries' gorgeous Byzantine architecture, quiet courtyards adorned with Macedonian frescoes, and museums housing paintings and religious artifacts. You can't stay in the monasteries, so return to Kalambaka for the night.

🚆 Kalambaka station has six direct services to Thessaloniki each day. For part of the route, the train runs along the Thermaic Gulf.

The Church of Agios Pavlos in Thessaloniki, at the end of the route

Thessaloniki

By this point, you'll have realized that Greece is a country where the past and the present sit side by side. And nowhere is that more true than Thessaloniki, a modern metropolis enclosed by crumbling Byzantine walls and studded with relics of its Greek, Roman and Ottoman past.

Start your visit on the New Waterfront, where modern sculptures sit beside a statue of Alexander the Great. Just around the corner is the superb (and wonderfully free) Archaeological Museum, which holds the Derveni Papyrus – Europe's oldest manuscript, written in the 3rd century BCE – and an open-air reconstruction of a Roman villa. To the north is the old commercial area of Valaoritou, which (in classic Greek fashion) has reinvented itself as a cosmopolitan nightlife hub.

EXTEND
YOUR TRIP

Thassos

Thessaloniki is about two and a half hours away from Kavala, from where you can take a ferry to the island of Thassos. Smothered in verdant vineyards and olive groves and skirted by gorgeous beaches, this is one of the most beautiful of the Aegean Islands.

44

The Baltics

Take an epic journey around the medieval-yet-modern Baltic states. United by geography and shared history, though still proudly individual, their captivating cities are home to picturesque old towns, pristine green spaces, hipster hangouts and budding foodie scenes.

- ● KLAIPĖDA LITHUANIA ○ TALLINN ESTONIA
- ◉ DISTANCES ARE SHORT AND PRICES ARE AFFORDABLE, SO THERE'S LITTLE BENEFIT TO BUYING A RAIL PASS (P258).
- ● 14-16 DAYS ○ 1,254 KM (779 MILES)

Klaipėda

4 hrs 40 mins

Kaunas

1 hr 20 mins

Vilnius

2 hrs 30 mins

Daugavpils

3 hrs 30 mins

Rīga

1 hr 10 mins

Sigulda

30-40 mins

Cēsis

1 hr 10 mins

Valga

1 hr 10 mins

Tartu

2 hrs

Tallinn

Klaipėda

LITHUANIA

Formerly known as Memel, the port city of Klaipėda has a distinctly German air – hardly surprising considering it was part of the Prussian Kingdom for hundreds of years. The buildings in the compact cobblestoned Old Town are built in the traditional German half-timbered style, and it's entirely feasible to explore them all in a morning. Reserve the afternoon for taking in the Old Town and Klaipėda's moat-protected castle, before leaving your starting destination and beginning your Baltic tour.

◒ There are four trains a day to Kaunas – ideally hop on the lunchtime one to make the most of your evening.

Kaunas

LITHUANIA

Lithuania's second-largest city and a European Capital of Culture for 2022, Kaunas sprawls along the banks of the converging Nemunas and Neris rivers. During the inter-war period, the city was the capital of Lithuania and it is still considered by many Lithuanians to be the true heart of the country.

The city's biggest draw is the delightful Old Town. Its main square is lined with 15th- and 16th-century merchant houses, overlooked by the picturesque tower of the town hall – dubbed the "White Swan" for its elegant form and pristine colour. Wedged between the Old Town and the Neris is the fascinating 14th-century Kaunas Castle.

Cobbled Vilniaus Gatvė, lined with restaurants and cafés, in Kaunas

Kaunas also has a plethora of unique museums and exhibitions, including the Devil Museum, packed with over 2,000 devil and witch figures; the MK Čiurlionis National Museum of Art, one of Lithuania's oldest and grandest galleries; and Sugihara House, where Japanese diplomat Chiune Sugihara – dubbed "Japan's Schindler" – saved around 6,000 Jews between 1939 and 1940.

🔁 Located to the west of the Old Town and city centre, Kaunas station has hourly services to Vilnius.

Vilnius

LITHUANIA

Vilnius may be the Baltic's least known and most underappreciated capital, but it is a city of immense verve. Beyond the cobbled streets and countless church spires of the UNESCO-listed Baroque Old Town (which happens to be Eastern Europe's largest), the city feels distinctly rebellious.

There's eye-catching street art around every corner, numerous hip cafés in weather-worn buildings and bizarre statues like the Frank Zappa Memorial on Kalinausko Street. The city's buzzing nightlife, meanwhile, reveals a kaleidoscope of countercultures, from goths and punks to upmarket clubbers and furry-boot-clad ravers. Then, there's the self-declared breakaway Republic of Užupis, a 0.6-sq-m (6-sq-ft) area of the Old Town that declared itself a separate state in 1997.

Vilnius is cheeky, charming, charismatic and confident – and

Vilnius is cheeky, charming, charismatic and confident — and above all, it will make you want to linger.

above all, it will make you want to linger, so consider spending around three days here to fully experience its wild side.

⊖ The Vilnius-Daugavpils train usually runs twice a day on weekends only. However, at the time of writing it's not operating across the border and it's not known when service will resume. In the meantime, there are up to five trains a day to the border town of Turmantas, from where there are regular buses that make the one-hour journey to Daugavpils.

Daugavpils

LATVIA

Daugavpils is an unavoidable stop on the journey from Vilnius to Rīga. Make the most of your layover by heading straight to the impressive riverside Daugavpils Fortress built on the orders of Tsar Alexander I. Other notable sights include the Mark Rothko Art Center, a multifunctional complex of contemporary art in honour of Daugavpils native Mark Rothko; the 1886 red-brick Lead Shot Factory, the oldest such tower in Europe; and the city's main synagogue, built in 1850 and attractively restored in 2005.

⊖ After whiling away a few hours, catch one of four daily trains to Rīga.

Rīga

LATVIA

Lively and cosmopolitan, Rīga is the largest of the Baltic capitals and, to be honest, the most captivating. The city is a heady mix of old and new, with Gothic spires dominating the skyline and a smorgasbord of contemporary art galleries, trendy bars and experimental kitchens serving up 21st-century flair at ground level.

The heart of Rīga is, like so many other stops on this tour, its UNESCO-listed Old Town. This is

Stalls selling fruit and vegetables in the vast Rīga Central Market

centred around Cathedral Square, where the imposing 13th-century red-brick cathedral houses one of Europe's largest organs. Enclosing the square is a delightful collection of cobbled lanes, multicoloured Art Nouveau buildings and sun-drenched courtyards, which fill up in the evenings as the cocktails begin to flow.

Just outside the Old Town is Rīga Central Market, housed in a series of five former Zeppelin hangars. It's Europe's largest market complex with over 3,000 stalls, attracting up to 100,000 shoppers a day. Rīga also has a growing craft beer scene in the Beer District (Alus Kvartāls), which has sprung up just a short distance northeast of the Old Town. A 2.5-km (1.5-mile) trail runs between a mix of brewpubs, microbreweries and even a beer embassy, offering the chance to sample over 200 Latvian ales.

 Take your pick from one of up to 13 daily trains to Sigulda.

DETOUR
Jūrmala

A short detour from Rīga will get you to Jūrmala, a series of white-sand beaches and 14 swanky townships backed by dunes and pine woods. Nearby are the wetlands of Ķemeri National Park, known for its tranquil nature trails and numerous outdoor activities such as hiking, rafting, stand-up paddleboarding and bogshoeing.

Sigulda
LATVIA

The quiet city of Sigulda is the main gateway to Gauja National Park, Latvia's largest protected area. The park's swathes of pristine forested wilderness are disturbed only by the languid flow of the Gauja river and the ancient sandstone cliffs lining its banks. This cherished natural landscape is Latvia's main outdoor adventure playground, with plenty of options for hiking, cycling and camping, as well as canoeing, caving and even bobsledding.

Turaida Castle, meaning "God's Garden" in ancient Livonian, is located just 5 km (3 miles) north of Sigulda. It's Latvia's most visited museum but still maintains an air of calm, even during the busy weekends and holidays. The 11th-century red-brick castle is surrounded by an assortment of outer buildings that have been transformed into exhibitions, including a smith house, wooden church and a Folk Song Garden featuring sculptures of Latvian heroes. There are also landscaped gardens, meadows of wildflowers and patches of woodland to stroll.

Within the city itself, the main draw is the 13th-century Sigulda Castle. The Livonian Order Castle was built between 1207 and 1209 by the Livonian Brothers of the Sword, a Catholic military order established in 1202 during the Livonian Crusade by Albert, the third bishop of Rīga.

 Five trains a day cover the short hop to Cēsis from Sigulda's centrally located station.

Cēsis

LATVIA

Still in Gauja National Park, adorable little Cēsis is probably Latvia's prettiest town. It's centred around St John's Church (the largest medieval basilica outside Rīga), an immaculate ornamental lake and gardens, and the sprawling Cēsis Castle complex. The latter site is actually made up of two castles: the dark-stone ramparts and towers of the restored medieval castle, and the elegant white-walled 18th-century manor house.

Founded by Livonian knights in 1214, the original castle was sacked by Russian tsar Ivan the Terrible in 1577 before undergoing frequent restoration in later centuries. There are several halls, dungeons and towers to explore, including one that requires visitors to collect a candlelit lantern in order to navigate the dark and eerie passageways. The "new" castle houses a collection of galleries and exhibits along with a series of restored and reconstructed rooms to explore.

Once finished with the main sights, take an hour or two to mooch around Cēsis's quiet streets and cute cafés before moving on.

🚊 Like everything in Cēsis, the train station is just a few minutes' walk from the castle. Catch either the lunchtime or evening train to the border town of Valga.

Valga

ESTONIA

For an example of shared Baltic history, look no further than Valga (meaning "walk" in German).

Until their separation in 1920, Valga in Estonia and the town of Valka in northern Latvia were one and the same. The history of the town stretches back to at least 1286, when it first appeared in the Rīga credit register and the regions of southern Estonia and northern Latvia belonged to the Governorate of Livonia. As such, Valga was the geographical centre of Livonia.

When the republics of Estonia and Latvia were formed after World War I, it was impossible to decide which country the town should become part of. The border issue was eventually resolved in 1920 by an Englishman, who was treated to a week-long reception in Estonia, then another with the Latvians. Equally charmed, he decided to divide the town in half on a map. Once both countries joined the Schengen Agreement in 2007, the towns became somewhat reunited when all border-crossing points were removed and roads and fences opened between the two countries.

The twin-town is the perfect border crossing, so take some time to stroll down to the Latvian-Estonian national boundary and enjoy the novelty of having one leg in Latvia and the other in Estonia. Other sights of interest are Valga Museum, situated in a handsome Art

Above
A cobbled street in Cēsis, with the spire of St John's Church in the distance

Below right
The Rotermann Quarter in Tallinn, featuring a blend of historic and modern architecture

Nouveau building, and Valga Prison Camp Cemetery, where an estimated 29,000 Russians died at the Nazi POW camp Stalag-351.

If you caught the afternoon train from Cēsis, then you'll have enough time to see the sights in Valga before jumping on the evening train to Tartu. If not, spend the night and catch one of three morning trains the following day.

Tartu

ESTONIA

Tartu, Estonia's second city, is often referred to as the nation's spiritual capital and said to have a special *vaim* (spirit). With its traditional wooden houses, 18th-century stately buildings, serene public parks and romantic river-front, it's also one of those cities where it's difficult to take a bad photo. Yet, it somehow manages to avoid the city-break tourism that can swamp places like Tallinn.

Despite feeling small and provincial (the population is less than 100,000), Tartu's sizeable student presence injects the leafy and historic city with boisterous exuberance – a perfect illustration of that Tartu *vaim* (particularly once the sun has set).

The railway station is a 20-minute walk from the centre with regular trains departing for Tallinn throughout the day.

Tallinn

ESTONIA

Tallinn, Estonia's capital, had to fight for its position on the world stage. It spent centuries being passed between various Danish, Swedish, Polish, German and Soviet rulers until 1991, when Estonia declared independence.

Since then, the city has changed considerably and continues to improve itself, as seen by its various accolades. (It was made European Capital of Culture in 2011 and won the European Green Capital Award for 2023.)

The best place to start your visit is in the Old Town. With its enchanting skyline ringed by medieval walls, this area is absurdly photogenic and bursts with fantastic sights, from the glorious Gothic St Nicholas' Church to the magnificent onion-domed Alexander Nevsky Russian Orthodox Cathedral.

You could spend days exploring the medieval streets alone, but Tallinn also has a modern dimension to it. With its ever-expanding 21st-century skyline, shiny shopping malls, cutting-edge art museums, emerging foodie scene and a futuristic train station due to open in 2030, the modern city counterbalances the Old Town's rustic charm. At the terminus of this eastern pilgrimage, use your last night to sample Tallinn's infamous nightlife and go out with a bang.

EXTEND YOUR TRIP

Narva

To experience the most un-Baltic place in the Baltics, take a two-and-a-half hour train to Narva. Estonia's easternmost city, separated from Ivangorod in Russia only by a narrow river, it is almost entirely populated by ethnic Russians. From the 15th-century castle, visitors can gaze across the river at the Russian equivalent, Ivangorod Fortress.

Right
Sitting at out-
door tables on
Haga Nygata in
Gothenburg's hip
Haga district

Below
Multicoloured
houses lining the
water in Nyhavn,
Copenhagen's
historic harbour

45

Best of Scandinavia

On this week-long rail trip around Denmark, Sweden and Norway's biggest cities, you'll discover the Scandinavian penchant for preserving the past while always striving for a better future.

○ Copenhagen (København)

3 hrs 20 mins–4 hrs

○ Gothenburg (Göteborg)

3 hrs 30 mins

○ Oslo

5 hrs 35 mins–6 hrs 30 mins

● Stockholm

◉ **COPENHAGEN** DENMARK ○ **STOCKHOLM** SWEDEN

◉ BUY INDIVIDUAL TICKETS FOR EACH LEG OF THE JOURNEY. LOOK FOR SNABBTÅG SERVICES IN SWEDEN – THEY ARE FASTER AND OFTEN CHEAPER (P260).

◔ 6–8 DAYS ◎ 1,258 KM (782 MILES)

Copenhagen
DENMARK

Frequently topping lists of the world's most liveable and happiest cities, the Danish capital is firmly on the map these days. When most people hear "Copenhagen", they probably picture Nyhavn. This 17th-century harbour was once the city's main shipping and fishing harbour, and one of the seedier parts of town, known for its drunken sailors and sex workers – a fact hard to imagine today now that its colourful townhouses,

cobbled streets and wooden boats are splashed on postcards and guidebook covers. It deserves a visit, of course, as do Copenhagen's other key sights, but if you want to find the locals, you'll need to venture out to the city's neighbourhoods.

Perched across the harbour from Nyhavn, and easily reached by ferry from there, is Refshaleøn. This formerly industrial area now houses craft breweries, the Reffen street food market and Copenhill – a waste-to-energy power plant topped with a dry ski slope.

Stockholm–Copenhagen Sleeper

Linking the two Scandinavian capitals in a seamless and sensible way (so typical of the region), the Stockholm–Copenhagen sleeper takes just seven hours to cover over 600 km (373 miles). Before the sky turns black, look out for moose as the green, forested scenery whizzes by the windows. You'll arrive as day breaks in a new city and country, ready for pastries and black coffee, local-style.

Another neighbourhood that reveals the real side of the city is Nørrebrø. A short bike ride to the north of the centre (if you want to blend in, you'll have to cycle), this residential area was rocked by riots from the 1980s to early 2000s. Today, it's still the place where any notable (peaceful) political protest kicks off, but it's also a hipster haven, full of skateboard ramps, streetwear stores and some of the city's most exciting restaurants. Whether you're after a hearty shawarma kebab or a bite-size smørrebrød (the classic Danish open sandwich), you'll find it here, so head to Nørrebrø for your last night in the city.

☻ Services between Københavns Hovedbanegård and Göteborg centralstation depart every 30 minutes or so. Soon after the train leaves Copenhagen, it runs along the Öresund Bridge, which connects Denmark and Sweden. Your documents will be checked once you cross the border.

Gothenburg

SWEDEN

Some call it gentrification, others a post-industrial renaissance. Whatever your politics, it's hard to deny that Gothenburg is passing muster as one of Scandinavia's new cool cities, thanks to an injection of cash and creative thinking. Around the old shipping harbour, still Scandinavia's biggest, former industrial buildings have had a lick of paint and a sharp refit. Inside, you'll find food trucks, craft breweries and hip, creative co-working spaces – just like Copenhagen's Refshaleøen.

The cityscape isn't all industrial though. Gothenburg has one of the prettiest centres in Sweden, with its broad avenues and elegant canals. Avenyn is the main boulevard and the cultural heart of the city. Here, you'll find the Concert Hall, City Theatre and Museum of Art, with its acclaimed Nordic collection. To the north, Haga (the Old Town) stretches towards the harbour. Once so run-down that demolition was on the cards, this area is now one of the city's hottest spots. Pop into one of its trendy cafés to indulge in *fika* (the Swedish tradition of making time for a coffee and cake).

☻ Catch one of the three trains that travel direct from Göteborg centralstation to Oslo sentralstasjon each day. The service is run by Vy. Passport control is carried out on board.

Oslo

NORWAY

Like almost everywhere in fjord-laced Norway, Oslo is oriented around the water. Founded at the end of an island-filled channel by the Vikings in 1040, the city's

If you only have time to do one thing during your stay in Oslo, make it a cruise on the Oslofjord.

The striking exterior of Oslo's Opera House, located at the head of the Oslofjord

atural port functions just like it lways has with wooden trading ouses replaced by sleek steel-nd-glass-sided buildings. If you nly have time to do one thing during your stay in Oslo, make it a ruise on the Oslofjord. As well as eeing the city from its all-mportant harbour, you'll visit slands with beautiful beaches, ature reserves and ancient ruins.

Back in the city centre, tick off ome of Oslo's biggest sights: the ast National Museum, contem-orary Opera House and the Nobel Peace Center, which xplores the prize's history.

One or two direct trains run between slo sentralstasjon and Stockholms entralstation daily, taking in some fantastic cenery en route. An alternative is to return o Göteborg centralstation and go on to tockholms centralstation from there, ut the route is far less scenic.

Stockholm

SWEDEN

Being spread across multiple slands has shaped Stockholm's istory and personality. People have come and gone over the centuries, from the Vikings to Hanseatic merchants, bringing wealth and new ideas with them. Creativity flourishes today, with start-ups and world-leading tech firms, such as Spotify, now calling the city home.

Each island has something to give, but you're here for the highlights so focus on the compact islands of Riddarholmen, Staden and Helgeandsholmen, which make up Gamla Stan (the Old Town). This web of narrow streets was made for strolling, particularly the areas around the Kungliga Slottet (17th-century royal palace), Riksdagshuset (parliament build-ing) and Storkyrkan (cathedral). Take every opportunity to head up side streets, where you'll discover worn cobbles, buzzing bars and faded coats of arms on old merchants' houses.

Once you've soaked up Gamla Stan's historic atmosphere, cross over the water to the buzzy down-town area of Norrmalm. It's here you'll find some of the city's cool-est restaurants, indie cinemas and clubs. What better way to end your visit to the home of Abba than with a dance?

EXTEND YOUR TRIP

Helsinki

The Nordic nation of Finland makes an interesting contrast to the Scandinavian countries, with its wildly different architecture and design. To get from Stockholm to Helsinki (the Finnish capital, *p234*) take the ferry. At over 16 hours it's a once-in-a-lifetime journey.

46

Aarhus

1 hr 35 mins

Odense

1 hr 10 mins

Copenhagen
(København)

Danish Design

Discover what makes Danish design so special on this rail trip. In the country's three key cities, you'll see examples of Denmark's finest interior design, architecture and urban planning.

○ **AARHUS** DENMARK ○ **COPENHAGEN** DENMARK

◉ INTERRAIL OR EURAIL DENMARK PASSES OFFER UNLIMITED TRAIN JOURNEYS FOR UP TO 8 DAYS A MONTH (P11). FOR INDIVIDUAL TICKETS, SEE THE DIRECTORY (P260).

🕐 4-6 DAYS 📍 328 KM (204 MILES)

Aarhus

Sustainability rules in Aarhus. Restaurants serve food grown just miles away, beehives sit on hotel roofs and coffee grounds from the many canal-side cafés are used to grow mushrooms on suburban farms. The city's architecture is similarly sustainable, making Aarhus the perfect place to begin your deep dive into Danish design.

The city is compact and eminently walkable, so you'll easily cover a lot of ground in a day. Spend the morning at Godsbanen, a railway yard turned cultural hub, ducking into its pottery, woodwork and graphic design workshops. Then follow the canal to ARoS Aarhus Art Museum. Potentially Aarhus's

most famous sight, the museum is crowned by Olafur Eliasson's *Your Rainbow Panorama*, a circle of colour that floats above the building's roof. At the end of the canal is the city's newest district, Aarhus Ø, where an out-of-use container terminal has been transformed into iceberg-inspired apartment blocks.

🚆 Catch the train from Aarhus Hovedbanegård to Odense Banegård. Services leave every 30 minutes.

Odense

Historic and modern design sit side by side in Denmark. Take Odense, where the redeveloped harbour district is just a stone's

Aarhus is the perfect place to begin your deep dive into Danish design.

throw away from the historic Old Town. This is where Danish writer Hans Christian Andersen was born and the area retains a fairy-tale vibe. Roses grow up pastel-coloured buildings and shopping streets have quirky alleyways and wonky, timber-framed buildings. But even here, contemporary architecture has taken root. Joined to the yellow-and-timber house where the writer was born is the H C Andersen Hus – a surprisingly contemporary curvaceous building, designed by Kengo Kuma.

Similar contrasts between old and new can be found all over the city: a futuristic bath floats in the historic harbour and a 100-year-old warehouse has been turned into Storms Pakhus, a trendy food hall. After all, contemporary Danish design isn't about doing away with the past – it's about reimagining it.

🚉 Services from Odense Banegård to Københavns Hovedbanegård (Copenhagen Central Station) depart every 30 minutes.

Copenhagen

Denmark's capital radiates out from its huge and historically important harbour. So what better way to get to grips with the city's architecture than from the water? Catch the Havnebuser (harbour bus) from Refshaleøen, a former industrial area that now houses street food stalls, craft breweries and Copenhill – a dry ski slope that swoops down the roof of a municipal waste building. Then, float along the water to the pot-bellied Royal Opera House, designed by Danish architect Henning Larsen in 2004, and the jenga-like Danish Architecture Center. Here, you can disembark to join a walking tour to learn more about the city's built history. Alternatively, strike out on your own, wheeling along the city's super-efficient bike lanes between buildings and popping into the many design stores along the way. You'll be amazed at how simple and stress-free it all is: this city, like all of Denmark, is designed for liveability.

The coloured panes of Olafur Eliasson's *Your Rainbow Panorama*, at the ARoS Aarhus Art Museum

47

Best of Norway

This two-week journey showcases the breathtaking landscapes, cosmopolitan cities and Scandinavian cuisine that help make Norway one of the most alluring destinations in Europe.

⊙ **OSLO** NORWAY ⊙ **BODØ** NORWAY

🛈 PLAN YOUR JOURNEY AND BOOK TICKETS WELL IN ADVANCE USING ENTUR (WWW.ENTUR.NO). FOR THE CHEAPEST RATES, LOOK FOR "LOW FARE" TICKETS, BUT BEAR IN MIND THAT THEY USUALLY CANNOT BE REFUNDED. DISTANCES ARE BIG IN NORWAY, SO CONSIDER BUYING A "FLEX TICKET" WHICH WILL GIVE YOU MORE FREEDOM WITH YOUR ITINERARY (P260).

🕒 14-16 DAYS ⊙ 3,282 KM (2,039 MILES)

Stavanger's iconic rock formation Preikestolen (Pulpit Rock)

Oslo

7 hrs 30 mins–9 hrs

Stavanger

14 hrs–16 hrs 30 mins

Bergen

15 hrs

Trondheim

9 hrs 50 mins

Bodø

Oslo

With its excellent international travel connections, the Norwegian capital is the obvious place to start your adventure. From culture and cuisine to nightlife and nature, the city has a lot to offer. Top of the list for most visitors, though, is the food. Oslo is the culinary capital of Scandinavia, so you'll want plenty of opportunities to dine here. The world's northernmost three-Michelin-starred restaurant (Maaemo) is located in the city, alongside a flurry of food halls, independent coffee shops and traditional restaurants. Local dishes are a must-try of course – think peel-and-eat shrimp and pølse (hot dogs) – but Oslo also has a penchant for pizza, sushi and fusion cuisine. Swing by any of the city's food halls to try everything from Japanese octopus balls to vegan-friendly Thai street food.

When you're not eating, take a walk around Oslo's museums. The Bygdøy peninsula is home to several unique ones including the Kon Tiki, Fram, Viking Ship and Norwegian Folk museums, all within a 15-minute walk of each other. In Gamle Oslo (Old Oslo), swing by the Munchmuseet, which opened in 2021 and houses the world's largest collection of Edvard Munch's work (some 28,000 items) – although not the most famous of the four versions of *The Scream*. You'll find this iconic image in the equally impressive National Museum, a short metro ride away in downtown Oslo.

Between the museums and mouthfuls of good food, be sure to squeeze in a drink. Fitting the city's Viking roots, Oslo hosts a burgeoning beer scene. Hunker down in a cosy bar or gastropub and order a locally made brew to toast the end of your time here.

🚊 There are up to four direct trains a day to Stavanger, leaving from Oslo S (Sentralstasjon/Central Station) located, as the name suggests, in the heart of the city.

Stavanger

Despite Stavanger's industrial credentials (it's home to the nation's largest oil company), the city has somehow managed to remain extraordinarily pretty. The 173 wooden houses of Gamle Stavanger are arguably the most handsome and best-preserved wooden buildings in Norway (many date back to the 18th century). Down on the historic wharf, colourful houses once used as storehouses for salt and herring have been transformed into a hive of bustling restaurants and bars.

Beyond the city limits the scenery is far less quaint. Here you'll find Norway's most famous vantage point, Preikestolen (Pulpit Rock), an extraordinary rock formation poised 604 m (1,981 ft) above Lysefjord. Be aware that you'll rarely have the view from here to yourself (the rock receives over 300,000 annual visitors); it's also a steep four-hour (8-km/5-mile) return hike, which is only accessible from May to October. The panoramic views of the fjords are very much worth the challenge though.

🚊 Catch the sleeper service to Drammen, where you can change onto the Bergensbanen to Bergen.

Bergen

Known for its seven fjords, seven hills and traditional fishing wharf, Bergen enjoys a spectacular setting. While it may be one of Europe's wettest cities (it rains on average 260 days a year), it is a vibrant place with easy access to the western fjords. So don't let the rain put you off.

Founded in 1070, Bergen was an important and wealthy seaport during the early Middle Ages, serving as Norway's capital from the 13th century to the 1830s. Today, it is the country's second-largest city. To soak up all of its history, make the UNESCO-listed Bryggen (wharf) your first stop. The bright and beautifully preserved Vågen Harbour is a chocolate box of 58 buildings dating from the 14th to 16th centuries; they now house an array of boutique cafés and art galleries. Another must-do is the hike (or funicular ride) up Mount Floyen. The city views up here are unmatched and the summit connects to a network of gorgeous hiking trails extending around the city's hills.

You're sure to have worked up an appetite on the trail and Bergen just happens to be a member of UNESCO's City of Gastronomy network. There's a long tradition of seafood here and, with that, some of the country's finest fish restaurants. Don't leave without trying the old Bergen classic *persetorsk*: cod first marinated in salt and sugar before being pressed and served.

🚉 There are at least four daily trains to Trondheim from Bergen, all requiring a change in Oslo. The most agreeable is the sleeper which arrives in Oslo early morning. After a 90-minute wait in the capital, the connection reaches Trondheim in the early afternoon.

Top
Waterfront houses on the Bryggen in Bergen

Above
A plate of fresh, locally caught seafood, Bergen's culinary speciality

There are three Michelin-starred restaurants in Trondheim and a wealth of high-quality spots offering unique and innovative dining experiences.

Trondheim

Norway's third-largest city is one of its most photogenic. Here, winding waterways and wooded hills form a backdrop to colourful warehouses and tiny timber homes. The wide avenues (which act as firebreaks) are the result of the city's redesign after a fire destroyed much of the centre in 1681. These sweeping streets now make for perfect cycling terrain (rental bikes are widely available).

Like many cities in Norway, Trondheim claims to have the best food scene. There are three Michelin-starred restaurants here and a wealth of high-quality spots offering unique and innovative dining experiences. You'll also find a bounty of farm shops and delis selling local specialities including craft beer and, of course, seafood.

Beyond the inventory of cafés and restaurants are curious sights such as the pop and rock music museum, Rockheim, and Europe's northernmost Gothic cathedral, Nidaros Domkirke.

There is one direct train a day departing Trondheim for Bodø. It takes around ten hours and usually leaves in the morning.

Bodø

Bodø's town centre was almost entirely rebuilt after being razed during World War II. The result is distinctly unexciting, but you haven't come to Bodø for the architecture. The city's allure lies in its surrounding scenery of wild peaks, vast skies and rugged islands that dot the horizon and support the world's densest concentration of white-tailed sea eagles. As such, Bodø is known as the "Sea Eagle Capital". Island-hopping, hiking, cycling, climbing and glacier trekking are just some of the outdoor activities on offer.

Bodø is also the northern terminus of Norway's railway system, a jumping-off point for the Lofoten Islands and the country's most accessible place to watch the aurora borealis. As Bodø is situated just inside the Arctic Circle, the Northern Lights are observable from September to April. Another result of the city's northerly position is the midnight sun, visible from the beginning of June to mid-July. Either the aurora or the midnight sun (unfortunately you can't have both) would make for an enchanting epilogue to your Nordic adventure.

EXTEND
YOUR TRIP

Lofoten Islands

Trains don't continue from Bodø, but that doesn't mean the end of your trip – the Lofoten Islands can be easily reached from Bodø by a three- to four-hour ferry. The approach is worth the fare alone: passengers come face-to-face with the islands' most amazing feature, the soaring jagged peaks of the Lofotenveggen (Lofoten Wall).

The northern lights dancing across the sky near Bodø

48

Malmö
3 hrs
Kalmar
5 hrs
Stockholm
38 mins
Uppsala

Green Sweden

Countries don't get much greener than Sweden. On this week-long tour, you'll tuck into zero-waste dishes, wheel around sustainable cities and get out into the country's verdant landscape.

▶ **MALMÖ** SWEDEN ○ **UPPSALA** SWEDEN

💰 SAVE MONEY BY BUYING AN SJ PASS, WHICH IS VALID FOR 7 CONSECUTIVE DAYS, RATHER THAN INDIVIDUAL TICKETS (P260).

⏱ 7–8 DAYS 📍 919 KM (571 MILES)

Malmö

Start your tour of southern Sweden in Malmö, which is perched on the other side of the Öresund Bridge to Copenhagen. Thanks to its position at a cross-roads, Malmö has long been a major metropolis for international cuisine and culture, something that's earned it the affectionate nickname Falafelstaden (Falafel City). Malmö is also leading the charge when it comes to Sweden's sustainable food scene, with chefs growing their own ingredients or using produce that would other-wise be thrown away. Get to grips with the city's culinary diversity at Malmö Saluhall, a covered food hall.

The heart of Malmö is arguably Gamla Väster (the Old Town), which is defined as the area between Lilla Torg ("little square") and Stortorget ("big square"). Here, you'll find Slottsparken and Kungsparken, two large public gardens with pathways, ponds, fountains and, in Slottsparken's case, the moat-ringed Malmöhus Slott – Scandinavia's oldest Renaissance fortress. These are but the first of a series of green spaces that you'll discover during your exploration of the region.

🚆 Travel direct from Malmö centralstation to Kalmar Centralstation on the nonstop Öresundståg service.

Kalmar

Next stop is the charming coastal haven of Kalmar. Built on a series of islands, with a long coastline

The industrial interior of Malmö Saluhall, the city's popular covered food hall

of bays and canals, the city is ideal for a couple of days spent outdoors. Popular activities here include hiking, cycling, kayaking and stand-up paddleboarding, with plenty of dedicated routes available to explore the surrounding landscape.

That's not to say that the city centre doesn't have delights of its own. Centralstation is located right on the peninsula that serves as Kalmar's main downtown. Here, surrounded by perfectly preserved architecture, you'll quickly discover why Kalmar has been awarded the Europa Nostra Award twice for its heritage conservation. One of the most impressive buildings is Kalmar Cathedral. Once a humble 12th-century fortress, it was refashioned in the 16th century by King Gustav Vasa into the imposing, copper-roofed Baroque jewel it is today.

🚆 Trains run on the hour from Kalmar Centralstation nonstop to Stockholms centralstation, from where the metro runs to other parts of the capital.

Stockholm

Of course, no visit to Sweden is complete without a stop in the lively and paradoxical capital of Stockholm. Metropolitan yet historical, modern yet traditional, a centre for technological innovation and forward-thinking design: Stockholm is somewhere you could explore for months and barely scratch the surface of what it has to offer. But you don't have time for that (and your

Inlandsbanan

Stretching for 1,288 km (800 miles) between Mora, 300 km (186 miles) north of Stockholm, and Gällivare in the Arctic Circle, "The Island Line" is one of Europe's most scenic summer rail journeys (the service runs between mid-June and August). Outside the windows, a parade of forests, meadows and lakes slip by as the *Inlandsbanan* glides north.

rail pass won't allow it). Instead of trying to see all of the 14 islands that make up this dynamic city, choose a few and explore them properly over three or four days. Djurgården, Stockholm's forested island, is a must; here you'll find some of the city's best-loved attractions: the Gröna Lund amusement park, ABBA Museum, Vasa Ship Museum and Skansen – Sweden's oldest open-air village.

Another worthy choice is Skeppsholmen. Once a military base, this island is now home to the Moderna Museet, the city's fantastic contemporary art gallery. Other barracks have been turned into restaurants and cafés.

To dip your toe into Stockholm's fantastic sustainable food scene, head to Gamla Stan – the city's concentrated centre. Here, ingredients are seasonal, locally sourced or even grown by the restaurants themselves. Others use "foodtech" to reduce waste and emissions, and become climate neutral or even positive.

➡ Ride the train from Stockholms centralstation to Uppsala centralstation. Services run every 30 minutes.

Uppsala

Your journey ends in Uppsala, repeated winner of WWF's national and international One Planet City Challenge. This prize is awarded to the municipal government that has best met the goals set out in the Paris Agreement each year. Uppsala has won it by collaborating with nearby cities to meet goals, and investing in public transport and renewable energy (it aims to be climate positive after 2050).

It's not surprising, then, that Uppsala leads the way when it comes to fighting climate change in Sweden. The city has been a hub for the best and brightest in Scandinavia since its university opened in 1477. Today, it's still the city's biggest attraction, with visitors flocking to its Gustavianum – a museum housing impressive artworks, Egyptian mummies and Nordic relics, with a unique 17th-century Anatomical Theatre on its roof.

It's thanks to Uppsala University's 41,000-strong student population that the city has a small-town, collegiate atmosphere and, like everywhere you've visited in Sweden, a green heart. You'll feel it as you play football golf (exactly how it sounds), cycle through the city on its fast paths and walk along the "green waterside" – a trail that tracks the coiling Fyrisån river.

EXTEND
YOUR TRIP

Gävle

The tiny town of Gävle is just a 45-minute train ride from Uppsala and offers a taste of rural Sweden. Visit a moose farm, walk the traffic-free cobblestone lanes of the Old Town or celebrate rail at the Swedish Railway Museum.

A bicycle in a cobbled square in Gamla Stan, Stockholm's Old Town

49

Explore Finland

Instead of speeding between Helsinki and Rovaniemi on the *Santa Claus Express*, take it slow on Finland's public trains. You'll be able to stop off where you want and take in the landscape during daylight.

○ **HELSINKI** FINLAND ○ **ROVANIEMI** FINLAND

● PRICES VARY ACCORDING TO THE SPEED OF SERVICE AND TIME OF PURCHASE – THE EARLIER YOU BOOK, THE CHEAPER THE TICKETS (P260).

● 4-7 DAYS ● 894 KM (556 MILES)

A herd of reindeer moving through a snowy winter forest, Rovaniemi

Helsinki

Sternly guarding the entrance of Helsinki Central Railway Station, Emil Wikström's tall granite statues set the Finnish capital's architectural tone. The city is dotted with 20th-century masterpieces, such as the Functionalist-style stadium, which hosted the 1952 Summer Olympics, and Alvar Aalto's shining white Finlandia Hall, which rises from the banks of Töölönlahti Bay to the north of the city centre.

These constructions were built to celebrate Finland's newfound independence after a century under Russian control. They stand in direct contrast to the city's Neoclassical brick buildings, which were modelled on St Petersburg's. Today, Helsinki still has a maritime feel that is more akin to Russia or Eastern Europe than anywhere else in Scandinavia.

After admiring the city's architecture, dive into its fantastic arts scene. The Kiasma, Ateneum, Helsinki Art Museum (HAM) and Design Museum are all excellent. Then, get ready to journey north.

● There are several services to Oulu from Helsinki each day, with the first one leaving in the small hours of the morning and the last one close to midnight.

Oulu

If you take the *Santa Claus Express*, you won't be able to stop off at Oulu, which would be a pity. The city has a fantastic cycle network, the largest in the country, making it the perfect jumping-off

point for exploring Finland's incredible scenery. Wheel out from the city centre to Hietasaari, which has a quintessential lakeland landscape of tall trees and still water. Alternatively, take your bike on the ferry over to the wild, windswept island of Hailuoto and explore its beaches and red wooden houses.

Trains to Rovaniemi run every two to four hours. Travel by day rather than taking the night train so you can admire the scenery out the window.

Rovaniemi

The landscape gets wilder and wilder as you cross into Lapland and approach the Arctic Circle, the most northerly of the five major circles of latitude on earth.

Here, tundra-like plains and deep forests seem to go on forever, just like the days during the months of the midnight sun (mid-May to mid-August).

Lapland's capital, Rovaniemi, sits slapbang on the Arctic Circle and is the only major city around these parts. It's profited from being so close to the North Pole by building a Santa Claus Village, which draws crowds of excited families during the Christmas season. But Rovaniemi is a fantastic place to visit at any time of year. The Arkikum, a museum and science centre exploring the Arctic region, is a year-round highlight, while the climb up to Kuninkaanlaavu is only possible in summer, when the snow has melted. From here, you'll have a fantastic view of Lapland's uninterrupted landscape.

Santa Claus Express

The night service from Helsinki to Rovaniemi is known as the *Santa Claus Express*. The double-decker train features comfortable sleeping compartments where you'll go to sleep in Helsinki and wake up 15 hours later above the Arctic Circle. It's understandably a very popular route in winter so book your tickets well in advance.

50

Top to Toe

Sometimes it pays to go a little off piste. Instead of crossing the continent from west to east, this tour stitches together stops from north to south – because why not?

○ **STOCKHOLM** SWEDEN ○ **NAPLES** ITALY

○ FOR A ROUTE THIS EXTENSIVE, IT MAKES SENSE TO INVEST IN AN INTERRAIL OR EURAIL PASS (P11).

○ 18-21 DAYS ○ 3,052 KM (1,896 MILES)

Kødbyens Fiskebar, a seafood restaurant in Copenhagen's Kødbyen area

Stockholm
SWEDEN

Most visitors to Stockholm confine themselves to Gamla Stan (the Old Town), but you want to gain a different perspective on the Swedish capital and for that you need to go to the city's southern island: Södermalm. Affectionately known as Söder, this island enclave is Stockholm's coolest neighbourhood.

Södermalm follows a similar story to other hip areas. Once a working-class district, Söder's cheap rents soon attracted an artsy and alternative community. Its most famous resident is its fictional one, Lisbeth Salander – Swedish writer Stieg Larsson's kooky crime-solving antihero. If you've read the books or seen the movies, you might imagine her sweeping through "SoFo", the grid of streets south of Folkungagatan that acts as Söder's epicentre.

During the day, Söder's eco-conscious boutiques and vintage design stores buzz with locals looking to snag the perfect piece. But the area really comes in to its own after dark, when its bars and clubs become the hottest spots in the city. Party the night away here and start your cross-continental adventure with a good boogie.

There are trains from Stockholms Centralstation to Københavns Hovedbanegård every one to two hours. Try to board a direct service to avoid changing in Malmö and adding more time to the journey.

Copenhagen
DENMARK

There's much more to Denmark's famously happy capital than Noma, the *Little Mermaid* statue and those much-photographed harbourside buildings. To experience the lesser-visited side of Copenhagen, head to Kødbyen in the Vesterbro neighbourhood, southwest of the railway station. Formerly the city's meat packing district, the area became the haunt of drug dealers and sex workers towards the end of the 20th century. With the dawn of the new millennium, though, start-ups and hipsters moved in, bringing with them art galleries, cool bars and boutiques. Check them out before lunching at Kødbyens Fiskebar, a restaurant housed in a former meat market.

Although it's far more conventional than it used to be, and can no longer claim to fly under the radar, Freetown Christiana still represents an alternative side of Copenhagen. This independent commune was founded in 1971 on a semi-abandoned military base in Amager, to the east of the station, by disenfranchised residents of a nearby neighbourhood. Since then, Pusher Street's open hash market has given people certain preconceptions about the area, even though these stalls are no longer tolerated. In reality, Freetown Christiana is still what it has always been – a wonderland of communal living.

This part of the city isn't about ticking off sights; it rewards aimless wandering. See where your feet take you, disappearing

Stockholm

5 hrs

Copenhagen
(København)

4 hrs 45 mins

Hamburg

4 hrs 30 mins

Nuremberg
(Nürnberg)

1 hr

Munich (München)

2 hrs–2hr 30 mins

Innsbruck

4 hrs 30 mins

Verona

50 mins–1 hr 30 mins

Bologna

3 hrs 45 mins–
4 hrs 15 mins

Naples (Napoli)

You'll find most of the city's highlights by the water, which has been Hamburg's lifeblood since the 13th century.

down side streets to check out street art, browsing second-hand shops for goodies and tucking into scrumptious vegan street food whenever you can.

🚄 Five direct trains a day run from Københavns Hovedbanegård to Hamburg Hauptbahnhof, with the last train of the day departing between 5pm and 5:30pm.

_____

Hamburg
GERMANY

For many visitors, Hamburg is simply sin city – a place of sex workers, dive bars and port-side grime. But, it's also seriously cosmopolitan. Hamburg is Germany's media capital and home to the most millionaires in the country. Thanks to these two distinct personalities, the city has dive bars and red-curtained theatres; a strong counterculture movement and a young, cool population; and a nightlife scene that is equal parts depraved and refined. It's a fantastic place to spend a few days.

You'll find most of the city's highlights by the water, which has been Hamburg's lifeblood since the 13th century. One of the most striking sights is the Elbphil-harmonie ("Elphi" for short), a thoroughly modern concert hall designed to evoke sails and waves. As you'll come to expect from this multifaceted city, it hosts both classical and contemporary musicians.

Hamburg's culinary scene is similarly far-reaching. Of course, you'll find plenty of hamburgers here (although donner kebabs are surprisingly more popular), but there are also swanky, multi-course and wine-paired menus a plenty, and no-frills spots serving up sailors' favourites. Try _labskaus_ (a hash made from corned beef, mashed potato, beetroot and pickled herring) or _aalsuppe_ (beef, eel and vegetable soup).

🚄 Though not the biggest, Hamburg Hauptbahnhof is the busiest station in Germany. You can keep your departure time flexible, since there are two or three direct trains from here to Nürnberg Hauptbahnhof every hour.

_____

Nuremberg
GERMANY

Despite its convincingly medieval, half-timbered centre, Nuremberg was almost entirely reconstructed after World War II. And this Bavarian city has worked hard to repair its image after the Nuremberg rallies, Nuremberg laws and postwar Nuremberg trials. It can never be entirely rid of the association, but the marvel of Nuremberg is how sensitively it handles its history. The old rally grounds, for example, now house the fantastic Documentation Centre, which explores the causes, background and effects of the Third Reich through regularly rotating exhibitions.

The buzzing Hacker-Pschorr beer tent at Oktoberfest in Munich

Other cultural highlights include the exhaustive Germanisches Nationalmuseum, which examines Germany's history, and the Albrecht-Dürer-Haus. The 15th-century artist was born and died in the city and painted some of his most famous works here.

⊋ Direct trains from Nürnberg Hauptbahnhof to München Hauptbahnhof depart every 20–30 minutes and take just one hour to reach their destination.

Munich
GERMANY

Like Nuremberg, Munich has a post-World War II façade. But unlike its Bavarian neighbour, the city that birthed the Nazi party has managed to shake off its associations in a way that Nuremberg can't seem to. Soon after the fall of the Third Reich, Munich became a cultural hub – its movie studios were Germany's answer to Hollywood and its record studios fostered the disco movement. Today, the city is home to some excellent museums, including the Pinakothek der Moderne, but Munich is more famous for its beer.

For two weeks each autumn, people from far and wide descend on Theresienwiese park for Oktoberfest. With thigh-slapping folk music, funfair rides, dirndl- and lederhosen-clad revellers, and foaming steins of limited-edition Märzenbier, this is the world's most famous beer festival for good reason. Don't worry if you miss out, Hofbräuhaus in Marienplatz, the city's long-and-thin main square, pours out steins year round.

⊖ München Hauptbahnhof is huge, so arrive in plenty of time to find your platform. Trains to Innsbruck Hauptbahnhof, either direct or via the Austrian town of Kufstein, depart hourly.

Innsbruck
AUSTRIA

Its proximity to the Alps might have put this Austrian city on the map, but Innsbruck isn't

The Arlberg Line

Austria's only east-west mountain railway connects Innsbruck with Bludenz, surging through spectacular scenery en route. This high-altitude train, which is part of the national network, stops at St Anton am Arlberg (p136), an appealing Tirolean town where you can go skiing in winter, and hiking or e-biking in summer.

just a haven for winter sports. Nestled in a valley of the Inn river, surrounded by snowcapped mountains and full of characterful 18th-century buildings, it's undeniably picturesque. The best views are had from the Hungerburgbahn funicular, which climbs the Nordkette range between curvaceous, futuristic stations designed by British architect Zaha Hadid.

🚆 Each day, there are four or five services from Innsbruck Hauptbahnhof to Verona Porta Nova via the Austrian town of Brenner (Brennero) or Italian city of Bolzano (Bozen).

Verona
ITALY

Thanks to William Shakespeare's *Romeo and Juliet*, the tale of two fated local lovers, Verona will forever be synonymous with romance. And a romantic air seems to imbue this city. You'll feel it in the Roman amphitheatre, which reverberates with opera each summer. And you'll feel it as you walk the cobbled streets, passing pretty squares and medieval buildings, some even embellished with balconies worthy of Juliet. If you want the "real deal", head for Casa di Giuletta, the balconied mansion of the Dal Capello family – the inspiration, possibly, for the fictional Capulets.

🚆 Direct trains from Verona Porta Nova to Bologna Centrale depart once or twice an hour and take just 50–90 minutes.

Bologna
ITALY

Rail travellers who choose Bologna for its useful connections may be pleasantly surprised by its dynamic, cultured atmosphere (and, perhaps less unexpectedly, its good food). The city is nick-named *"La Dotta"* ("The Learned") and *"La Rossa"* ("The Red") because of the colour of its buildings, ancient university and left-leaning politics.

Below left
Verona's centre, split in half by the meandering Adige river

Below right
Casa di Giulietta, the medieval house said to have inspired Shakespeare

from Centrale station, you simply have to cross the road to breach what remains of the city's once impenetrable walls, which envelop all of Bologna's main sights. First, you'll reach the university district, where you'll find 11th-century lecture halls, MAMbo (one of Italy's most important contemporary art museums) and the Finestrella. This tiny window, which always seems to have a long queue, grants a glimpse of one of the many canals that secretly run beneath Bologna's streets.

Further south is the Basilica di San Petronio, an unfinished cathedral which has a unique two-phase look, and the Due Torri. These twin 12th-century towers are all that remains of a forest of fortifications that once defended the city, and the taller of the two can be climbed for fantastic (though leg-shaking) views of the red-roofed city below, with its long stretches of porticoes.

● Bologna Centrale is one of Italy's busiest stations. Direct trains speed south to Napoli Centrale three to four times an hour.

Naples

ITALY

You've travelled across Europe from top to toe, so why not end your tour by exploring Naples from top to bottom? The delights of raffish Naples never fail to deliver – fine museums, hard-to-resist pizzerias, pulsating street life – but underground is another world entirely, a honeycomb of ancient aqueducts, secret escape routes and sacred catacombs.

Subterranean Naples sprawls below the city and, as such, exploring it involves visiting several sights. Discover plumbing as it was in the Roman times at Napoli Sotterranea; a vast spider web-like network of tunnels and refashioned cisterns at Galleria Borbonica; and Naples' oldest and most sacred catacomb at Catacombe di San Gennaro, a place of pilgrimage for Christians through the ages. From nervous kings seeking escape from revolting subjects to Neapolitan locals taking refuge from World War II bombs, stories are vividly brought to life beneath the surface. You'll no doubt emerge onto Naples' streets, squinting in the light, ready to make some stories of your own.

EXTEND YOUR TRIP

Pompeii and Herculaneum

Mount Vesuvius is a brooding presence in Naples. Experience its might at the fascinatingly preserved ruins of Pompeii and Herculaneum, Roman cities that were famously buried beneath volcanic debris in AD 79. Take the Circumvesuviana, a local train that departs Napoli Garibaldi station 2–3 times each hour. It takes just 35 to 40 minutes to reach Pompei Scavi-Villa Misteri.

Directory

Europe's rail network is wonderfully well connected and the integrated pass system makes travel from country to country, and island to mainland, a breeze.

Many things hold true through-out the continent (p8), but there are some ways in which places differ and that's where this directory comes in.

Over the following pages, you'll find essential information for each country's train network. We've also included helpful advice, money saving tips and network maps showing the main lines and stations in each country. You can use these to craft your own adventure; the 50 rail trips in this book are just the beginning.

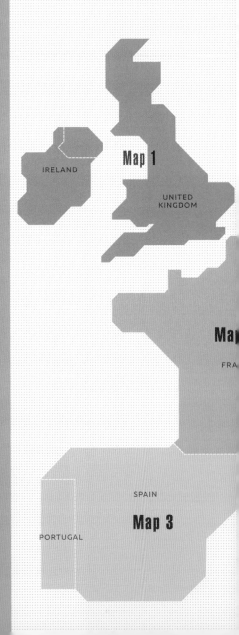

IRELAND

Map 1

UNITED KINGDOM

Map 2

FRANCE

SPAIN

Map 3

PORTUGAL

Map 1

England, Scotland and Wales
www.nationalrail.co.uk

Great Britain's rail network is run by over 20 private train companies. Fortunately, the companies all work together under the umbrella group National Rail, with coordinated fare and ticketing structures. Tickets and timetables are available at stations, company websites and via National Rail.

There are four types of fare: Anytime, Off-Peak, Super-Off-Peak and Advance. Anytime tickets (the most expensive option) can be used on any service; Off-Peak tickets are valid outside of the Monday to Friday commuter window; Super-Off-Peak tickets are only available on certain services; cheaper Advance tickets are only valid for pre-booked trains, with limited or no changes or refunds allowed.

Ireland
www.irishrail.ie

Iarnród Éireann or Irish Rail is the national rail operator of the Republic of Ireland. There are three types of tickets available online: Low, Semi-Flexible and Flexible. Low tickets are the cheapest and amendable up to 48 hours in advance of departure for a fee; Semi-Flexible are amendable up to 24 hours in advance for a smaller fee; Flexible tickets can be amended for free up to 60 minutes before departure. You can also buy a ticket at the station on the day, but it will be more expensive.

Tourist tickets are also available online and come in two forms: Trekker (allowing four consecutive travel days) and Explorer (for five days of travel within 15 days).

Northern Ireland
www.translink.co.uk

Translink operates Northern Ireland Railways (NIR), as well as Ulsterbus and Metro. Note that there is no cost advantage to booking in advance online.

If you are planning on making great use of the country's bus and train services, you might save money with an iLink. This smart card provides unlimited bus and rail travel within specified zones in the region.

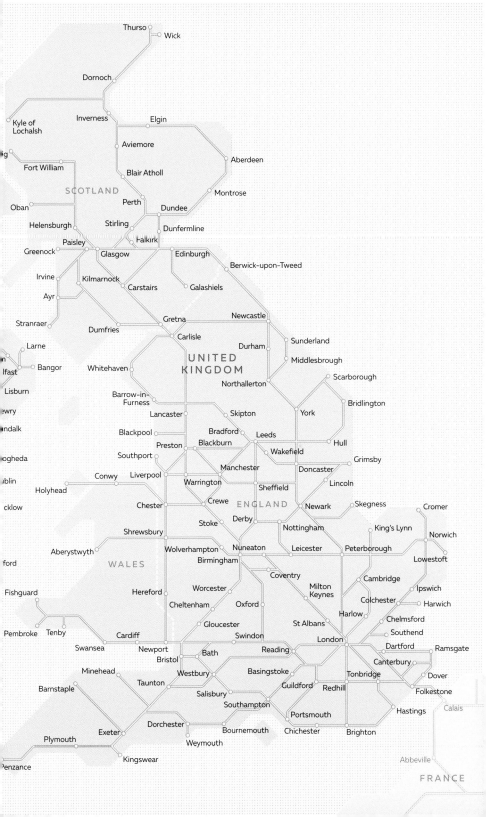

Map 2

France and Monaco

www.sncf-connect.com

Société Nationale des Chemins de Fer (SNCF) operates France and Monaco's rail networks. The SNCF's fastest trains are the Trains à Grande Vitesse (TGV), which run on long-distance routes. Ouigo trains are cheaper versions of the TGV services. Intercités are slower long-distance trains, while the infrequent Intercités de Nuit are overnight sleeper trains. Trains Express Régionaux (TER) cover local regions.

Tickets in France are fixed-price and can't sell out, so there's no need to buy an advance ticket. Always remember that French train tickets (except e-tickets) must be validated before you board the train in the yellow machines marked "Compostez votre billet" at the platform entrance. You may be fined if you don't validate your ticket.

Luxembourg

www.cfl.lu

Public transport is wonderfully free in this tiny nation. Tickets are only required for first class and can be purchased on the Société National des Chemins de Fer Luxembourgeois (CFL) website.

Switzerland

www.sbb.ch

Switzerland's rail network is super efficient. Swiss Federal Railways (SBB in German, CFF in French or FFS in Italian) runs most mainline routes, but private operators run some regional trains.

In most cases, you can just turn up at the station, buy a ticket and hop on a train. For some long-distance journeys, Super-saver tickets are available online. These fares can be as little as 30 per cent of a full-price ticket, and the further ahead you book, the cheaper the fares are.

There's also the Swiss Travel Pass, which grants unlimited travel across the country for 3, 4, 8 or 15 days. Be sure to compare the cost with an Interrail One-Country Pass, though, as these can sometimes be cheaper.

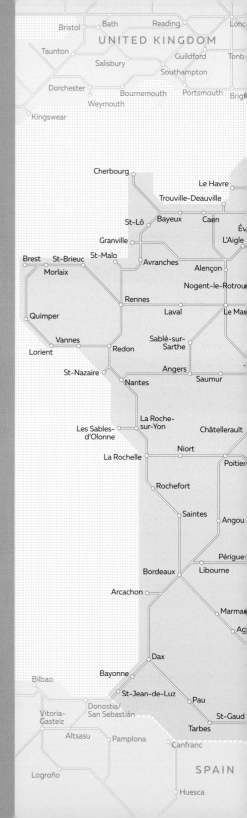

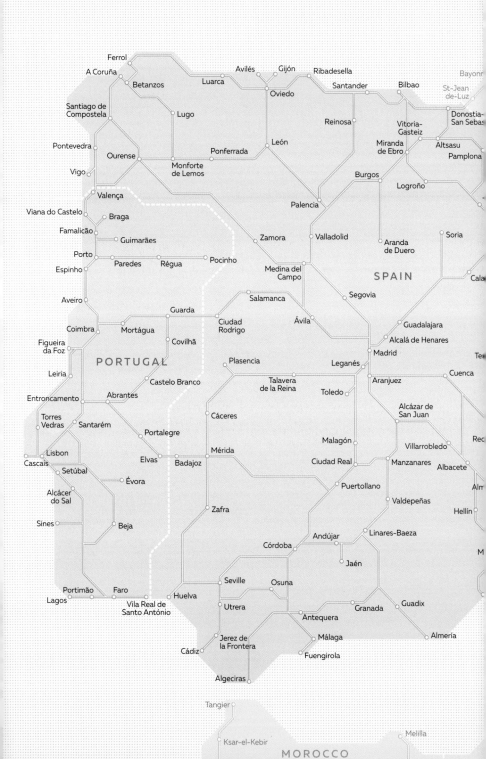

FRANCE

Aurillac
Marmande
Cahors
Agen
Rodez
Montauban
Albi
Millau
Toulouse
Pau
Pamiers
Carcassonne
Tarbes
St-Gaudens
Narbonne
Canfranc
Jaca
ANDORRA
Perpignan
La Pobla de Segur
Puigcerdà
Figueres
Huesca
Girona
Vic
Monzón
Balaguer
Manresa
aragoza
Lleida
Terrassa
Montblanc
Tarragona
Barcelona
Caspe
Reus
Sitges

Castellón de la Plana
Soller
Sa Pobla
Sagunto
Palma
Manacor
Valencia
Gandia
Dénia
Alcoi
Alicante

rtagena

Algiers

Blida
Chlef
Oran
Rellzane
ALGERIA
Sidi Bel Abbès

Map 3

Portugal
www.cp.pt

Portugal's national rail operator is CP (Comboios de Portugal). CP runs urban rail services (*urbanas*), Regional and InterRegional trains, Alfa Pendular (fast and comfortable long-distance services) and Intercidades (long-distance trains which are older, cheaper and stop regularly).

Seat reservations are mandatory on all Alfa Pendular and Intercidades services; pre-book tickets online or at stations. A conductor will validate tickets onboard and will often ask for ID.

Tickets for *urbanas* can be bought at the station prior to departure and should be validated at the ticket machines on the platform before boarding.

Spain
www.renfe.com

Renfe is Spain's national rail operator and has absorbed many regional train operators, including FEVE, which runs the rambling narrow-gauge network along the north coast. A few smaller regional operators still remain though: Euskotren runs trains from Hendaye and Irun to San Sebastián and Bilbao, and the FGC local railway operates in Barcelona. Renfe also faces competition from two other high-speed operators: Ouigo Spain and Avlo. For long-distance journeys, compare ticket prices for all three.

All long-distance trains and even some shorter regional services require a seat reservation. Places are usually available on the day of travel but at peak times, such as Easter and Christmas, trains can be full days in advance. To avoid missing out on a seat, and to take advantage of cheap advance fares, always pre-book your train.

Interrail and Eurail one-country passes are not recommended in Spain as pass-holder reservations can't be made online and an additional fee is levied on every booking. Consider buying Renfe's Spain Pass instead. It can be used for either 4, 6, 8 or 10 one-way journeys of any length in a one-month period on all of Renfe's long-distance and medium- distance trains.

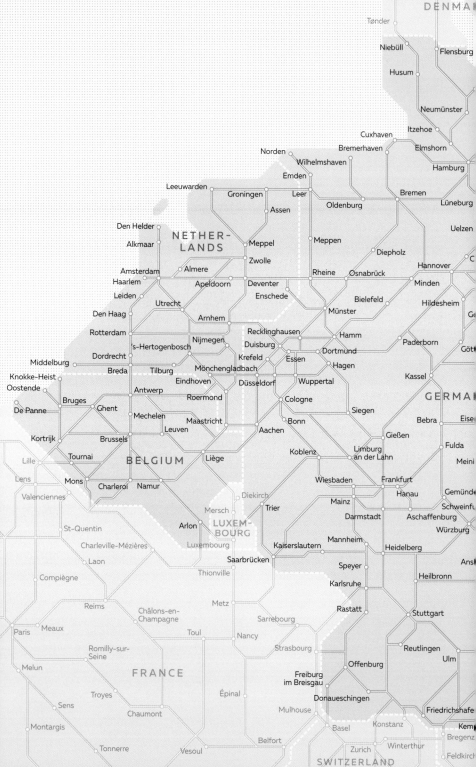

Map 4

Sassnitz
Stralsund
Wismar · Rostock · Świnoujście
Greifswald
Bad Kleinen · Szczecin
Waren · Pasewalk
Ludwigslust · Neustrelitz
Wittenberge · Angermünde
Oranienburg
Stendal · Rathenow · Berlin
Potsdam · Frankfurt (Oder)
Magdeburg · Jüterbog
Dessau · Cottbus
Halle · Leipzig · Riesa
Ruhland
Dresden · Görlitz
Gößnitz
Jena · Chemnitz
Zwickau
Ústí nad Labem
Hof · Chomutov
Prague
Coburg
Cheb · Karlovy Vary
Bamberg
Marktredwitz · Plzeň
Nuremberg · Weiden · CZECH REPUBLIC
Schwandorf · Klatovy
České Budějovice
Treuchtlingen · Regensburg
Donauwörth · Plattling
Ingolstadt · Passau
Augsburg · Landshut
Mühldorf am Inn · Linz
Wels
Munich · Rosenheim · Salzburg
Vöcklabruck
Garmisch-Partenkirchen · Bischofshofen
Wörgl · AUSTRIA
Innsbruck

vendborg · Næstved
kov · Nykøbing Falster
eck · chwerin · zwedel · rsburg · nschweig · rhausen · urt

Belgium

www.belgiantrain.be

Belgium has an extensive rail network run by Société Nationale des Chemins de Fer Belges (SNCB). There's no need or cost advantage to booking train tickets in advance here, as prices are fixed and based on distance. Simply turn up, buy a ticket and hop on the next train.

Germany

www.bahn.de

An efficient train network, largely run by Deutsche Bahn (DB), operates throughout Germany's vast regions. The fastest trains – InterCity Express (ICE) – connect the largest cities. If you have more time on your hands, the cheaper InterCity (IC) trains also travel between cities – they're just a fair bit slower. When travelling shorter distances it is often quicker to take Regional Express (RE) trains.

It is always cheaper to buy tickets in advance in Germany. There are three types of tickets: Flexpreis are the most expensive but can easily be amended; Sparpreis are valid only for a select service; and Super-Sparpreis are the cheapest, with only a limited number available for each route.

Netherlands

www.ns.nl

Ever-punctual, the Netherlands' trains are operated by Nederlandse Spoorwegen (NS). NS domestic trains come in two types: Intercity for speedy city-to-city connections and Sprinter on local routes with multiple stops.

Ordinary train fares are calculated by the kilometre with the rate reducing the further you travel. If you are staying in the country for a while, it's worth buying an OV-chipkaart (a rechargeable smart card), as it offers significant savings around the country's network.

Map 5

Bosnia and Herzegovina

www.zfbh.ba; www.zrs-rs.com

The country's fairly limited railway network is operated by two companies. Željeznice Bosne i Hercegovine (ŽFBH) runs the railway in the Federation of Bosnia and Herzegovina (the south and west of the country), while Željeznice Republike Srpske (ŽRS) operates in the Republika Srpska (the north and east of the country). Reservations are compulsory for regional trains and tickets can be bought at stations or online.

Until 2017, a daily train linked Sarajevo (the Bosnian capital) to Zagreb (the Croatian capital). It was due to be modernized, but a disagreement between the two countries' rail companies led to the service ending. It is not clear when any direct train service will resume, and as a result, Bosnia is cut off from the European rail network.

Croatia

www.hzpp.hr

Due to Croatia's terrain, the country's rail network (operated by Hrvatske željeznice or HŽ) mainly runs inland rather than along the coast. There are two types of domestic trains: passenger *(putnički)*, which are slow and stop frequently, or intercity (ICN), which are faster and pricier.

Purchase tickets at the station before boarding rather than onboard, where you might incur a surcharge.

Italy

www.trenitalia.com

Trenitalia runs Italy's comprehensive rail network. There's no cost advantage to pre-booking regional services in Italy and no reservation is required for these trains. All you need to do is buy a ticket at the station and validate it in the little green validating machines (there's a fine if you don't).

For long-distance services, buy your ticket in advance to reserve a seat (a must) and secure a cheaper fare. You don't usually need to validate your ticket for long-distance trains.

As an additional fee is levied on each booking, Interrail and Eurail one-country passes can be more expensive than individual tickets in Italy. Trenitalia offers its own pass, but it can't be used on regional trains and only covers a set number of journeys. If you're going to use multiple trains a day, an Interrail or Eurail pass can be cheaper.

Slovenia

potniski.sz.si

The national railway operator, Slovenske železnice (SZ), runs an efficient service, with routes snaking out from Ljubljana to most areas of the country. There are three types of service: Inter-City Slovenia (ICS), which link the country's cities; InterCity (IC), which cover long-distance routes; and Regional (RG or LP) trains, which stop at every station on the line.

Ticket prices are calculated based on distance covered and, unusually, trains are often cheaper than buses here.

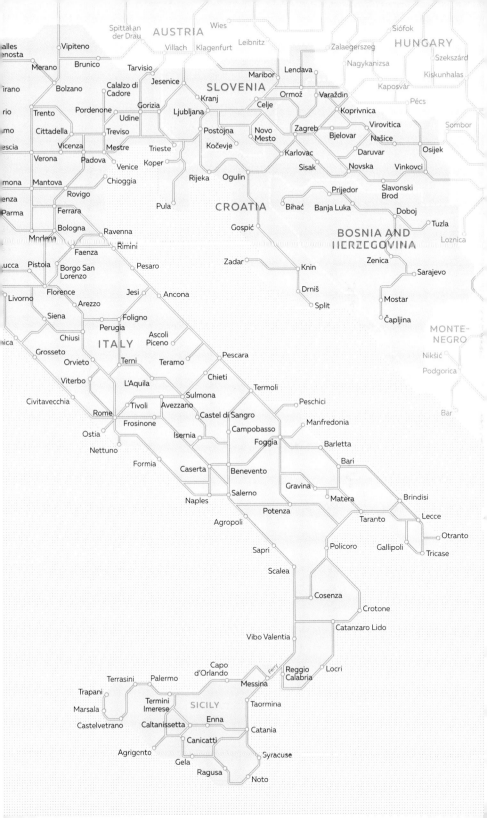

Map 6

Pervomals'k
UKRAINE
Podilsk
ngheni
Voznesens'k
Chisinau
MOLDOVA
Tiraspol
Odesa
ad
Artsyz
Galaţi
la
Tulcea
Constanţa
Kardam
orich
Varna
as
ezkoy
Istanbul
Sakarya
andırma
Bilecik
kesir
Eskişehir
TURKEY
Kütahya
sar
Afyonkarahisar
Uşak
Isparta
Denizli

Bulgaria

www.bdz.bg

Bâlgarski Dârzhavni Zheleznitsi (BDZ) runs Bulgaria's rail network. There are three types of trains in Bulgaria: *patnicheski* (slow), *barz* (fast) and *ekspresen* (express). Buy tickets for all three types of service at stations or on the BDZ website.

Greece

www.hellenictrain.gr

Greece's railway infrastructure is owned and run by Hellenic Train (formerly known as TrainOSE until 2022). There are three types of service: InterCity, Tréno (regional) and Proastiakos (suburban). All services require a seat reservation, so book tickets in advance on the Hellenic Train website or at stations.

Montenegro

www.zcg-prevoz.me

Montenegro's rail network is run by Željeznički prevoz Crne Gore (ŽPCG). There are two types of service: Local and InterCity. You don't need a reservation for either and it's impossible to buy tickets online, so simply turn up at the station on the day.

North Macedonia

Mzt.mk

Makedonski Zeleznici (MZ) operates North Macedonia's rail network. There are three types of service (Regional, Regional Express and InterCity), none of which require a reservation. Buy tickets at stations; it is not possible to buy them online.

Romania

www.cfrcalatori.ro

The Romanian rail network is the fourth largest and most dense in Europe – even the smallest villages are serviced by a train station. The network is run by Societatea Nationale a Cailor Ferate Române (CFR).

There are four types of domestic train in Romania. The slow Regio (RE) trains connect small towns and villages. Inter-Regio (IR) are faster and cover longer distances. Intercity (IC) services connect the main cities and link to international destinations. Special (S) are tourist trains that run specific routes.

Buy tickets at stations or on the CFR website or app. Ticket prices depend on when you book. Save 10 per cent on tickets purchased 11 to 30 days in advance of departure, and 5 per cent on those purchased 6 to 10 days in advance.

Serbia

www.srbvoz.rs

Both Zeleznice Srbije (ZS) and Zeleznice Cme Gore (ZCG) run Serbia's sizable rail network. You cannot buy tickets online, but they are easy to come by at stations and on trains.

Turkey

www.tcddtasimacilik.gov.tr

Istanbul can be reached by a night train from Sofia (Bulgaria). If you're travelling by train in Turkey it's best to book your tickets in advance on the Türkiye Cumhuryeti Devlet Demiryollan (TCDD) website. Tickets are usually available at the station, too.

Map 7

Austria

www.oebb.at

Situated at the heart of Europe, Austria has great international rail links, with regular high-speed trains, such as Railjet, linking Austrian cities with neighbouring countries. Early booking is advised, especially on overnight sleeper trains.

Austria has an excellent national rail network, too, with most services run by Österreichische Bundesbahnen (ÖBB). There are several types of ticket. Standard tickets can be valid for two days and amended up to 24 hours before travel. Komfort tickets can only be used on a specific service and can be amended up to 15 days before. Sparschiene, the cheapest, are valid only for a specific service and cannot be amended. Buy tickets online, via the ÖBB app or at stations.

Czech Republic

www.cd.cz

The railways here are run by České Dráhy (ČD) and include the *rychlík* (express) trains for longer distances and the slower *osobní* (passenger) local trains. Tickets can be bought in advance or at the station, but be aware that queues at ticket booths

can be long. Reservations for international services are essential.

On the timetable, an "R" in a box by a train number means you must have a seat reserved on that train. An "R" without a box means a reservation is recommended. If you are caught in the wrong carriage, you will have to pay an on-the-spot fine.

Hungary

www.mavcsoport.hu

All trains in Hungary are operated by Magyar Államvasutak (MÁV). Fast InterCity services stop only at major towns and cities. Gyorsvonat and Sebesvonat are slower and make more stops. Személyvonat stop at all stations and are very slow.

Prices for all trains are relatively cheap, and tickets can be bought from stations or online from MÁV. InterCity services require a prior seat reservation.

Slovakia

www.zssk.sk

Slovakia's rail network is extensive, and has particularly good links with the Czech Republic. Železničná spoločnosť Slovensko (ZSSK), Slovakia's national rail company, runs several rail services: Regional Expres (REX) and Osobný Vlak (Os) regional commuter trains; Expres (Ex), Rýchlik (R) and Regionálny Rýchlik (RR) long-distance trains; and Eurocity (EC) and InterCity (IC) services between large cities.

Map 8

Estonia

www.elron.ee

Train operator Edelaraudtee runs Estonia's intercity passenger services while Elron, a government-owned operator, runs local electric trains.

You can save money by buying your ticket online in advance. If you are planning on travelling extensively around Estonia, consider buying an Elron Farecard, an electronic card which you can preload with money to buy tickets. The card gives a 10 per cent discount on all tickets purchased at station machines in Estonia.

Latvia

www.pv.lv.

Latvia's rail network is run by the state-owned Pasažieru Vilciens company. Tickets can be purchased at stations, on the train and on the Pasažieru Vilciens website and app. Fares are priced on a zonal basis, meaning that the further you travel, the more you pay.

Tickets are available for single trips, unlimited journeys over one, two, three, four or five days, or for travel during an entire month. If you are carrying luggage with you, you will need to buy a specific "baggage ticket". Note that for most trains it's not possible to reserve a specific seat.

Lithuania

ltglink.lt

Lithuania's national rail network is run by Lietuvos Geležinkeliai

(Lithuanian Railways), and you can buy tickets on the company's website and at stations. Prices vary according to the distance travelled, number of changes and speed of service. As a rule, the faster the service is, the pricier the tickets. Reservations are not mandatory though they are recommended for the busy Vilnius to Klaipėda route.

Poland

www.intercity.pl

The sprawling Polish rail network is operated by a variety of companies. PKP InterCity runs the express services between Warsaw, Kraków and other big cities. TLK, part of the same company, also runs an express service; it is cheaper than InterCity but trains are slightly slower and carriages older and cramped. PolRegio runs a variety of cross-country and local trains, and is a useful way of getting to regional towns. Trains operated by regional companies such as Koleje Mazowieckie (central Poland) or Koleje Dolnośląskie (south-western Poland) connect smaller places within the relevant region.

Buy tickets at stations or online from the individual rail companies or Polrail *(www.polrail.com)*. This Polish train ticketing agency can arrange tickets for travel within Poland or for international trains starting in Poland.

Map 9

Denmark

www.dsb.dk

Denmark's various islands are well connected by the national railway company Danske Statsbaner (DSB). Timetables, ticket information, transport maps and more can be obtained from the DSB website. Standard tickets are valid for travel at any hour, on the day specified. They also include free travel for two children under 12 per adult ticket. You can save money by buying a travel card or "orange ticket", available online only and up to two months in advance.

Finland

www.vr.fi

Finland's rail network is run by the State Railroads of Finland (Valtion Rautatiet, or VR), and connects the major cities. Advance reservations are recommended for long-distance, intercity (IC) and express (EP) trains. Fares for regional and suburban trains are fixed-price and tickets can be bought on the day.

Norway

www.nsb.no

Norway's epic landscape is traversed by Norwegian State Railways (NSB). Intercity trains provide frequent services between the main cities; regional trains serve smaller stations; and commuter trains run hourly or semi-hourly on select lines.

It's often easiest (and cheapest) to book tickets on NSB's website or app. Tickets are also available from machines at most main stations, at ticket counters and onboard.

Sweden

www.sj.se

The state-run Statens Järnvägar (SJ) operates most services in Sweden, including Snabbtåg (high-speed), InterCity (the most expensive), Regional (the cheapest) and Night trains. Buy tickets directly from the SJ website or app or at stations. A select number of discounted tickets are available for each journey.

Index

Acknowledgments

DK Eyewitness would like to thank the following contributors for their words:

Nicola Brady

Nicola is an award-winning travel writer based in Dublin. She's contributed to countless print and digital publications, including the *Irish Independent*, *CNN Travel* and *Dublin Like a Local* for DK Eyewitness.

Jon Bryant

British by birth, Jon has lived in the south of France since the millennium and has written extensively about his adopted home. His family has accompanied him on many iconic trains around the country, including *Le Petit Train Jaune* in the Pyrenées-Orientales, the *Swallows' Railway* in the Jura and the *Train des Pignes* steam locomotive to Digne-les-Bains.

Marti Buckley

An award-winning author, journalist and cook, Marti has lived in San Sebastián since 2010. She is passionate about the city's food scene and is the author of the acclaimed cookbook *Basque Country*.

Kiki Deere

Brought up between England and Italy, Kiki writes travel stories in both English and Italian. Her byline regularly appears in such publications as *The Guardian*, *Grande Cucina* (an Italian food magazine) and *The Telegraph*, where she's the Italian Lakes expert.

Steph Dyson

Addicted to getting truly off the beaten path, Steph splits her time between the UK and Latin America and runs the award-nominated website www.worldly adventurer.com. She's written about sustainable travel for many big names, including *CNN*, *The South China Morning Post* and *The Independent*.

Emma Gregg

Few people can claim to have visited all seven continents, but this acclaimed travel journalist has done just that. Emma specializes in responsible and sustainable tourism, and is never happier than when embarking on a new, low-carbon adventure, especially when it's by train.

Gavin Haines

Taking the train from London to Beijing convinced this writer of the merits of rail travel long ago. He's been penning articles in carriages ever since, for the *BBC*, *Lonely Planet*, *The Telegraph* and others.

Laura Hall

Based in Copenhagen, Laura regularly writes articles on Scandinavia for *Vogue*, *Condé Nast Traveller* and *The Sunday Times*. She's also acted as a consultant for several Nordic tourist bodies, including Visit-Denmark, VisitCopenhagen and Visit Faroe Islands.

Paula Hotti

Finnish born and bred, Paula writes about travel, gin and coffee (sometimes all at the same time). Her work has appeared in *BBC Travel*, *The Times* and Finnish print media.

Phoebe Hunt

Phoebe's words have appeared in *GQ*, *SUITCASE* and *Condé Nast Traveller*. She lives between Italy and the UK and penned parts of *Florence Like a Local* for DK Eyewitness.

Sophie Ibbotson

A writer, tourism consultant and chair of the Royal Society for Asian Affairs, Sophie once rode the entire Trans-Siberian Railway three times back to back – something few can claim.

Wailana Kalama

Originally hailing from Hawaii, Wailana now calls Vilnius home. She writes about science and travel and has contributed to the likes of *Deep Baltic, BBC Travel* and *Culture Trip.*

Stuart Kenny

This Scottish outdoor and travel journalist loves nothing more than exploring his homeland by rail. Currently the editor of the *Much Better Adventures,* Stuart's byline regularly appears in *The Guardian, Metro* and *VICE.*

Mike MacEacheran

Based in Edinburgh, Mike is an award-winning travel writer who has reported from an eye-watering 108 countries. You'll find his words in the likes of *The Times, National Geographic* and *Monocle,* as well as several DK Eyewitness and Top 10 guides.

Kate Mann

Kate is a freelance writer specializing in food, culture and travel. She's been based in Munich since 2017 and spent the summer of 2022 travelling around Germany on a €9 train ticket (part of a government initiative to get more people travelling by train).

Shafik Meghji

An award-winning travel writer, Shafik has penned more than 40 guidebooks, including a few DK Eyewitness guides. His latest release is *Crossed off the Map: Travels in Bolivia.*

Tristan Rutherford and Kathryn Tomasetti

Tristan and Kathryn write about train travel for the likes of *The Guardian* and *The Times.* Their latest rail adventure was from London to Croatia with their three young children in tow.

Regis St Louis

A full-time travel writer since 2000, Regis's byline regularly appears in *The Telegraph, The Manual* and *Lonely Planet.* He's written about journeys all over the globe and goes by train wherever possible.

Dan Stables

Dan has contributed to more than 30 travel books, including many DK Eyewitness guides. You'll also find his work in *BBC Travel, National Geographic Traveller* and *The Independent.*

Somto Ugwueze

Somto is a Nigerian-American travel writer based in Los Angeles. An avid solo traveller, she has traversed most of Spain and Portugal by train and looks forward to having many more adventures by rail.

Peter Watson

Founder of the outdoor travel blog www.atlas andboots.com, Peter has visited over 90 countries, including 40 European nations, and makes many of his journeys by train.

The publisher would like to thank the following for their kind permission to reproduce their photographs

Key: a-above; b-below/bottom; c-centre; f-far; l-left; r-right; t-top)

123RF.com:
Sorincolac 140c

Alamy Stock Photo:
26cb, 103tl, 110c, 151cb, 171cb, Walter Bibikow / Hemis.fr 231ca, Michael Brooks 40, Pocholo Calapre 74-75b, Ian Dagnall 131cb, Ian G Dagnall 220ca, Have Camera Will Travel / Europe 122-123c, Frantic 148cb, Prochasson Frederic 65ca, Horst Friedrichs 24-25cb, Andy Gibson 94ca, Glenn Harper 30tl, Hemis 29tl, 72-73bc, Krasnevsky 36tl, Aliaksandr Mazurkevich 202ca, Alan Novelli 102bl, ronstik 218, Alex Segre 29crb, Stockbym 64cb, Boris Stroujko 145br, Martin Thomas 112cb, Uskarp 158cb, Zoonar GmbH 53c

ARoS Aarhus Art Museum:
Anders Trærup 225ca

AWL Images:
27cb, Robert Birkby 101c, Marco Bottigelli 228tc, 240cb, Davide Camesasca 55cb, Click Alps 177c, ClickAlps 144cla, Matteo Colombo 21cb, 57tr, Kav Dadfar 157clb, Danita Delimont Stock 206bl, Guy Edwardes 195ca, Hans Georg Eiben 50ca, Michele Falzone 210c, Hemis 75cra, 128-129ca, 132-133ca, Francesco Ricardo Iacomino 168cra, imageBROKER 152-153c, Christian Kober 143cr, 159ca, Karol Kozlowski 190ca, 219br, Francesco Ricardo Iacomino 168cb, Jason Langley 18c, Sabine Lubenow 23br, 149tr, 54c, Stefano Politi Markovina 56cb, Jan Miracky 193ca, Chris Mouyiaris 156-157ca, Nordic Photos 183tr, 239tr, Doug Pearson 160ca, Ben Pipe 63ca, Maurizio Rellini 120cra, Baden Wurttemberg 163bl

Belmond Management Limited:
Martin Scott Powell 30c

Dreamstime.com:
Natallia Babok 37br, Dziewul 188bl, Valerijs Jegorovs 93ca, Patryk Kosmider 129br, Marinv 198-199c, Nanisimoval 223cla, Eldar Nurkovic 58-59c, Pytyczech 192cb, Alexander Tolstykh 182cb

FishMe Fisketorget:
228cr

Getty Images:
118-119cra, 126cb, 143ca, 162ca, Fadzrulnizam Ahmad / EyeEm 189ca, John Alexander 90-91c, Alxpin 78ca, 241br, Atlantide Phototravel 216crb, Allan Baxter 181tr, Patrik Bergström 34c, Walter Bibikow 22tr, Massimo Borchi 179ca, Andrei Bortnikau / EyeEm 213tr, Daniel Bosma 124-125cb, Marco Bottigelli 172c, Cavan 212cb, Cavan Images 170tl, Matteo Colombo 33cla, 146ca, Luis Dafos 47tl, Drazen 2-3c, Julian Elliott 7c, Samere Fahim 117cb, John Finney 82-83c, Shi Han 84bc, George Karbus 114-115cra, Kolderal 51br, Sigfrid López 67ca, Irene Lorenz / EyeEm 226ca, Maremagnum 28ca, Didier Marti 135cb, Meinzahn 147br, New Zealand Transition 89cla, Andrea Pistolesi 113tl, John and Tina Reid 81cb, Peter Richardson 97tr, Roberto Roberti 108c, Michael Roberts 96cb, Jonas Rudolph 235cla, Jan Rzaczek / EyeEm 127tl, Alexander Spatari 204-205cr, 220cb, Achim Thomae 180cb, LOIC VENANCE / AFP 69ca, Angel Villalba 215c, Peter Zelei Images 167cb

Getty Images / iStock:
42-43tc, 71tr, 86c, 98-99tc, 136-137ca, 201c, afinocchiaro 121cb, Paul Antonescu 206-207cra, Encrier 77ca, Gatsi 49ca, Ross Helen 174-175tc, Kolbjorn 229br, Mike Mareen 187cla, Michael Mulkens 60-61cb, Nikada 33br, Sean Pavone 38-39cla, Roberto Rizzi 233c, RossHelen 165cb, Greg Sullavan 197cb, no_limit_pictures 161br

Glacier Express:
Stefan Schlumpf 138c

Golden Eagle Luxury Trains:
Rizsavi Tamás 184c

The Luxury Train Club
www.luxurytrainclub.com:
44c

Shutterstock.com:
Lukasz Pajor 105ca

Unsplash:
Victor Malyushev 39cra

UV Arts C.I.C:
107tl

Wikimedia Commons:
Rašo 209cb

Wonderful Copenhagen:
236ca

Cover images: Back Flap:
AWL Images: ClickAlps tc, Baden Wurttemberg cr; Getty Images: cl; Getty Images / iStock: Ross Helen bc

All other images © Dorling Kindersley

Project Editors Elspeth Beidas, Rebecca Flynn
Senior Designers Ben Hinks, Laura O'Brien
Editor Lucy Sara-Kelly
Designers Jordan Lambley, Donna-Marie Scrase, Stuart Tolley
Proofreader Kathryn Glendenning
Indexer Helen Peters
Senior Cartographic Editor Casper Morris
Senior Cartographer Mohammad Hassan
Picture Researcher Laura Richardson
Publishing Assistant Halima Mohammed
Jacket Illustrator Asahi Nagata
Jacket Designers Laura O'Brien, Sarah Snelling
Senior Production Editor Jason Little
Senior Production Controller Samantha Cross
Managing Editor Hollie Teague
Managing Art Editor Sarah Snelling
Art Director Maxine Pedliham
Publishing Director Georgina Dee

First published in Great Britain in 2023
by Dorling Kindersley Limited
DK, One Embassy Gardens, 8 Viaduct Gardens,
London, SW11 7BW.

The authorised representative in the EEA is
Dorling Kindersley Verlag GmbH. Arnulfstr. 124,
80636 Munich, Germany.

Published in the United States by DK Publishing,
1745 Broadway, 20th Floor, New York, NY 10019.

Copyright © 2023 Dorling Kindersley Limited
A Penguin Random House Company
24 25 26 10 9 8 7

The publishers cannot accept responsibility for any consequences arising
from the use of this book, nor for any material on third party websites, and
cannot guarantee that any website address in this book will be a suitable
source of travel information.

A CIP catalog record for this book is available from the British Library.
A catalog record for this book is available from the Library of Congress.

ISBN: 978 0 2416 1602 4

Printed and bound in China

For the curious
www.dk.com

The rapid rate at which the world is changing is constantly keeping the
DK Eyewitness team on our toes. While we've worked hard to ensure that
the train routes, times and attractions described in *Europe by Train* are
accurate and up-to-date, timetables and services change, routes become
impassable, places close and new ones pop up in their stead. Always
check services and fares for your own dates of travel, using the websites
suggested. If you notice something wrong or have a suggestion, we want
to hear about it. Please get in touch at travelguides@uk.dk.com